CENTRAL CITY'S
JOY AND PAIN

CENTRAL CITY'S JOY AND PAIN

SOLIDARITY, SURVIVAL, AND SOUL IN A BIRMINGHAM HOUSING PROJECT

JEROME E. MORRIS

THE UNIVERSITY OF GEORGIA PRESS
ATHENS

Published by the University of Georgia Press
Athens, Georgia 30602
www.ugapress.org
© 2024 by Jerome E. Morris
All rights reserved
Designed by Kaelin Chappell Broaddus
Set in by 10.5/13.5 Miller Text Roman by Kaelin Chappell Broaddus
Illustrated maps by Dan Zettwoch
Front cover image courtesy Richard Lee Morris Jr.

Most University of Georgia Press titles are
available from popular e-book vendors.

Printed digitally

Library of Congress Cataloging-in-Publication Data

Names: Morris, Jerome E., author.
Title: Central City's joy and pain : solidarity, survival, and soul in a
    Birmingham housing project / Jerome E. Morris.
Description: Athens : The University of Georgia Press, 2024. | Includes
    bibliographical references and index.
Identifiers: LCCN 2023028630 | ISBN 9780820365749 (hardback) |
    ISBN 9780820365756 (paperback) | ISBN 9780820365763 (epub) |
    ISBN 780820365770 (pdf)
Subjects: LCSH: Morris, Jerome E.—Family. | Public housing—
    Alabama—Birmingham—History—20th century. | Low-income
    housing—Alabama—Birmingham—History—20th century.
    | African Americans—Alabama—Birmingham—Biography. |
    Birmingham (Ala.)—Social conditions—20th century.
Classification: LCC HD7304.B5 M67 2023 | DDC 363.5/109761781—dc23/
    eng/20230717
LC record available at https://lccn.loc.gov/2023028630

To my mother, Joann Steele Morris (1942–2001), whose deep and abiding commitment to her children, presence, wit, intelligence, courage, determination, and love personified the wholeness of being human. You truly changed the world.

CONTENTS

PREFACE   Reconciling Real-Life Research
in a Black Southern City   ix

Key Places, People, Relationships, and Terms   xiii

Maps   xvi

CHAPTER 1   The Poorest Zip Code in America   1

CHAPTER 2   Before the Projects   12

CHAPTER 3   Convergence   27

CHAPTER 4   A Link in the Chain   34

CHAPTER 5   Blue Black   40

CHAPTER 6   Sankofa   46

CHAPTER 7   Black and Proud   53

CHAPTER 8   Fists, Knives, Neck Bones, and Collard Greens   65

CHAPTER 9   Going to School   78

CHAPTER 10   The Sugar Jets   97

CHAPTER 11   First Impressions   109

CHAPTER 12   Inner-City Church Joys and Pains   118

CHAPTER 13   April Fools' Day   125

CHAPTER 14   Player No More   131

CHAPTER 15   The Joys and Pains of Central City   151

CHAPTER 16   Black Consciousness   159

CHAPTER 17	Chocolate or White Milk?	168
CHAPTER 18	Big Meaty	175
CHAPTER 19	Building Some New Apartments for Y'all	182
CHAPTER 20	That's Home	193
	Conclusion	199
	Epilogue	203
	Acknowledgments	207
APPENDIX	Participants, Residents, and Interviewees	209
	Notes	211
	Index	233

PREFACE   RECONCILING REAL-LIFE RESEARCH IN A BLACK SOUTHERN CITY

In 1968, my family moved into Central City, a housing project in Birmingham, Alabama. By the late 1990s and early 2000s, along with other low-income Black families, we were forced to leave Central City when the local housing authority began demolishing the public housing community. The Birmingham Housing Authority had partnered with private developers to build a new housing complex called Park Place. In addition to displacing low-income families unable to afford the increased rent, a major criticism of Park Place was that the new development would have significantly fewer units. The displacement of former residents exacted a devastating toll on many families, including mine, which I describe later in the book.

During the early 1990s, shortly after completing college and eventually attending graduate school, I no longer lived in Central City but my family remained. I would later go on to complete my doctorate in 1997 at Vanderbilt University and accept a faculty position at the University of Georgia (UGA). Beginning in 2005 and while at UGA, I led a research project in Birmingham to capture the perspectives of those Black families who had been forced out of Central City to make way for the mixed-income housing development.

I secured Institutional Review Board approval and, funded by a seed research grant from UGA's Institute for Behavioral Research, traveled to Birmingham during the summer of 2005 to begin the study. Data collection for the project would continue over several years. Given what I had known about my family's experiences in Central City, I sought to learn more about how events had unfolded for other Black families forced to relocate. For example, how were the evictions communicated to residents? Where did families go, who was allowed to return, and under what conditions? Finally, what effect would this move have on the families and children who once lived there? These questions began shifting my relationship to Central City away from an insider's role and toward a researcher's role with an insider's understanding. As someone who was researching a community where I had lived and that I still viewed as "home," I found myself between two worlds.

I had led and participated as a member on research projects in communities and schools in St. Louis, Nashville, and Atlanta. However, the "Central City Research Project" was very different from my previous work—both professional *and* personal. I was forced to examine my identities, experiences, assumptions, and beliefs at a much deeper level, while learning about my relatives' and neighbors' experiences and views. I had to be reflexive by acknowledging how my experiences growing up in a Birmingham housing project, educational experiences at Black K–12 schools and then predominantly white universities, and positionality and identities (academic, male, movement into the middle class) shaped the research and how the book unfolded.[1]

A unique feature of the Central City Research Project was that I acted as researcher, former community member, friend, and family member. While interviewing (my) people, hearing their stories, and conducting research at the public library, I eventually found myself reaching beyond the research study and delving into what life was like for me growing up in Central City. That awareness further shifted my focus away from solely a research project to one that also included autobiographical accounts and narratives. The Central City Research Project, initially focused on the displacement of Black families from the public housing project, evolved into a book-length manuscript. The latter years of Central City (the late 1990s) and the razing of the housing project were no longer the central focus. The study had become a historical and sociological analysis of Black community life in a southern public housing community, filtered through my lens as a Black male growing up there. Extending across time, I began to weave my autobiographical experiences into this analysis of a predominantly Black southern and urban public housing community.

During the writing of this book, I shared draft chapters with former Central City residents, family members, university colleagues, and graduate students. I presented scholarly papers and talks at various academic meetings and research societies, including the American Sociological Association, the Southern Sociological Society, and the American

Educational Research Association. Every time I traveled to Birmingham (initially from Atlanta and then from St. Louis) I would stop where Central City once stood, observe the people there, and engage in conversations about life and sometimes the book. Almost any time of day, I could find former Central City residents in the nearby Marconi Park who readily talked about the *old* Central City. During the mid-1980s, Central City was renovated and renamed Metropolitan Gardens. However, many of the architectural features and residents remained, and we still referred to the community as Central City until the entire area was demolished in the early 2000s and replaced with a new complex named Park Place.[2] While in Marconi Park, someone would always inquire about the Central City book that I was writing. I would respond that though I was not finished, I could read draft sections. While sharing passages, a small crowd would gather to listen for references to particular individuals or events, or even themselves. When I got something wrong in the retelling, the former residents would correct me.

People from Central City trusted that I would accurately capture what they remembered as their community. When I could not make the journey back to Birmingham, I telephoned key people to check the stories' and events' accuracy. Data sources for this book included more than forty interviews (see the appendix), library and other archival data, sociological data, secondary sources such as books and articles, family stories and photos, field notes from annual Central City reunions, high school reunions, funerals, and birthdays, as well as my experiences living in the community for more than two decades.

I changed some names, locations, and identifying characteristics to protect interviewees' and research participants' confidentiality and privacy. In some parts, the dialogue comes from actual interviews with participants. In other sections, I re-created dialogue from informal conversations and observations over several years with community residents and other research participants, friends, acquaintances, and family members. I made all efforts to place these stories within a broader historical, economic, and sociopolitical context. I used endnotes when necessary to elaborate or provide additional scholarly background for the reader.

These stories from Central City reflect the sadness, hope, and triumph we hear within African American spirituals. Like the blues, they create feelings of nostalgia, happiness, and sadness while reminding us of the realities that those at the economic and racial bottom of U.S. society must wake up and face every day. These stories, coming from our souls, would embody our dreams—dreams that are realized by some and swallowed up for others in the larger historical, social, economic, and political context of African Americans' experiences during and after the Civil Rights Movement. *Central City's Joy and Pain* depicts what life is like for people who live and die at the intersection of race and poverty in a rapidly evolving southern urban center.

KEY PLACES, PEOPLE, RELATIONSHIPS, AND TERMS

Central City: Public housing project, three blocks east of Birmingham's City Hall, built in 1941. The area was renamed **Metropolitan Gardens** in the 1980s and then razed in the 2000s. **Park Place**, an entirely new complex, was built on the land where Central City once stood.

Marconi Park: Park across the street from Central City (later renamed Metropolitan Gardens and Park Place).

Powell Elementary School: Originally named the Free School in 1874 and built for white children, the present school was completed in 1888. Black children began attending in the late 1960s. Powell Elementary is located adjacent to where the Central City housing project resided. The author, his siblings, and other children from the Central City housing project attended this school.

Phillips High School: Adjacent to Central City and where children from the housing project were zoned to attend. The author graduated from Phillips in 1986.

The Alley: Considered a "slum" area of Birmingham, this all-Black area consisted of shotgun-style houses. Located near Twenty-Sixth Avenue and Seventh Avenue North in Birmingham, the Alley sat a few yards from a set of railroad tracks that ran almost parallel to the shotgun houses.

Twenty-Ninth Court and Seventh Court (pronounced "coat" in African American Vernacular English): Located near the railroad tracks and considered "slums" of Birmingham, these areas consisted of communities of Black residents who lived in shotgun-style houses. Black residents seamlessly flowed between the Alley and the Court, although separated by a few blocks, and related families often lived between the two.

Terminal Station: Former railway station, demolished in 1969. Once located adjacent to Central City.

Downtown Farmers Market: Located at Twenty-Sixth Street and Second Avenue North.

Collins Hotel: Boarding house run by the author's maternal grandmother (Oceola Steele Collins), nicknamed "Collins Hotel" by Black residents. The building once stood on the corner of Twenty-Sixth Street and Second Avenue North.

Carruba Grocery: Italian-owned grocery, near the Alley and Central City and located on Twenty-Sixth Street and Seventh Avenue North.

Hardie Tynes Foundry: Located on Twenty-Eighth Street and Eighth Avenue and a few yards from the Twenty-Ninth Court community where the author's immediate family and other Black residents lived, the foundry produced industrial equipment for the iron industry and large water-related public works projects such as Hoover Dam.

Jones Valley Urban Gardens: Located along Seventh Avenue and Twenty-Fifth Street North, the gardens emerged in the early 2000s.

One Stop Convenience Store: Adjacent to Phillips High School and the Central City public housing project, this convenience store was owned by an African American couple, James and Leola Goldthwaite, during the 1980s and 1990s.

Beulah Missionary Baptist Church: Located at 1616 Eighth Avenue North (now called Rev. Abraham Woods Jr. Boulevard), this church hosts a scene from chapter 12.

Willie's Super Market: Grocery store approximately three blocks from Central City owned by a Jewish man known as Mr. Willie. The building sat on the corner of Second Avenue and Twenty-Fifth Street North near downtown Birmingham.

Red Mountain Expressway: Expressway shaped by a geological cut into Red Mountain integral in developing Birmingham's suburbs. It runs alongside Twenty-Sixth Street North and adjacent to the one-time location of Central City.

Joann Steele Morris: A central protagonist and the author's mother. Her children, from oldest to youngest, include Ronald Steele, Richard Lee Morris Jr., Kenneth Morris, Michael Morris, Maurice Morris, Jerome E. Morris, Steve Morris (died during childbirth), and Shelda Morris.

Richard Morris Sr.: Spouse of Joann Steele Morris and father of Kenneth Morris, Michael Morris, and Maurice Morris; stepfather to Ronald Steele, Richard Lee Morris Jr., Jerome E. Morris, and Shelda Morris. He would move out from the family home when the author (Jerome) was born.

Mama (aka Oceola Collins and Ms. OC): Author's maternal grandmother and mother to Joann Steele Morris, Maxine Steele Collins Wright, Eddie Steele Collins, Sandra Collins, Brenda Green, and Alonzo Collins.

Joe Steele Jr.: Author's maternal grandfather.

Charlie Ray Clency Jr.: Author's biological father.

Charlie Ray Clency Sr.: Author's paternal grandfather.

Papa Slim: Man who impregnated Joann (author's mother) when she was a teenager.

Ronald Steele: Author's oldest brother by his mother; Joann Steele Morris's firstborn son.

Richard Lee Morris Jr.: Joann Steele Morris's second-born son.

Kenneth Morris: Joann Steele Morris's third-born son.

Michael Morris (aka Big Meaty): Joann Steele Morris's fourth-born son.

Maurice Morris: Joann Steele Morris's fifth-born son.

Jerome E. Morris (the author): Joann Steele Morris's sixth-born son.

Steve Morris: Joann Steele Morris's seventh son, who died at childbirth.

Shelda Morris: Joann Steele Morris's only daughter and eighth child.

Panky: Author's eldest brother, a sibling on his biological father's side.

Map 1. The city of Birmingham situated within the state of Alabama, featuring key historic landmarks and communities, including Central City's placement within the city's center.

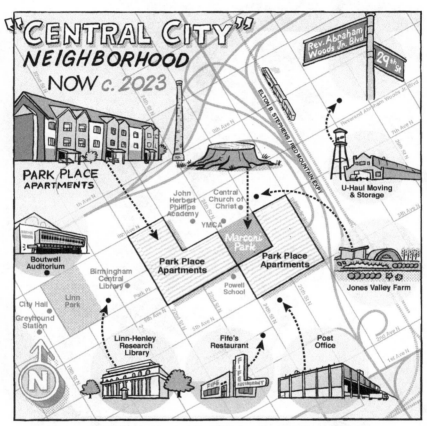

Map 2. The Central City neighborhood now, around 2023. The map illustrates how contemporary physical structures such as the Park Place Hope VI development, Jones Valley Farm, Rev. Abraham Woods Jr. Boulevard, and U-Haul Moving and Storage have replaced former communities, structures, and symbols such as Central City, the Alley, the Court, and the tree in Marconi Park.

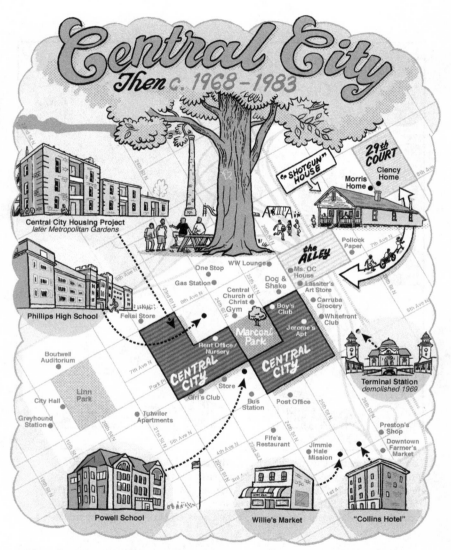

Map 3. The Central City community as it appeared between 1968 and 1983, with a particular emphasis on key landmarks mentioned throughout the book.

CENTRAL CITY'S JOY AND PAIN

CHAPTER 1   THE POOREST ZIP CODE IN AMERICA

Block parties, freeze cups, shooting marbles, the best girls' softball team, the Sugar Jets football team, kissing in the hallways, fighting, borrowing butter and eggs, Powell School, my mama, five older brothers and a younger sister, the free summer lunch program, the Double Dutch Bus, Mr. Hooks's store, the Electric Poppers and the CC Poppers, free school breakfast and lunch, due bills, and the music of Frankie Beverly and Maze. This was the Birmingham so many of us knew. This was the Central City housing project.

If I ever told someone from outside the South that I was born in 1968 in Birmingham, Alabama, however, I would remind that person that Birmingham holds the distinction of being the U.S. epicenter of the Black Freedom Movement of the 1960s. People generally know about Birmingham's infamous title as "the most segregated city in America."[1] They might also know about the bombing of Sixteenth Street Baptist Church, a vicious act of racism and murder that cost four little Black girls (Addie Mae Collins, Carol Denise McNair, Carole Rosamond Robertson, and Cynthia Wesley) their lives.[2] While talking, we would summon the imagery of Black children forced into police vans, police officers beating Black protesters, and dogs tearing into human flesh. Iconic images of firefighters spraying Black bodies have become etched in the public's mind.

Occasionally, someone would ask, "Jerome, how was it to grow up in Birmingham?," as if I had been raised in the segregated South of the forties and fifties. To many people, Birmingham was still in the past—literally and figuratively. Consequently, I found myself too often informing people instructively about how Birmingham's segregation and poverty today are similar to those among Black people in cities like Cleveland, Baltimore, Oakland, Chicago, and St. Louis—where they experience segregation in just about *every* area of their lives, also known as *hypersegregation*.[3]

People with some familiarity with Birmingham might ask me which part of town I lived in or where I had attended school. I usually told them that I grew up downtown. They would often probe deeper. "Where exactly?" they'd ask. I'd answer Central City, a public housing project. "How did you get out of the projects and become a professor?" was the typical follow-up question. I tailored my response to the audience and reminded them of a more appropriate question: *Why do so many Black people, after deep sacrifices and fights for freedom over hundreds of years, even have to deal with the idea of trying to get up out of the "hood"?* Had not the blood, sweat, and tears that our ancestors shed been enough to ensure that we would no longer have to endure such horrific living conditions?

I was born on March 22, 1968, less than two weeks before Dr. Martin Luther King Jr. was assassinated. I, and millions of other Black children like me, would grow up in the ghettos of the United States, and my six siblings and I would suffer through extreme poverty for the next two decades. We were those children whom the Civil Rights Movement of the fifties and sixties had forgotten. The movement's leaders' focus on projecting an image of respectability so that white people would see Black people positively would limit them from supporting young people like Claudette Colvin in Montgomery, Alabama. Claudette refused to give up her seat on a bus before Rosa Parks, but movement leaders, due to their penchant for respectability politics, placed their support behind Rosa Parks instead. Although Birmingham had been the chief battleground for the movement, thousands of Black children still attended financially neglected inner-city schools and lived in impoverished public housing.[4]

In 1986, I graduated from Phillips High School, which sat across the street from Central City. Built in 1923 exclusively for whites, Phillips High is where fiery Birmingham-based civil rights icon Rev. Fred Shuttlesworth and his wife Ruby were beaten in 1957 trying to enroll their children.[5] By the time that three out of five of my older brothers had attended Phillips between the late 1970s and early 1980s, the student population was predominantly Black. At the time that I graduated from Phillips in 1986 and our younger sister attended later that fall, the student population was 99 percent Black, and at least 90 percent of us were on free or reduced-price lunches.

Altogether I have nine brothers, all of whom are older than me—five on my mother's side with whom I was raised in Central City and four on my biological father's side. I am the only one of the ten to never see the inside of a jail or prison. I also have a younger sister with whom I was raised in Central City and two older sisters on my biological father's side. I survived the streets of Birmingham, but not because of any special qualities. In fact, many of our teachers would have expected a couple of the brothers I grew up with to be most likely to write this book. They were intelligent, and one even skipped a grade in elementary school. I survived Birmingham and Central City because caring people, educational experiences, and opportunities allowed me to see another world—beyond Central City, beyond the inner city's enclosed world, and beyond Birmingham and Alabama. These opportunities allowed me to begin to see—sort of from a bird's-eye view—what it meant to be Black and poor in a southern U.S. city.

One such opportunity arose in 1985 when I was one of four high school students—two Black males, a white female, and a white male—selected for a summer study abroad program in Hitachi City, Japan. Birmingham City and public school officials selected us because of our academic achievement and leadership. As "ambassadors" for the city and school system, we were expected to testify to Birmingham's commitment to education, opportunity, and equality. Our selection supposedly demonstrated how Birmingham had moved beyond the turbulent fifties and sixties. For two weeks, the four of us, along with the two white women chaperones, traveled throughout Japan and became immersed in Japanese culture and society through visits to historic sites, family homestays, language classes, and lectures. The Mayor's Office, Birmingham public school system's leadership, and the Birmingham Sister City Commission jointly funded the program's entire cost.

A little less than one year after traveling to Japan, and during my senior year of high school, I received another opportunity for summer travel abroad. I became one of thirty-one high school students from across the United States to be selected as Malcolm H. Kerr Scholars. The program's intent was for scholarship recipients to return to the United States and offer a more balanced view to the misunderstanding and misrepresentation of people of Arab descent in U.S. society. Sponsored by the National Council on U.S.-Arab Relations in Washington, D.C., the Kerr Scholarship Program honored Malcolm H. Kerr, the president of American University in Beirut, Lebanon, who had been assassinated in 1984. The thirty-one scholarship recipients traveled to one of three countries: Egypt, Tunisia, and Jordan. The program's administrators chose Jordan for me to visit.

During the Jordan trip in the summer of 1986, I learned that only a month earlier more than two thousand college students had protested against Jordan's Yarmouk University administrators because of the school's high academic fees and the university's dismissal of thirty-one students who protested U.S. air strikes against Libya. Police units killed at least three of the students, and many more were injured. While in Jordan that summer, I witnessed hope and despair at Baqa'a refugee camp, which was home to approximately one hundred thousand Palestinian refugees. I stood along the Jordan River, viewed as sacred due to the biblical story of Jesus's baptism there. I trekked through the magnificent Nabataean city of Petra. At the University of Jordan, I learned about Islamic society and culture, inside and outside the classroom. I became further informed by numerous speakers whose wide range of topics included "the role of women in Arab society and culture" and "the politics of the Arab-Israeli Conflict."

After completing the study abroad program to Jordan in mid-July of 1986, I once again left Birmingham and Central City. It was early August when I left for summer football camp and enrolled at Austin Peay State University—a small public school in Tennessee that I had never heard of until the football coaches there offered me an athletic scholarship to play quarterback. I went to Austin Peay with the hope of continuing my dream of playing quarterback in college and "going as far as I could." Like many determined Black quarterbacks over the years such as Hall of Famer Warren Moon and Super Bowl winner Doug Williams, I was determined to make my mark at the position. Honestly, I was disappointed that major universities like Alabama and Auburn did not offer me a "full ride" football scholarship, even though I was one of the top quarterbacks in the state of Alabama that year. I was not informed enough (and did not receive the guidance) to apply to various universities, given my strong academic record and numerous achievements. Like so many Black males growing up in extreme poverty and with community pressures to get my family out of poverty, my athletic dreams—rather than academic potential and aspirations—shaped my decision about which undergraduate college I would attend.[6] Years later I would join with other scholars and research and write about the experiences of Black male "students who play sports."[7]

Once enrolled in college and playing football, however, I would find myself trying to reconcile my identification as an athlete with what I felt were more pressing matters facing Black students at the university. I eventually left the football team at the beginning of my junior year and became deeply involved in Black student organizations and politicizing efforts. In May 1990, I graduated with a bachelor's degree in political science and a minor in engineering technology. A month later I traveled to Cairo, Egypt, to participate in a summer internship, which was also sponsored by the National Council on U.S.-Arab Relations. This opportunity placed me with the Ain Shams Community Centre, which serves an impoverished area on the outskirts of Cairo. During the summer of 1990, and for three days each week, I taught English classes to a group of Muslim and Christian women and men.[8]

While in Egypt that summer I visited the pyramids of Giza and other historic places. I also befriended Black Sudanese Christian refugees who—along with thousands of others like themselves—sought asylum and refuge in Cairo because of an impending genocide being waged against them and other African ethnic groups by the Arab and Islamic government of Sudan.[9]

I lived in an apartment in an area of the city known as Heliopolis. In conversations with my four roommates and fellow interns, all white male college students, I discussed human rights issues and U.S. race relations. Outside of these conversations, I spent time with Ghanaian and Tanzanian migrants whom I had met in Cairo. We discussed the relationship between Africans on the African continent and people of African descent throughout the diaspora. Moreover, I met with Palestinian youth who told stories of being watched, harassed, and beaten by Israeli soldiers, many of whom were youth themselves. After approximately three months in Cairo, I returned to the United States in August 1990—just as U.S. naval ships were making their way to the Persian Gulf in response to Iraq's invasion of Kuwait.

These earlier international experiences further educated and politicized me about global, ethnic, racial, religious, class-related, and gender dynamics and inequities. I tell of these experiences because it is important for young Black people who are growing up in impoverished communities to know that they can imagine and engage with a world that exists outside of their immediate surroundings. They just need opportunities like I received to experience other places. Although living in the Central City housing project in Birmingham, I had become fascinated with political issues in the United States and on a global scale. These opportunities to travel internationally began teaching me about the injustices experienced by people, especially Black and other marginalized groups, globally. I was also beginning to connect the dots between what my family, friends, and I were experiencing in Central City and Birmingham with what Black and oppressed people experienced globally.

After returning to the United States from Egypt in August 1990, I moved back into Central City—into my mother's apartment—at the age of twenty-two and became reimmersed in the day-to-day dynamics of living and surviving in what many people termed "the hood." The crack-cocaine epidemic was sweeping the United States. Unheralded waves of violence were terrorizing inner-city neighborhoods across the nation as young Black males like some of my own brothers, cousins, and friends competed for gang and drug turf. The Central City of 1990 was becoming very different from the one I had grown up in throughout early and middle childhood. The violence in Central City had emerged from a deadly combination of government neglect, unemployment, miseducation, crack cocaine, guns, and hopelessness. The despair and violence were taking a devastating toll on our communities, friends, and families. While the media and those within the academic community would often focus on challenges facing inner-city communities in northern and midwestern centers such as New York, Philadelphia, and Chicago, impoverished and predominantly Black urban communities in southern places like Birmingham, Memphis, and New Orleans were also reeling.[10]

In the fall of 1990, while living in Central City, I ran for and was elected the vice-president of our public housing community's tenant council. The president at the time, Joe Harris (nicknamed Sugar Man), had been my peewee football coach. Sugar Man and I were excited to be working together. But all we could do was attempt to make sense out of what was taking place. Daily, friends and family in Central City gathered in the neighborhood park under the large oak tree. While catching up on the latest news, playing cards or dominoes, we discussed the connection among poverty, drug-related crimes, and Central City killings to some of our people's increasing sense of hopelessness and *pain* as a result of what we were going through; some people call this the blues.[11] During my late teens and early twenties (late 1980s and early 1990s), Central City's poverty rate was a shocking 72 percent. Birmingham's white and Black civic and business elite had forgotten about Central City and the city's other predominantly Black public housing projects such as Collegeville, Gate City, Tuxedo Court, Kingston, and Elyton Village.[12] This neglect was evidence that the so-called Modern Civil Rights Movement had not fully engaged issues around Black poverty in a tangible way.

While others were celebrating how far Black people had come since the 1960s, the Black poor were looking at what legal scholar Derrick Bell refers to as the "bottom of the well."[13] We were trying to figure out how to get out.

I tried to stay encouraged while back living in Central City between 1990 and 1991, and I used that time to prepare for my future. But I had to be sure to stay alive while living in Central City. From September 1990 to May 1991, I worked a part-time job in the children's department of the public library in downtown Birmingham and regularly substituted at my former elementary and high schools, both located across the street from where we lived. Going back to Powell Elementary and Phillips High to substitute teach and earn a little money allowed me to see the changes within the schools and community since I had left for college. I began to envision myself as an *educator* in the broadest sense of the word. I continued mapping out my next moves in life and thought about whether I should continue to pursue my interests in international relations, attend law school, or go to graduate school. No matter which route I pursued, I needed much more money than I was making as a substitute teacher and part-time librarian. I knew that whatever I did in life it had to focus on human rights and social justice for Black people living in the impoverished communities I knew so well.

I first applied to law schools but was not admitted to those I wanted to attend. I then enrolled in a summer program for prospective law students at Saint Louis University (SLU). But after a few weeks in the program, I was no longer motivated to become a lawyer. I lost interest in the course and began to think that a future as a lawyer could be too constraining for someone like me. Consequently, I did not fare well in that course. I was still not sure as to what route to go in life. After the summer law program at SLU, I stopped to visit Mary (my girlfriend at the time, now my spouse) in Nashville, where Mary was completing her undergraduate degree at Tennessee State University. That stop in Nashville became an extended one. I had decided that I was not interested in law school nor ready to go back to Birmingham. I moved into Mary's apartment that year.

During the fall of 1991, and while living with Mary in Nashville, Vanderbilt University's Television News Archives hired me in a part-time position to catalog and write abstracts for CNN's complete coverage of the Persian Gulf War. Although the work was mundane and tedious, I was excited to use my experiences and knowledge of the Middle East in a meaningful way. Between lunch breaks and writing abstracts, I stopped by academic departments at Vanderbilt University to inquire about scholarship opportunities that would fund graduate school. In early 1992, I was encouraged to apply to the Master of Education program, which included a yearlong internship teaching in a Nashville public school, and gained acceptance. Later that year Mary and I got married, and the following year I enrolled in a Vanderbilt doctorate program in educational policy. I completed my PhD in 1997 and accepted a tenure-track faculty position in the College of Education at the University of Georgia.

After graduating from Vanderbilt University, my family in Birmingham was proud that I had, in their words, "done well for myself." However, I was still troubled because my mother, siblings, extended family members, and close friends remained in poverty among Birmingham's housing projects. Like my family, so many Black people were still limited in where they could live, work, and go to school. And the situation in Central City and other public housing projects had become dire. It was the late 1990s, more than three decades after the Modern Civil Rights Movement had begun. For some Black people, the changes associated with the movement were evident because they could take advantage of educational and economic opportunities that were closed to so many of them a generation or two earlier. A few had even risen to new political and financial heights. But this was not the case for the majority of Black people.

The social and economic elevation of a few of us did not mean that if more of those Black people at the bottom had worked harder, they too would be able to partake in the so-called American Dream. It meant that some of us from the bottom had become beneficiaries of a scarcity of opportunities from which only a small number of Black people living in poverty are allowed to benefit. This was clear to me during my many visits to Birmingham (to see family and later conduct research) as well as from conversations with former residents and friends from Central City. They were proud that I had "gotten up out of the hood," but they often blamed themselves and felt that they should have worked harder. I informed my childhood friends that we all did not have the same opportunities and that our families had suffered through adverse economic conditions for generations.[14] I told them that there were only so many slots for some of us to ascend out of poverty, akin to a lottery. They seemed shocked when I told them that we had all grown up in the *poorest zip code in the United States.*[15] Many did not know how intergenerational economic and racial trauma were shaping so much of our futures.[16] I tried to be as convincing as I could about how interventions, opportunities, and people in my life helped me as an individual.

Unfortunately, those who wrestle with the devastating effects of enslavement, cultural erasure, ongoing discrimination, and persistent economic inequities rarely hear this message. Whereas there is a powerful counterstory of enslaved Black people—and those of us who are descendants—surviving racial, physical, and psychological trauma, these traumas have resulted in scores of Black people today experiencing poverty, racial inequality, and psychological stagnation.[17] It is imperative to tell those who suffer through these traumas the truth: *opportunities are often scarce, unlike the aspiration and will to do better and to "make it."*

Today, my frequent trips to Birmingham often bring about a sense of bliss, memories of friendship and love, and a renewed appreciation for the education I received inside and outside of the community where I had once lived. Whereas I have always had this strong kinship with Black people in Birmingham, I still think about the numerous events that caused distress and agony for those growing up in and experiencing poverty and racial inequities throughout Birmingham and in similar locales across the United States. I think about the stigmatization that came with living in "the projects," coded language for poverty and so-called moral decay.

Even those who lived in housing projects often blamed themselves for the difficulties they encountered.[18] They, too, have been fed the idea that *personal responsibility can lead to upward mobility*. Rarely mentioned is the relationship among whiteness, privilege, and wealth accumulation over decades and centuries and how these shape immense financial and social opportunities for some and vast social and economic inequality for others.[19] Few have connected the dots leading from enslavement and economic exploitation to mass incarceration, systemic racism and discrimination, and the conditions that Black people in impoverished communities face today.

As Black people whose ancestors lived on the African continent only a few generations ago, we must remember that we already had families before enslavement. We had already lived in communities where we could thrive and create a living for ourselves, where we learned about the sciences, arts, and folklores in these communities and among kinfolks and neighbors.[20] Enslavement, however, disrupted our ancestors' worlds, communities, and families, and ultimately even our lives. Living in a housing project and experiencing poverty were not magical events, curses, or outcomes due to Black people's shortcomings. Instead, a series of historical events contributed to our presence in housing projects like Central City. This history includes the forced ripping of Black people from their communities and families, the torturous trek to the slave dungeons, the horrific Middle Passage, centuries of enslavement where Black people endured rape and death, and legalized segregation and discrimination for close to another century. White supremacist ideologies and practices were reinforced through racist laws and policies that ultimately confined Black people to neglected areas of the city, otherwise known as ghettos.[21]

As a former Central City resident, I would go on to earn tenure at the University of Georgia, achieve the status of full professor there, and later accept a position as an endowed professor of urban education at the University of Missouri–St. Louis. Whenever I travel to Birmingham today, I still experience conflicted feelings about Central City and Birmingham—a deep sense of connectedness mixed with a piercing hurt. In trying to understand these feelings, I find solace in the soulful words and sounds of the rhythm and blues group Maze—featuring Frankie Beverly. Especially during the summertime, the music from the soulful group would permeate every Black community in Birmingham, and beyond. In one of the group's iconic songs, "Joy and Pain," Frankie Beverly, the lead singer, described how "joy and pain are like sunshine and rain."[22] Both represent the same feeling and come from the same source.

I have begun reconciling these feelings of *joy and pain* when remembering childhood, family, community, school, and friends. I was not fond of the precarious places that too many Black people occupied, which spoke to the reality of the U.S. racial and poverty-caste system.[23] Yet I admired how many of Central City's Black residents had held on to a sense of dignity and humanity. We had formed a community despite— or because of—such an oppressive social, political, racial, and economic structure. This, too, is what I witness when I go back to Central City. To me, this is an illustration of the resilience and the dogged determination within *The Souls of Black Folk* that W. E. B. Du Bois described more than a century ago.[24]

Growing up in Central City and later being able to view the community through a researcher's eyes, it became more clear how that particular section of Birmingham represented a microcosm of impoverished Black people's experiences throughout the United States. I witnessed parallels between our experiences and those of other marginalized and oppressed people worldwide and across history. I no longer saw a so-called ghetto or inner-city community as something endemic to Black and poor people in the United States.[25] Groups throughout the world, including African people in Brazilian favelas and South African townships, have been relegated to neglected areas of a city due to their physical, cultural, and religious characteristics. Historically, ghettos were associated with Jewish people. Throughout Europe, Jewish people were once stigmatized and segregated into ghettos.[26] Unfortunately, today Palestinian people in Israel have become ghettoized due to Jewish settlement over the past few decades. No longer did I see the unprovoked killing of Black people by police officers as an isolated phenomenon. It did not matter if I was in Jordan or Japan, Jamaica or Ghana, Egypt or Kenya, Zimbabwe or South Africa, Atlanta or St. Louis. It was clear: people who had been colonized, displaced, enslaved, and deculturalized had suffered similar educational, social, health-related, psychological, and economic fates.

Thus, after seeing Central City from elsewhere and experiencing other central cities and ghettoized areas throughout the world, I became more emboldened to understand the stories of our people, many unnamed. I realized the importance of telling the stories of those who experience the pangs of hunger and poverty and whose life stories too often go untold. They may not be well-recognized names on the pages of books and magazines or on street signs or boulevards. Nevertheless, they also are important. Despised by many, these people have names and experiences worth knowing and noting. Too often their names emerge only during moments of crisis and crime, and their heroic deeds are rarely mentioned in the daily news.

I began to write *Central City's Joy and Pain* also because of the sense of community, strength, and resilience and Black people's ability to take so-called slums and housing projects and remake these spaces into a community that offers us a sense of warmth and family. I wanted to share the stories about Black people's adaptive vitality *with* our people and beyond.[27] I wanted to share the universal messages enveloped in the experiences of those of us who called Central City *home*. Central City—a public housing complex consisting of 910 units across approximately twelve square blocks near downtown Birmingham—is where some of our spirits, souls, and understandings of community, family, education, and the world began to form.

CHAPTER 2   BEFORE THE PROJECTS

Constructed in the early 1940s, Central City initially housed low-income and working-class white families. Some of these white families were part of the hundreds of thousands of families throughout the United States unable to pay their mortgages and who lost their homes during the Great Depression. In 1932, for example, approximately 273,000 families fell into homelessness.[1] In response to this national housing crisis, President Franklin D. Roosevelt's New Deal program created the Home-owners Refinancing Act of 1933 and the National Housing Act of 1934, which offered low-interest loans and made homeownership more affordable for white families. Black people, however, faced discriminatory tactics that prevented homeownership. Such tactics included *redlining*, in which mortgage lenders would draw red lines around maps of a neighborhood in which they were unwilling to make loans. Another tactic, *racial steering*, involved real estate agents deliberately directing Black people to primarily Black neighborhoods. In addition, exclusionary zoning laws that had been used to maintain property prices effectively discriminated against Black people seeking to move into suburban or, more recently, urban areas.[2]

To further support white families' homeownership, Congress passed the Housing Act of 1937, which created the United States Housing Authority; this agency facilitated the creation of 302,000 public housing units.[3] Although it was later modified in 1949 and 1954, the Housing Act of 1937 laid the foundation for public housing for millions of U.S. families.[4] These laws allowed local officials such as the Birmingham Housing Authority to build and manage public housing.

The first public housing complexes in Birmingham included Smithfield Court in 1937 for low-income Black people and Elyton Village in 1938 for low-income white people.[5] Smithfield consisted of 81 one- and two-story buildings that could house 544 Black families. This number of units was insufficient due to the large numbers of Black families throughout the city, many of whom had migrated into Birmingham from rural Alabama in search of employment. Elyton Village, on the other hand, exclusively housed 555 white families.

Despite the need for more housing for Black people, the Birmingham Housing Authority built another housing complex for whites, Central City. Construction began in 1941 and was completed by 1943. Central City would house 910 white families in one-, two-, and three-story brick buildings. As the name suggests, Central City sat in the middle of Birmingham's downtown business center with convenient access to the public library, city parks, the Greyhound Bus Station, and the Terminal Railroad Station. As late as the 1960s, downtown Birmingham was the epicenter of Alabama's commercial and entertainment districts. Central City's white residents lived only a few blocks from amenities that included two adjacent schools, Powell Elementary School and Phillips High School, in addition to a Boys Club.

Many Black families living in Birmingham's housing projects had arrived there due to a series of circumstances, sometimes by choice and at other times by force. Whenever white business and civic leaders wanted land for white families and businesses, they employed white urban planners who would then declare "Negro" sections of a city to be blighted.[6] Like Negro sections of St. Louis and Chicago, this is also what happened to the Negro section on Birmingham's South Side. As part of national urban renewal efforts across the United States during the 1950s and 1960s, the University of Alabama at Birmingham (UAB) Medical Center displaced hundreds of Black families from the South Side to expand its footprint in the city.

Black community leaders such as Ruby Hurley of the local National Association for the Advancement of Colored People (NAACP) and Emory Jackson, editor of the city's Black newspaper, *Birmingham World*, fought against these plans to displace the Black families. Still, UAB's expansion resulted in the forced removal of 484 Black families. Of those eligible for public housing, only 76 moved into existing Black public housing communities such as Loveman Village (built in 1952) and Southtown Court. Another 112 families eventually moved back into sub-

Potential residents touring the newly built Central City apartments,
reserved exclusively for white families (early 1940s).
(Courtesy, Birmingham Public Library Archives.)

Central City and Phillips High School aerial view amid downtown.
The rectangular-shaped buildings in the center of the photo
constitute the Central City housing project.
(Courtesy, Birmingham Public Library.)

standard housing.[7] The Birmingham Housing Authority created and maintained segregated racial boundaries in public housing units for another two decades.

For a short time, Mama—our family's maternal grandmother—was among the Black residents who lived on the South Side. But our family mostly lived in the Alley and Twenty-Ninth Court, located east of downtown Birmingham. These were considered slum areas consisting of rows of shotgun houses. The shotgun houses in the Alley have since been demolished, and the Red Mountain Expressway now runs through the area. The shotgun houses in Twenty-Ninth Court have also been demolished, and a sign naming a street after Birmingham Civil Rights icon Rev. Abraham Woods now marks the area.

The Carruba family, Italian immigrants, owned some of the shotgun houses in the Alley where Mama once lived. The Carruba family, like many other European immigrant families, was hoping to achieve their American Dream by renting the units to Black families. On the other hand, Black people's prospects for homeownership throughout the South were not as favorable as those for recent European immigrants. As the descendants of involuntary immigrants, Black people were relegated to the racial and economic bottom of U.S. society. Furthermore, white Americans' banishment of entire communities of Black people, racially restrictive housing covenants, inequitable employment practices, and bankers' unwillingness to loan money to Black people collectively kept generations of Black people from homeownership.[8] Many Black residents in Birmingham would rent houses from the same landlords for years, even decades, without the possibility of ownership. This inability to build wealth would have consequences for homeownership and wealth disparities between white and Black people for decades to come.

Birmingham and other cities throughout the United States maintained rigid housing segregation laws. Still, some police officers recognized the impracticality of enforcing these laws, mostly when there was money to be made. The Carruba family owned a home adjacent to the Alley and alongside Black families. Italian immigrants were generally embraced as "white" within the city's power structure only when supporting white supremacist efforts at limiting Black people's opportunities. However, when they acted in their own group's interest, they were relegated to "immigrant" status.[9] Like several Italian immigrant families throughout Birmingham, the Carrubas owned a small grocery store and sold fruits, vegetables, and other items to Black residents. The Carruba family, however, eventually left the area. Like numerous southern and

Historical photo of Carruba Grocery at the corner of Twenty-Sixth Street and Seventh Avenue North in Birmingham, Alabama. The Elton B. Stephens / Red Mountain Expressway now runs alongside this area.
(Courtesy, Birmingham Public Library Archives.)

eastern European immigrants before them, ghettos like the Alley would become a temporary stopover in their American experience. While southern and eastern Europeans initially faced open hostility and discrimination, Black people faced hostility and discrimination that were much more severe and persistent.[10] A temporary stopover in America's slums would not be the case for most Black people.

Given Black people's social and economic status in the United States, their wealth could not lie in material resources. Instead, their sense of wealth would have to become embodied in the relationships, the interdependence, and the community they formed with one another. According to one former resident of the Court, "Everyone in the Alley and the Court knew each other and counted on one another in order to survive; it was a village and we were village children."

In Birmingham, the Alley and the Court (we pronounced it as "coat") were ghettos created by a U.S. power hierarchy that prized profits over people and white over Black. Located about three blocks from each other, the Alley and the Court were two different residential areas that both consisted of shotgun-style houses. They sat a few yards from a set of railroad tracks that ran almost parallel to the shotgun houses. Black residents seamlessly flowed between the Alley and the Court, although separated by a few blocks, and related families often lived between the two.

Unlike the Black poor residing in places like the Alley and the Court, those who worked as teachers in the segregated schools or who preached in the local Black churches in Birmingham were able to shield themselves and their children, to a certain degree, from racial hatred. Some of these working-class and lower-middle-class Black people rented or owned their homes. Another group, Black professionals, built a vibrant community for themselves, most notably the Smithfield Community. Built in the early 1900s, Smithfield was home to prominent residents such as Alabama's first Black millionaire, A. G. Gaston, as well as political activist Angela Davis.[11] Smithfield is featured in the National Museum of African-American History in Washington, D.C. But most Black people in search of housing in Birmingham had no choice but to contend with the racial and social class structures that drove a wedge between Black and white people.

⬱

Our immediate family (at the time my mother, five older brothers, and myself) lived in one of Birmingham's slum areas known as Twenty-Ninth Court. Our maternal grandmother, Mama, lived a few blocks away in the Alley. As children, we did not use the title "Mama" in reference to our mother. Instead, we called her by her first name, Joann, a practice that Ronnie, the firstborn son, started and the rest of us mimicked.[12] Ronnie was born when our mother (Joann) was sixteen and still living in the household with her mother (Mama). That household included our mother and her newborn son and our mother's five younger siblings (Maxine, Eddie, Sandra, Brenda, and Alonzo). There was only one Mama in that household. After our mother married Richard Morris Sr. and began renting a house with her new husband, Ronnie continued to live with Mama in the Alley.

Uniformly painted a light green or brownish-gray color, rows of shotgun-style houses lined the Court's and the Alley's dusty grounds.[13] The Hardie Tynes Foundry that produced industrial equipment for Birmingham's iron industry sat just a few yards from the house where we lived. Its smells and noises were constants. In the house where we lived, like the other houses in the Court, a couple of wooden chairs always sat

Twenty-Ninth Court in Birmingham. As an infant, I lived with my family in the house in the photo where the three males (two of whom are my biological brothers) are playing basketball. The Clency family (my biological father and his family) lived in the house where the couple is on the porch and the two children are in the doorway. (Photos courtesy of Clara Clency Moorer.)

on the narrow front porch. The house's four rooms were directly behind each other; there were no hallways. The furniture included two beds, a chifforobe to hang and store clothes, a rubboard our mother used to wash our clothes, and a card table that doubled as a dining table. The house where Mama lived was similar. In one of the rooms sat a juke-box that she used to play music for everyone in the area who was in a partying mood. A bathroom was attached crudely to the back part of the house. At the very back, behind where Mama lived, residents would keep a fire going, often burning old trash in a heap on the ground.

Families assembled in the first room where the potbelly stove kept them warm in the wintertime. To avoid the searing summer sun, young and old sat on front porches to stay cool and catch up on the latest gossip. The houses' layouts were conducive to conversation, whether on the porch or in the front room. Children played and adults walked the dusty alleyway.

Inside the Alley's shotgun houses is where Mama served as a local midwife delivering Black babies in familial environments, offering an alternative to the cold hospital basements that were designated for "colored" people. As Mama practiced the ancient tradition of midwifery, her second oldest daughter, Maxine, watched her every move and sometimes assisted in the deliveries of the babies. Mama was a community midwife, having delivered many of the children in the Alley and the Court, including two of our mother's children.

Mama (known as Ms. OC—short for Oceola Collins—by local residents) was born around 1916, purportedly in Akron, Ohio. While she would later change her name to Oceola, her birth name was Alice. Moses DeYampert and Adella Thomas were listed as her father and mother, respectively, although it was believed that they were not her actual birth parents. It was suspected that they informally adopted her—not an uncommon practice for Black people at that time. Oceola (whom we referred to as Mama) lived an itinerant home life throughout childhood, having lived between blood and nonrelated family members in Akron, Birmingham and Tuscaloosa, Alabama, and Washington, D.C. One nonrelated family was the Collins family in Alabama, who allowed her to live with them when she was about eleven years old. The Collins family listed her on the 1930 U.S. census as their daughter. They also had a son named William Collins, a childhood friend with whom Mama would enter into a common-law marriage. According to family lore, Mama had once attended the famous Dunbar High School in Washington, D.C., where she lived for a few years with a step-grandfather. She then returned to Birmingham and attended Industrial High School (later renamed A. H. Parker High School)—the first public high school in Birmingham built for Black people.[14]

My maternal grandfather—Joe Steele Jr.—was born in 1920 in Birmingham to Lula Smith and Joe Steele Sr., who had migrated from Selma, Alabama, to Birmingham to work in the city's steel mills and foundries. Nonunionized labor by Joe Steele Sr., and other Black men from the state's rural towns, would lead to the astronomical growth in Birmingham's steel mills and blast furnaces at the latter part of the nineteenth century and the beginning of the twentieth. This growth earned Birmingham nicknames such as "Magic City" and "Pittsburgh of the South."[15] Joe Steele Sr.'s path from the rural landscape to Birmingham's foundries would mirror that of thousands of other Black men.[16] They had left the Black Belt in droves, escaping the former plantations in search of an opportunity to build a new life.[17]

My maternal grandmother and grandfather separated when my mother was a toddler—shortly after he had returned from the military. They eventually divorced when my mother was a young girl. My maternal grandfather, Joe Steele Jr., remarried and started another family. Mama never officially remarried after she and Joe Steele Jr. divorced. However, she would maintain a common-law marriage with William Collins, the young man whom she had grown up with. They would go on to have three children together. By the time my mother was a preteen, her contact with her father had decreased significantly. Sometimes her father and his new wife, Emma Carr Steele (nicknamed "Baby Love") would drive over to pick my mother up and take her to spend time with them and their children. At other times Mama would send my mother (Joann) to her father's workplace, the American Cast Iron Pipe Company (ACIPCO), to get money from him. It was common back then for Black mothers who did not live with their children's father to send their children to get money from him. This would especially be the case if the father had another wife and family.

Mama earned money during the 1950s and 1960s by renting out rooms to boarders, mostly Black men, in a house that she leased from a white man. Mama's common-law husband, William Collins, and his older brother, "Uncle C," each had a room in this boarding house. People in the Alley and the Court who frequented the boarding house nicknamed it the Collins Hotel. The Collins Hotel served as one of the few places where the Black underclass on that side of town could get a room for the night. Otherwise, Black people across class levels stayed in similar establishments throughout the city because of racist hotel policies or would bunk up for the night with friends and relatives.[18] The Collins Hotel stood on the corner of Twenty-Sixth Street and Second Avenue, less than two blocks south of where Birmingham's main post office is presently located. Customers paid weekly rent, usually around seven dollars. Mama and her children occupied some of the rooms. She rented the other rooms to nightly, weekly, or monthly guests. Mama had to keep an eye on the numerous men who frequented there, especially those who couldn't keep their eyes off her two oldest daughters.

In addition to renting rooms, Mama sold shots of whiskey to customers and used some of the earnings to employ Black women who helped clean the rooms and cook. The money also allowed Mama to pay some of the tuition for her three oldest children to attend Our Lady of Fatima Catholic School, part of the city's Black Catholic school system, for a few years.[19] After finishing eighth grade there, my mother and her siblings attended Immaculata Catholic High School, the city's Black Catholic high school. Mama's second-oldest daughter, Maxine, took pride in her schooling: "We went to good schools, and Mama paid for our books; we didn't have to use the books from the public schools," said my Aunt Maxine.

While running the boarding house and bootlegging whiskey, Mama shopped for food, cooked for the boarders, laundered their clothes, and delivered babies as a midwife. This labor of love and risk taking offered some semblance of stability and normalcy for her children. Like other Black women of the time, Mama did this work while contending with pervasively harmful racial and gender ideas about Black women, particularly those from the underclass.[20] As a participant in the informal labor economy as an entrepreneur, and what some scholars who have studied similar groups of Black women in New York describe as "off the books laborer," Mama worked to earn money not just for her own survival but also for her children's futures.[21] Maybe the loss of six babies earlier in her life due to miscarriage and stillbirth—before Joann, her seventh child, was born—drove Mama to take whatever risks necessary to ensure a decent living for herself and her children. Sending her children to Catholic schools for a time represented one way of ensuring their futures.

With beaming eyes, my mother would speak admiringly of her teachers at the Catholic schools, the nuns. At one time my mother aspired to join their ranks in the Church. My mother's other dream was to become a professional secretary because of what many described as her nearly flawless penmanship. When my mother was a teenager, her step-grandfather, who lived in Washington, D.C., sent money for her to purchase a typewriter. My mother prided herself on her writing and speaking abilities during grade school. She would boast of the time that she "earned two As for my impeccable and verbatim recitation of President Abraham Lincoln's Gettysburg Address." Unfortunately, my mother's schooling abruptly stopped when she became pregnant with her first child in 1958. She was sixteen and a sophomore at Immaculata High School.

The man who raped my mother when she was a teenager was in his mid-fifties and a regular overnight guest at the Collins Hotel. He was known as Papa Slim, and he was a "friend of the family" who would often pat her on her legs and say, "Oh, your legs so pretty!" Born around 1900, Papa Slim was a tall and dark-brown-skinned man whose daily attire included overalls, workman boots, and a farmer's hat. He always carried a newspaper in one hand and would have a pipe in his mouth that he occasionally smoked. Papa Slim was nearly toothless—except for two canines on the top and two incisors on the bottom. He worked as an independent laborer with Grayson Lumber Company, based in Alabama, and sometimes hired other Black men to work for him. Papa Slim was known to keep money, and he would often loan it to his coworkers at low interest rates. Papa Slim owned several cars, regularly flashed his cash, and frequently doled out money to women, especially the young ones.

Shortly after my mother's pregnancy began to show, she withdrew from Immaculata High School because administrators prevented pregnant girls from attending. My mother would have transferred into Parker High School, the oldest public Black high school in Alabama, but she felt stigmatized and embarrassed about her predicament. This thrust into motherhood and the judgment that followed resulted in my mother withdrawing from high school altogether.

Over the years, my mother regretted not finishing high school. Rather than casting blame on others, she assumed responsibility for the pregnancy. She absolved Immaculata's administrators' strict beliefs about pregnancy from her having to leave school prematurely. She did not criticize her mother or father. She did not even blame Papa Slim: "That was my decision; I knew what the hell I was doing!" is how she responded when asked about the circumstances surrounding the pregnancy and the rape. Maxine, my aunt, however, would provide a different perspective. She described how Papa Slim had been "like a member of the family; he was Mama's friend."

When Aunt Maxine and my mother were much younger, Papa Slim would drive them around in one of his many cars, often taking them out for ice cream. Papa Slim represented an extension of the family, later allowing Aunt Maxine and her husband, Monroe, to borrow one of his cars when they got married until they could purchase one of their own. In addition to giving them treats like ice cream when they were young, Papa Slim allowed the young girls to earn spending money by paying them to clean up his room in the boarding house. My mother used the extra money to buy *Archie* comic books, which she loved. My mother cleaned Papa Slim's room much more than Maxine did. There was a trust that had been built between Papa Slim, Aunt Maxine, and my mother—a trust that would ultimately make them as young Black girls vulnerable to men like Papa Slim. For example, Aunt Maxine talked about how Papa Slim "got us used to him when we were young, and I guess he slowly got Joann to trust him. Men back then always would give little girls money to try to get to them, you know what I mean?" After Aunt Maxine told me about what really went on, I was not shocked because I had seen similar behavior when I was growing up in Central City. This grooming could be between adult men and teenage girls as well as between adult men and teenage boys.

While renting rooms at the boarding house and bootlegging whiskey provided opportunities for Mama to earn a living while raising her children, these activities also placed the children in very vulnerable positions with the adults who frequented the boarding house. Whereas Black mothers in Mama's predicament knew the risks of engaging in illegal activities out of the view of white people and law enforcers, they generally could not turn to legal authorities when things went awry. So street justice was the only way to punish perpetrators.[22] Shortly after the news of my mother's pregnancy, William Collins—my Aunt Maxine's father—confronted Papa Slim with a butcher's knife. Mama and my mother's merciful pleading prevented Collins from killing Papa Slim, who fled out of the hotel. Papa Slim returned only after things had simmered down. Upon his return, he apologized to Mama, Collins, and my mother. Then he vowed to them that he would take care of the baby.

Aunt Maxine also talked about how my mother's lighter complexion was one reason my mother and one of her close friends, Laura Jane, were very vulnerable to many older men's sexual desires. My mother sometimes described how people jokingly called her "Salt," due to her light-brown complexion, and Aunt Maxine "Pepper" because of her dark-brown complexion. In the *color-struck* world that Black people lived within, the lighter a person's skin color, the more beautiful a person was perceived, especially in girls and women. While growing up in the 1970s and 1980s, we used the word "color-struck" when describing some Black people's emphasis on skin complexion.[23]

The idea of being color-struck, however, is rooted in much deeper ideas about racial superiority created by white people that placed white over Black and created a structure within Black communities that would lead to our placement of lighter community members over darker ones. Academics today use the word "colorism" when referring to what we called color-struck.[24] Historically, colorism has advantaged lighter-complexion Black people who were more likely to gain greater access to social, economic, and educational opportunities than those with a darker hue. This phenomenon is evident in the earliest members of the "Black middle class" arising out of enslavement, people who were overwhelmingly lighter skinned.[25] But having lighter skin did not protect young girls like my mother from the sensual desires of adult males.

The pregnancy dashed my mother's hope of becoming a nun or a secretary. The growing baby inside was a reminder that she would soon become a mother. Upon her first child's birth in 1959, my mother moved out of the room she shared with her sister Maxine. She occupied a separate bedroom in the boarding house with Ronnie, her new baby son.

Less than a year after Ronnie's birth, my mother began dating a young man who was a few years older. He was a tall, slender, and brown-skinned man with a slightly reddish hue and dark curly hair. My mother thought that they could have a meaningful relationship. This young man's actions, however, would indicate this was not the way he felt. Not long after they had begun seeing each other, my mother would become pregnant by the young man. After revealing that she was pregnant by him, he stopped visiting the boarding house. He didn't tell my mother about the other young woman that he was seeing and also impregnated.

My mother would later meet Richard Lee Morris Sr. (Richard Sr.), a Korean War veteran. Richard Sr. had moved to Birmingham from the nearby rural town of Columbiana. He was thirteen years older than my mother and occasionally stayed in the Collins Hotel when seeking seasonal work in Birmingham. A dark-skinned man with curly hair, Richard Sr. had a quiet disposition. He proposed to marry my mother, all the while knowing that she had a son who was a little more than a year old and knowing that she was pregnant by another man. Before my mother and Richard Sr. would marry, Mama pleaded for my mother to leave Ronnie with her, instead of taking the toddler into the marriage. Mama, instead of my mother, would raise Ronnie during the first few years of his life. Mama also had a son (Alonzo) who was one month younger than Ronnie.

My mother and Richard Morris Sr. married in 1961. Eighteen at the time, she would give birth to a second baby boy. The new couple named the baby boy Richard Jr., although the baby was not Richard Sr.'s biological son. Richard Sr.'s willingness to marry my mother and to name the baby after him was likely shaped by the fact that when Richard Sr. was a little boy growing up in Columbiana, he was raised by his mother and a man who was not his biological father.

After my mother and Richard Morris Sr. married in 1961, they moved into the Court. They would have three sons together (Kenneth, Michael, and Maurice). Richard Sr. would take care of the family through his work in the lumberyard. Papa Slim, of all people, had hired him. My mother described how Richard Sr. entrusted her with the money from his paycheck, boasting about how he would give her the entire check and she would pay the bills, buy food, and buy clothes and household items, and then she would give him a little bit of the money back so that he could "go to the whiskey house and buy himself some beer or a shot or two of whiskey."

⌐

A couple of years after the birth of my mother's and Richard Sr.'s third son, Maurice, they would separate due to my mother's pregnancy by another man. Rumors began circulating in the Alley and the Court that a man by the name of Charlie Ray Clency was secretively visiting the house to see my mother. They lived in shotgun houses located directly across from one another.

As he vividly noted how we lived in a "little bitty shotgun-type house," Ronnie, my oldest brother, casually described how "dudes" like Charlie Ray would "hone in on when a woman was struggling financially." Charlie Ray, according to Ronnie, was one of those dudes who came around when our mother needed help to buy food for her five boys. Always one to add a little humor to a very serious situation, Ronnie said that "short, fat, Black, and ugly Charlie Ray would come over to our house and bring the five of us some sweets from the bakery and give Joann some money to help pay her bills. Jerome, when you were born I knew by your head that Richard wasn't your daddy. Charlie Ray was your daddy!"

My mother had had a husband who would come and go. And Charlie Ray Clency had a family, which included his wife, four sons, and two daughters. Charlie Ray was almost twenty years older than my mother, and his other children were teens and young adults at the time of my birth in 1968. Gossip spread quickly that my mother and Charlie Ray had had a child together. While Charlie Ray did all he could to keep this information quiet, my mother told me the truth about my birth: "I ain't going to lie and put you on somebody else. Charlie Ray is your daddy, Jerome."

Charlie Ray supported his wife and their children through gambling, bootlegging whiskey, and serving as a "police pimp." It was common knowledge that rogue white police officers relied on Charlie Ray and other Black informants to keep them abreast of the happenings in the Alley, the Court, and different Black sections of town. To avoid incarceration, Charlie Ray and other bootleggers—Black and white—would pay off the police officers. It was customary for so-called bootleggers to provide white police officers in Birmingham with a payment during Christmastime. Even Mama gave them money and gifts. This way, she too avoided incarceration. But Mama was forced to stop selling liquor once the police began harassing her. She suspected that someone in the Alley or the Court had snitched on her.

CHAPTER 3   CONVERGENCE

Downtown Birmingham—specifically Central City—is approximately 250 miles from Memphis, Tennessee. But what happened in Memphis on April 4, 1968, would reverberate throughout Central City, Birmingham, the United States, and the world. On that day, a sniper's bullet tore into Dr. Martin Luther King Jr.'s flesh, as he stood tall on the balcony of the Lorraine Motel in Memphis. King had been advised by other members of the Southern Christian Leadership Conference (SCLC) to focus on issues of greater importance than striking Black sanitation workers. Nevertheless, Dr. King went to Memphis to support the workers who were grossly mistreated and underpaid. The deaths of Echol Cole and Robert Walker, two Black men crushed in the back of a garbage truck while seeking shelter from a torrential Memphis storm, galvanized more than a thousand striking Black sanitation workers. The strike not only highlighted Memphis's overwhelmingly large and impoverished Black community but also raised awareness about economic and human rights injustices facing folks living in poverty.[1]

A day after King's assassination, Black discontent was further set ablaze throughout the urban United States, resulting in a Black rebellion in more than a hundred cities from coast to coast. The social unrest following King's murder brought immense national attention to how poverty, segregated housing, and educational inequalities resulted from racial and economic injustices. One week after King's assassination, and to calm the Black uprising, Congress quickly passed, by a wide margin, Title VIII of the Civil Rights Act of 1968, commonly referred to as the Fair Housing Act. This act prohibits discrimination in the sale, rental, and financing of housing based on race, religion, and national origin.

Decades prior to its hurried passage in 1968, members of Congress fili-
bustered fair housing bills and never treated it as a serious issue.

Amid the racial and social class tensions of 1968, everyday Black
people still had to live their lives. They went to work, took children to
school, shopped for groceries, took care of family members, buried the
departed, and celebrated birthdays. December 5, 1968, was my mother's
twenty-sixth birthday and the day she signed the lease to move my five
older brothers and me into a three-bedroom apartment in Central City.
I was eight months at the time. Our family's opportunity to move into
Central City directly emerged from the unrest following the assassination of Dr. King on April 4, 1968. Like others searching for better living
conditions, my mother sought consistent heat, reliable appliances, hot
water, and paved sidewalks—taken-for-granted conveniences missing
from many of the shotgun houses in the Alley and the Court. Separated
from her husband, Richard Morris Sr., and with no verifiable income
other than a welfare check and food stamps, my mother enthusiastically
signed the lease as a sort of birthday present for herself and with a sense
of pride and accomplishment as the mother of six sons. She described
how everything in Central City was "immaculate." She awed at the por-
celain sinks and bathtubs, the clotheslines that hung in the backyard,
and the laundry facilities in the basement if she needed to use them.

"Whoo chi'd! Joann kept that apartment clean when y'all were little
growing up there. She wasn't nasty; can't nobody say that 'bout her," said
Aunt Sandra, one of my mother's younger sisters. The milkman, who
was white, would deliver bottles of locally owned Barber's milk that was
placed inside a plastic crate. He placed the filled bottles of milk on the
apartment steps in exchange for the empty bottles. Moreover, whenever
the grass had gotten too high, Central City's maintenance staff promptly
mowed. The mostly white residents in Central could count on maintenance workers' timely repairing and painting of the premises.

My two older brothers, Ronnie and Richard Jr., vividly recalled our
family's move out of the Court. They remembered the drastic change
from wood-burning stoves and the poorly insulated dwellings in the
Court to the comforting warmth of the radiator heat in Central City.
They cherished the memories and lasting friendships with their Black
peers in the Alley and the Court. They also remembered playing and
laughing with their new white peers in Central City and what Richard
Jr. described as the "peace between Black and white people." According to Ronnie, Central City was "paradise." The sense of peace and par-

The Central City apartments during legalized segregation (1957).
(Courtesy, Birmingham Public Library Archives.)

adise that Richard Jr. and Ronnie felt during those early days, however, quickly vanished as the numbers of Black people moving into Central City increased. Black people began experiencing backlash and white rage from some white people who resented these minor civil rights gains.[2] We were, according to Ronnie and Richard Jr., the second Black family to move into Central City, and other Black families who knew us would follow. White people keenly watched the Black families move in. At first, there were only a few Black families in Central City, and Ronnie and Richard Jr. felt welcomed by the white families and children. Then other Black families moved in, and white parents began to show their rage as my mother described during an interview I conducted with her in 1998, a few years before commencing the research project: "This little white girl pushed Richard off his bicycle; Richard then hit her. The girl's mother called the police on Richard. I then yelled to the woman and asked her why would she call the police on a seven-year-old child. He's just a little boy." Our mother then asked Richard why he hit the girl, and Richard reminded our mother that she had taught him to hit back if anyone ever hit him.

A white exodus began. Consumed with rage related to the fear of Black advancement, white families began to leave Central City and also resorted to pulling their children out of Powell and Phillips. They used concerns about the quality of the neighborhood and fears of Black crime as reasons. Ronnie and Richard Jr. would be the few Black children in the neighborhood for no more than two years. As white families with children fleeing the neighborhood reached a "tipping point," and the white elderly were the only white people who remained.[3]

One of the first Black persons to move into Central City was Ms. Washington, an elderly woman who also attended the all-white Central Church of Christ adjacent to Central City at Seventh Avenue and Twenty-Fifth Street North. Over the years, my brothers and I would take out Ms. Washington's trash, help change the sheets on her bed, and go to the store for her. We cherished the dime and the Nabisco graham crackers that Ms. Washington gave us for helping her. By the early 1970s, many more Black families had moved into Central City.

Ms. Rosie Lee Jackson and her son represented one such family. They moved into Central City in 1973 after the death of her uncle, whom she had lived with at the time. She was a single mother raising a son named Roderick. Like many of the city's Black residents, Ms. Jackson's family had come to Birmingham from the state's rural areas and found some refuge in the shotgun houses. Ms. Jackson, now in her nineties, has since been relocated to Smithfield Court, the first and oldest public housing complex in the city of Birmingham. While sitting in her Smithfield Court apartment watching an Auburn University football game on television, Ms. Jackson addressed my interview questions only during commercial breaks. She enthusiastically described how she and her family had first migrated from a rural area known as Snowhill, Alabama, in the early 1900s. Ms. Jackson's family, like millions of Black people, fled the rural South for southern, northern, or western cities. Her mother's folks stopped in Birmingham.

Ms. Jackson was born in 1929. When she was a little girl, her uncle, her mother's brother, saw the living conditions she was having to endure by living with her mother and siblings on "Thirty-First Street North [in Birmingham]." Ms. Jackson's family lived approximately four blocks from the Court, and it was "not too far," as Ms. Jackson said, "from the Buffalo Rock Plant [located on Tenth Avenue and Twenty-Sixth Street North]. . . . My uncle passed by our house on Thirty-First Street and he got me from my momma and he raised me." While being raised by her mother's brother, Ms. Jackson helped out financially as soon as she was able to work. She even washed clothes and cleaned white folks' houses when she was a teenager, generally being paid fifty cents for four hours of work.

Ms. Jackson would go on to graduate from Parker High School, but she still found herself having to clean white folks' houses because of the limited job opportunities for Black women in the forties and fifties. Her uncle eventually moved the family into a house in an area of the city known as Inglenook (near the present Birmingham-Shuttlesworth International Airport). After being there a short time, her uncle died and she became sick. Ms. Jackson, with a keen memory and the ability to switch between the interview with me and the Auburn game, described how she was able to move into Central City during the early 1970s: "I couldn't work at the time, but I had a child. I didn't have the money to pay the rent; that is why I was able to move in [into Central City later on]."

As Black families like Ms. Jackson and her son moved into Central City in increasing numbers, white people quickly left. Even the mostly white Central Church of Christ would lose members and eventually shut its doors. Nonetheless, if white people had remained in Central City alongside their increasing numbers of Black neighbors, their decisions to stay could have symbolically represented some degree of civic and civil rights progress for Birmingham and the larger national story of integration in public housing. However, those white families living in poverty and that could flee into nearby suburbs with the assistance of federal housing vouchers and other kinds of support were intent on holding on to whatever little valuable commodity they possessed, namely the unearned but psychological wage from having white skin. Whiteness has historically operated like money and serves as a kind of property and a psychological wage for white people.[4] White people convert their whiteness into tangible and intangible benefits across many areas, including employment opportunities, schooling, housing, the legal system, and many more.[5] The notion that whiteness is a wage or property did not begin or end with Central City, or Birmingham, or the state of Alabama. Throughout U.S. history, white people have taken measures to ensure they maintain their majority status in the most desired jobs, neighborhoods, and schools.

The federal government's unwillingness to support policies that could potentially contribute to racially diverse neighborhoods in suburban communities further demonstrated the Kerner Commission's realization that the United States had become "two nations."[6] Supported by banks and real estate agents who would spread fear among white people

Three residents in Central City. Note the managerial neglect as demonstrated by the deteriorating conditions once Black residents moved into Central City (undated). (Courtesy, Birmingham Public Library Archives.)

about Black people's arrival, white residents' decisions to flee central cities throughout the United States are not very different from those that occur today. However, this consistent departure of white people away from Black people in housing and schooling often becomes framed with coded language that substitutes social class for race. Demographic shifts reify entrenched racial patterns of segregation and economic inequality. The racial stigmatizing of Black people and the fear that white home values will plummet with the presence of Black people represent some of the key reasons why white people desire to maintain racially segregated neighborhoods, even if some of them say they would like to live in more racially diverse areas.[7]

As the complexion of Central City's residents changed by the early 1970s, maintenance crews mowed the lawns and tended to the premises less frequently. There is the general perception held by some that the overwhelming presence of Black people in a community eventually "brings it down." Embedded in this thinking is the notion that Black people do not take care of the communities where they live. I assert that it is not so much about Black people bringing an area down. When Black people primarily become renters, instead of homeowners, landlords and city officials are not as responsive to their complaints as they are to white families' complaints. Still, the fleeing of white people from Central City did not cramp our style. Used to functioning away from their everyday gaze, those of us in Central City adjusted to what would become a reality and became even more committed to making Central City *our community*, even if the white people were leaving.[8]

CHAPTER 4   A LINK IN THE CHAIN

Though no longer living with us, my mother's husband and my stepfather, Richard Morris Sr., continued to visit us in Central City during the early years, between 1969 and 1975. Christmastime was especially memorable. Richard Sr. would bring a small gift for everyone in the household, including me. He and our mother played music throughout the day, ate the delicious chicken and dressing that our mother had prepared, drank beer, and reminisced about the good times. Richard Sr. also drank the whiskey that he had stashed in his coat pocket. My mother and Richard Sr. sat and listened to the songs on the record player. One of the most memorable songs for me was "Please Come Home for Christmas" by the legendary blues singer Charles Brown. As a child, I always thought the song was titled "Bells will be ringing, the sad, sad, blues. . . ." Richard Sr. and our mother hugged and laughed, and everybody appeared happy. But those pleasant times would be fleeting. Richard Sr. eventually stopped coming around regularly. He would make one unexpected visit to Central City when I was about ten years old. At the time, he had recently been released from the hospital and still had some bandages on his forehead. He informed my mother that a couple of white police officers had beaten him up.

Over the years, Richard Sr. moved in and out of boarding houses and wandered throughout the city, often along railroad tracks. He lived the life of a hobo, seemingly traveling without a destination. We had always suspected that he was probably shell-shocked—a condition that later became classified as posttraumatic stress disorder (PTSD) resulting from combat and war-zone exposure during the Korean War.[1] Richard Sr. withdrew from confrontations and anything else that seemed to stress him. Even some of his family members in Columbiana, Alabama—a rural town only forty-five minutes southeast of Birmingham—rarely heard from him. To get in touch with him, Richard Sr.'s siblings would drive to Birmingham and search the various boarding houses.

But Richard Sr. rarely talked about his time at war and never got medical help or treatment for PTSD, although researchers have found PTSD in 80 percent of Korean War veterans who have sought psychiatric help.[2] Unfortunately, Black military veterans like Richard Sr. disproportionately served on the front lines of battles, and despite experiencing PTSD at higher rates than other racial and ethnic groups, they have seldom received adequate psychiatric treatment.[3] Black military personnel, in every U.S. war, have fought an enemy abroad and racism and discrimination when they returned to the United States.[4]

Our mother raised the six of us, her sons, alone. However, now and then, she wanted some time to relax. To get away, she occasionally visited a local juke joint, the WW Lounge, to hear some good music. As the youngest of the six boys, I often went with her when she had to go out. One particular day she had Ronnie and Richard Jr., the two oldest, watch Maurice, Kenneth, and Michael. Holding my hand, our mother pulled me along as we walked across Seventh Avenue and Twenty-Fifth Street, four blocks east of downtown Birmingham. We walked a little more than one block from our apartment to the WW Lounge on Eighth Avenue North. Still, she kept me close to her. My three-year-old legs struggled to keep pace with her. She moved quickly, and I did my best to keep up. With a perfectly shaped sandy-brown Afro, hoop earrings, a white blouse, a short dark skirt, and high-heeled shoes that accentuated her muscular calves, our mother knew that she "looked good" when she strutted down the sidewalk.

"How is everybody doing?" our mother asked upon entering the WW Lounge. Once inside the dimly lit and small air-conditioned building, I whiffed the mixed aroma of fried fish, French fries, and beer. I clung to our mother's legs, and then she heaved me up and placed me on a barstool. "Stay right here, Jerome," she commanded while making her way over to the Rock-Ola. Looking around at everyone, I noticed a few familiar faces, particularly Ms. Chubby, who was about our mother's age.

Our mother inserted some coins into the Rock-Ola and carefully selected a stream of hit songs, including "What's Going On" by Marvin Gaye, "Have You Seen Her" by the Chi-Lites, and "Clean Up Woman" by Betty Wright. As the grown folks' music blared across the small hole in a wall, I asked my mother if she could "play me sumthin." She scrolled through and selected "ABC" by the Jackson Five. Sitting on the barstool with my feet dangling, I began to bob my head to the rhythmic beats. Our mother then placed her order: "Chubby, let me get a bag of onion rings, a bottle of Grapico, a can of Schlitz beer, and a plain bag of Golden Flake potato chips. Also, hand me a paper towel," my mother requested, as she gave Ms. Chubby the money. After ringing everything up on the bulky cash register, Ms. Chubby placed the items on the table. Enjoying the music, I became exceptionally cheerful when my mother handed me the bag of onion-ring chips and a bottle of Grapico—a purple-colored and grape-tasting soda mainly sold in Louisiana and Alabama. Out of habit, she then wiped the beer can's rim with a paper towel before she took a sip. After I had devoured the bag of onion ring chips, Ms. Chubby turned toward me and said, "Hey baby, here's one on the house," while handing me another bag of chips. Excited, I couldn't wait to tell Maurice, my brother who was two years older than me, that I had eaten two bags of chips!

Shortly, a side conversation between my mother and Ms. Chubby ensued for a few minutes but in a whispering tone: "Joann, what in the hell were you trying to prove by telling Janice that you and Slick been going together? You think you gonna just disrespect me like that?" My mother immediately countered, "Don't bring that shit up to me, Chubby. In fact, I can do whatever in the hell I want and be with whomever I want!" With the pitch rising in her voice, my mother continued, "I came over here to get me a beer and sit and listen to my music, but you're going to bring up something you know nothing about!" My mother walked toward the bar to retrieve another paper towel but came away with a handful of blood oozing from the back of her head. "I told you heifer! I don't care if you think you're going with him, or whatever you call it. Slick's my man!" shouted Ms. Chubby. I looked up and saw Ms. Chubby holding a gun in her hand. She had hit my mother in the back of her head with the gun's butt. This seemed odd to me because minutes before Ms. Chubby had treated me nicely.

My mother appeared hysterical after being struck in the head. "Jerome, come here quick!" she shouted, after gaining her composure for a moment. I dashed over to hold her hand. There she was, lying on the floor in a pool of blood, and there was little that I could do. Ms. Chubby had a gun! My new Charlie Brown–style zigzagged shirt was becoming bloodied. My mother struggled to get up and while holding my hand made her way to the front of the building. She opened the door and immediately fell on the ground between Twenty-Fifth and Twenty-Sixth

Street North. With my new yellow and black Charlie Brown shirt now pinkish-red, I held on to my mother's hand. "Stay close to me," she said. "Stay close to me," all the while crying.

As we sat outside on the sidewalk, passing onlookers in cars paused while others walking stopped to see what was going on. A woman, whose name I couldn't remember but someone whom I had seen before, put her arms around me. "Where the ambulam?" I asked. "Get the ambulam," I pleaded. A crowd began to form and through it emerged Kenneth, one of my brothers, running frantically, apparently after hearing the news that something terrible had happened to our mother. Kenneth came screaming from around the corner after crossing the Seventh Avenue side of Central City. He was crying uncontrollably, something I had never seen before.

It seemed like we sat there for eternity. Then, against the dusky sun and the Birmingham skyline, red lights twirled while wailing sirens blared—slowly making their way toward us. Two white males— the driver and passenger—got out of the ambulance and placed my mother—now covered in a bloodstained blouse—into the vehicle. By then Ronnie and Richard Jr. had arrived to pick me up and take me home. Michael and Maurice were also with them.

My mother eventually filed charges against Ms. Chubby. The white male judge charged her with "one count of battery." After hearing the facts of the case, the judge told my mother, "You are a lover and not a fighter." I was clueless about what this phrase meant when my mother would laughingly tell people that the judge had said this to her in the courtroom. About six months after being hit in the head, my mother delivered a stillborn son named Steve Morris. Steve was buried in an unmarked grave in a local cemetery, without a funeral. My mother would receive no record of his birth because the state of Alabama did not provide birth certificates for babies considered stillborn.

A dark brown and relatively short male—nicknamed Slick—was a playboy in the area and the alleged father of several babies by different women. Proudly, my mother had told everyone it was Slick's baby that she was carrying, which made Ms. Chubby and a few other women upset. A little more than a year after the altercation and the stillbirth of her son and our brother, my mother became pregnant again and eventually gave birth to a healthy baby girl named Shelda. My mother told everyone that Slick was also Shelda's father.

❏

During the early to mid-1980s, my teenage years, Central City was given a facelift and renamed Metropolitan Gardens as part of an effort to beautify downtown Birmingham. Despite the name change, those of us living there still referred to the public housing complex as Central City, and so did Black people throughout the city. After the renovation, Ms. Chubby and her two teenage daughters had moved into a Central City apartment near Twenty-Fourth Street and Sixth Avenue North, only a couple of blocks from us and directly across the street from Powell Elementary School. They, too, had moved out of the Alley.

As a teenager, I often walked past Ms. Chubby's apartment on my way to the neighborhood convenience store, and I would see her on the new front porch. "How you doing, Jerome?" she would ask. I always reciprocated with a smile and "I'm fine Ms. Chubby, how is everything going with you?" Even though the incident had happened years earlier, I had vividly remembered the events. I liked Ms. Chubby a lot as a child; but shortly afterward, I began to think that she was a mean person because of what she had done to my mother some years earlier. I always wondered if Ms. Chubby felt that I was just too young at the age of three to have remembered what took place that day back in 1971. Despite my mother's and Ms. Chubby's earlier animosity toward one another, Ms. Chubby was always pleasant toward my siblings and me. She and my mother still talked when they saw each other. They were linked. For years, our families had known each other, having come up together out of the Alley and the Court. However, the insidious competition for attention from one young man had turned two young women from neighbors into temporary enemies.

Slick's "ladies' man" reputation increased after this incident, so much so that many of the younger boys in the area were in awe at how Slick "dealt with the ladies." They all laughed at and admired the courage Slick displayed to get with women—once jumping out of a second-floor bedroom window when one woman's husband had arrived home! But most of the time Slick did not have to go through such measures. The numbers were in his favor, and he, like some of the other young men in the area, did not have to obligate himself to any particular woman. Given the scarcity of available males, he had little competition. Mortality rates, drugs, joblessness, the police, and prisons took a toll on many of the young Black males who had grown up in the Alley and the Court. Consequently, sharing a man would sometimes occur, very often to other women's chagrin.

Mrs. Joann
Steele Morris,
the author's
mother, standing
in Metropolitan
Gardens (formerly
Central City).
(Source: Author's
collection.)

As the years passed by, the memories and pains had begun to leave scars on my mother. To soothe the hurt, she turned to her music. Whenever her favorite songs would come over the radio, she stood and began singing and dancing, snapping her fingers, swaying her hips, and clapping her hands in a syncopated manner to the soulful sounds of hits such as Aretha Franklin's "Chain of Fools."

CHAPTER 5   BLUE BLACK

My mother had always told me that a man named Charlie Ray Clency, and not Richard Morris Sr., was my biological father. I do not remember exactly when she told me, but I was very young at the time, possibly around three years old. Whenever she told me, it was not a major revelation or occurrence at any particular moment. Even if my mother had not told me, I had already heard my older brothers' many stories and jokes about Charlie Ray, particularly about his physical features. They described him as being a very dark-skinned man, what we called *blue black*. I could only laugh along with my brothers because I had no reference point for how he looked. We had few photos in the house, and definitely not one of him. Because my brothers were a number of years older than me and remembered vividly seeing Charlie Ray in the Court, I first relied on their descriptions. Around the age of eight, I decided that I wanted to see how this man looked—this man whom my brothers connected me to and whom they said I resembled by the head. His presence was not something that I missed in my life. I was just curious to know about this person whom my brothers sometimes mentioned in their jokes, particularly when targeting the jokes toward me.

Charlie Ray, at that time, lived about four blocks away from Central City in an area referred to as the Huli Hole and NatNalley, where he sold his whiskey and gambled. He had moved out of the shotgun house in Twenty-Ninth Court where our families once lived. To see how Charlie Ray looked, I would have to cross over to the other side of the railroad tracks some kind of way. These tracks, and the trains that passed on them, separated not only the Central City housing project from the Court and Alley but also me from a past I had not known. Surely, I could learn about this man whom everyone tied me to if I crossed over those tracks, I thought to myself.

A boy who lived in the Huli Hole and who was good friends with my brother Maurice allowed me an opportunity to cross those tracks. Maurice and I would cross the tracks and play with this boy (whom I refer to as CW). I also knew that CW was Charlie Ray's grandson. It was early summer 1976, and Maurice and I strolled toward the area, picking up different rocks along the railroad tracks and hurling them at passing-by trains. The American Freedom Train—painted red, white, and blue—had arrived and stopped near Central City. It was a celebration of the U.S. Bicentennial. Everyone, including Maurice and me, stopped to admire the train. As the train rested on the tracks with its caravan of decorated boxcars, a crowd of white people who had driven from the other sides of town took out their Polaroid cameras and began taking pictures, instantly able to see whether they got the shot they wanted. About thirty years earlier in the 1940s, there had been another train that also celebrated "American freedom." But that particular train did not stop in Birmingham or Memphis because white city officials in those cities insisted on segregating Black and white people whenever they toured the train.[1]

Maurice and I got lost in amazement from touring the American Freedom Train. The people working on the train welcomed us aboard, for free. They showed us the Liberty Bell, George Washington's copy of the U.S. Constitution, and Abraham Lincoln's Emancipation Proclamation, and then told us stories of how "important and great America is." Jesse Owens's and Dr. Martin Luther King Jr.'s personal items were also on display.

After Maurice and I had finished walking alongside the tracks and touring the train, we made our way into the Court. Our arrival at this place seemed like a trip back in time. The difference between the Court and Central City was stark. The Court looked like a photo from a *National Geographic* issue that I had seen in the downtown library. The ground was unpaved and dusty, and the light brownish-gray shotgun houses had a small front porch where the neighbors would sit and chit-chat. Although the Black and brown faces in the Court looked worn with age and their bodies appeared beaten down from years of over-work and stress, everyone seemed friendly and immediately knew who Maurice and I were. "Y'all Joann's babies, ain't y'all?" asked a dark-brown lady sitting in a chair on a front porch eating some food. "Yes ma'am," Maurice and I responded together. A couple of greasy-looking dogs would pass us, quickly gnawing and then devouring the scraps of bones thrown on the ground. They seemed to know who would throw out food to them.

Maurice and I caught up with CW who was shooting basketball with another boy named James. For the basketball goal, they used an old bicycle tire rim that was nailed to a tree alongside some houses. "What y'all playing"? Maurice asked. "Nuthin," responded CW. "Let's play 21," said CW, while gesturing to James—who was deaf—with his hands the numbers two and one. James nodded his head. In a game of 21, the first person to score 21 points, from a combination of shots from the basketball court, which counted as two points, and free throws, which counted as one point, is the winner. I was an okay basketball player earlier on. CW and Maurice were decent basketball players, but they dribbled a lot. We did our best to imitate the Harlem Globetrotters, who seemed to come to Birmingham every year. Everyone wanted to be Curly Neal, the bald Globetrotter who would dribble close to the ground while on one knee, or Meadowlark Lemon, the trickster and lead showman known for his fantastic hook shot. A couple of years younger than everyone, I was just happy when I scored a few points. James, a good shooter and dribbler, quickly finished off the games, winning all three.

After basketball and playing outside for about an hour, the four of us had grown tired and thirsty. Luckily, a hosepipe attached to a faucet provided water to keep us from becoming dehydrated in the scorching sun. Only when exhausted would we think about eating. "Let's go to my house and get some grub," said CW. Seeing that we were leaving, James took his ball, dribbled away, and stepped onto his family's porch. Maurice and I followed behind CW. After jumping onto the tattered porch with its loose planks, I was delighted to see bottles of Royal Crown (RC) Cola sitting inside a large metal tub. Each of us grabbed an RC and used the can opener attached to the string on the metal tub to open our soda that we referred to as a "drank." Maurice and I trailed CW as he opened the screen door, which made a squealing sound, and slammed back swiftly because of a broken hinge. CW then pushed open the adjoining door.

Inside the house, in the front room near the sidewall, sat a wood-burning potbelly stove. A stocky built and blue-black-looking man with a cleanly shaved head and face emerged. "Daddy," CW began to ask. "Can me and my friends get some honey buns?" "Let me go back here and get y'all some," said CW's granddaddy, barely looking at Maurice and me. I peeked around the corner and saw that CW's granddaddy had gone to the back part of the house to talk to another person, a man with

Charlie Ray Clency—the author's biological father—sitting on his car in the Court community in Birmingham, 1966. (Courtesy, Clara Moorer Clency.)

only one leg who was sitting in a chair drinking a brown liquid out of a clear miniature glass. An old and beaten-up crutch sat beside him. "Walter," said CW's granddaddy to the one-legged man, "hand me three of 'dem honey buns over dere so I can give to CW and his friends." Walter reached to his right, grabbed the honey buns, and handed them to CW's granddaddy, who then returned with three honey buns in his hands, one for each of us. I closely examined CW's granddaddy's facial and physical features, searching fervently for some clues to see if my brothers' descriptions matched what I was witnessing. He was wearing dark brown pants and a white sleeveless T-shirt.

"Man," I said to myself, "jest like they said—short, kinna fat, bal'-headed, blue-black—and ugly?" He had on some house shoes, so I couldn't tell whether it was true or not what my oldest brother Ronnie said about Charlie Ray having only three toes! "Uhn unh, I don't look like him, I favor my mama!" I exclaimed quickly but to myself. Well, we both had a gap between our two front teeth. I was staring at Charlie Ray Clency, the man who my mother had told me was my "daddy." Only after seeing Charlie Ray in person was I then able to visualize the story that my oldest brother, Ronnie, would often share when he wanted to get a good laugh out of everyone: "Do you remember that story about Charlie Ray [knowing that I did not since I had not been born or was too young]? It's about that time when Charlie Ray was running from the police. Man, Charlie Ray got butt naked and started running along the railroad tracks so the police couldn't see him!" I finally saw Charlie Ray. Maurice and I never mentioned anything to CW about Charlie Ray being my biological father or about me being CW's uncle.

Later that summer, I would begin walking across the tracks by myself to play with CW. Whenever CW and I finished playing, he would always ask his granddaddy for something sweet. If he didn't have honey buns, CW's granddaddy would give us those big yellow moon pies, the kind in which two cookies encased a sweet marshmallow filling. But CW's granddaddy said few words; he would bring out the honey buns or moon pies and hand them to CW, who would pass one of the treats to me. After some time, probably when I was about eight and a half years old, I realized that Charlie Ray would not look at or say a word to me. He talked only to CW or gave him what he desired. I stopped making the short trip across the tracks. However, CW and I would still play together at Powell Elementary School, where we both attended. I recalled seeing Charlie Ray a few other times when he would drive past Central City and some of my friends and I would be outside playing. But he never spoke.

Eight years later, while a sophomore at Phillips High School, the news broke in my journalism class. A classmate of mine solemnly made her way over toward my desk, looking anxious to tell me something. A look of sadness covered her face when she began to speak to me:

"Jerome, have you heard?"

"Heard what?" I asked.

"That Daddy died."

I responded with a question to this student's morbid statement:

"You mean Charlie Ray is dead? Is that what you're tryin' to say?"

"Yeah, Daddy died yesterday, and I just wanted to let you know," she continued.

"Thanks for letting me know," I said.

This particular student, her younger sister, and her older brother all referred to their grandfather, Charlie Ray, as "Daddy." To them, he was genuinely perceived as a loving daddy figure and someone who took care of his family. They talked about the things that he would do for them. But in that journalism classroom that day, I found it strange to hear the word "daddy" being uttered to me by someone who had been a classmate of mine since first grade. Until that moment, we never talked about being related during the entire time we had gone to school together. How long had she known we were related? These thoughts raced through my head.

My classmate (who was also my biological niece) was sad at the death of her granddaddy. Yet I didn't feel sad or a sense of loss for someone I considered a stranger. I am sure the moment affected me, but it was in a way that elicited only curiosity. At that time in my life, and because of other influential male figures in my life such as teachers, coaches, and others from the community, I had just about forgotten about Charlie Ray's existence as my biological father. However, I was reminded that day of his existence. After my classmate's pronouncement and having left school for the day, I arrived home and told my mother about Charlie Ray's death. One of my brothers overheard our conversation and thought he should offer his input on the matter. Jokingly and with a wry smile, he asked, "Jerome, man aren't you going to your daddy's funeral?" Our mother interjected before I could utter a single word. "Jerome doesn't have to go to his goddamned funeral! Don't put that on him. Charlie Ray hadn't done shit for Jerome but gave me five motherfucking dollars to buy some *Pampers* when Jerome was born!"

Protectively, my mother did not want me to feel obligated to reach out to Charlie Ray and his family. She believed that a man who knew he had fathered a child should take the lead. Like so many Black women in that era and in that area of Birmingham, my mother did not force the men she had babies by to support the children they had fathered. The women often assumed full responsibility for their children because they also knew the judgment Black women faced when having a baby by a man, especially if he was already married to another woman. There was nothing else to say after our mother's profound response to my brother. While in our mother's presence, no one in that apartment dared ask me anything about my connections to Charlie Ray Clency or the Clency family.

CHAPTER 6   SANKOFA

For years I blocked out the Clency side of my family because my mother taught me and my siblings to "never kiss anybody's ass to get them to accept you." However, for this project I would have to connect the past to the present. I would have to go beyond Charlie Ray, the person, to understand the Clency family's story and part of my story. In doing so, I would become better equipped at telling our people's stories in places like Birmingham and beyond.

Charlie Ray Clency Jr.'s paternal grandfather (my paternal great-grandfather) was born into slavery around 1850. The earliest recorded Black person near Birmingham with the last name Clancy/Clency was a "Negro" female born around 1810. In the slave census of 1860, a white slave owner in Perry County (located adjacent to Jefferson County, where Birmingham is located) had the last name Clancy.[1] He had also been a Confederate soldier during the American Civil War. This slave owner was named Thomas G. Clancy, which was an Irish last name. He owned four enslaved Black people: two females (fifty and twenty-eight years of age) and two males (thirty and twelve); the twelve-year-old was most likely the Black Clancy/Clency family's earliest known patriarch, Nathan Clancy.[2] The couple was most likely Nathan's parents and the fifty-year-old female his grandmother.

The young "Negro" Clancy male who was reportedly twelve years of age in the 1860 slave census reported in the 1900 U.S. census that he was forty-nine, worked as a farmer, and lived in Jonesboro Precinct 2 in Jefferson County. His name was Nathan Clancy. Like so many Black people, shortly after slavery the Black Clancy/Clency family members left rural southern communities (Marion, Alabama). They moved a few miles east to Jefferson County. Between 1880 and 1900, the Black population in Jefferson County increased from 5,053 to 56,334.[3]

Nathan Clancy married a young woman named Annie in 1892. Less than thirty years prior, countless other Black couples across the U.S. South zealously pursued marriage—or legally formalized their relationships—after having marriage denied to them during enslavement. Annie, whose listed birth year is 1861, birthed eight children, with six surviving. One of Nathan and Annie's children was Charles Ray Clancy Sr., born around 1898. He was my biological paternal grandfather.

Charlie Ray Sr. worked in Birmingham in the sheet metal and construction industries. He was also a deacon in the church. During the early 1900s, companies like Tennessee Coal and Iron, a steel manufacturer that specialized in mining coal and iron ore, refused to hire Black men. Instead, industrialists used Black prison labor to increase their profits.[4] Often, Black men would be arrested due to Alabama's vagrancy laws. City and county officials would then lease these "victims who committed no crime" to a coal or steel company, where they would have to work off their penalties. This neo-slavery formed the world that Charlie Ray Sr. and many other Black people in Birmingham would come to know.

Charlie Ray Sr. and his wife, Lillian, had four children, including Charlie Ray Jr., born in 1924. But for Charlie Ray Jr., the racial caste system of the South would mold him into a man who would learn about the world not in a church or classroom but in the streets. Instead of holding down what some might consider a regular job, Charlie Ray Jr. learned how to earn money as a hustler, gambler, and bootlegger. For many Black males in Birmingham, employment choices were few and far between. They could acquire some skill that allowed them to make a living. If not, they could seek temporary work in the mines, the steel mills, or the foundries or on the railroad and become underpaid and cheated out of a fair salary by white foremen and supervisors. Those who did not go these routes hustled. Charlie Ray Jr. would take the hustling way. He stopped attending school around the fifth grade.

Charlie Ray Jr.'s children saw how their father and his friends gambled, conspired with and avoided the police because of illegal activities, and womanized. For some Black males, such behaviors became perceived as normal and worthy of imitation. Some had gotten accustomed to seeing Black women's mistreatment and abuse, whether on plantations, in slave quarters, in the city while working for white people, or at the hands of other Black males.[5] Consequently, some Black men perpetuated the mistreatment of Black women. With a knack for hustling, Charlie Ray Jr.'s turf included the Alley and the Court, where he would flex his muscles and stick out his chest. According to anyone and everyone who knew him, "Mr. Charlie Ray ran the alleys and was a bad man!" He always maintained two houses—one where his wife and their children lived and another where he would gamble and sell whiskey.

All four of Charlie Ray's sons born to him and his wife would inherit his very dark complexion and their mother's height. Each of the four sons is over six feet tall. On the other hand, Charlie Ray Jr. was about five feet nine inches, slightly shorter than me. My complexion is a cross between his darker and my mother's lighter complexion. For various offenses, including armed robbery, shoplifting, and battery, Charlie Ray Jr. and his four sons were incarcerated at one time or another. Rather than attributing their incarcerations to endemic racism and discrimination, some Clency family members believed that the Clency males had made bad decisions or were just cursed. One of my Clency sisters had talked about how I was the only "Clency" male not to go to jail or prison. I informed her that it was not because of a curse but due to the environment and a criminal (in)justice system that vilified Black men. Panky, the eldest of the Clency siblings, showed how the family "curse" could be broken. He just left Birmingham.

In 1969, Panky left behind the Alley, the Court, Birmingham, and the U.S. South because he felt that the "environment there was pulling me into a life of petty crime." He had been arrested and served time in jail because of what he said was "on a humbug." Panky, who graduated from Birmingham's Hayes High School and was the only young man in the Alley or Court to get a job at United States Steel, felt obligated to make his mother proud.[6]

However, Panky had a small rap sheet. After being arrested, he no longer wanted to live the life he had experienced in the Alley and the Court. Fearing that he would face a stiff prison sentence, Panky "walked away" from a prison work release site in 1969 with detailed plans on how to get to Buffalo, New York, where his fiancée's family awaited him.

He fled on a plane to deceive the guards and police, who expected a Black person to catch a bus. After boarding the plane, Panky sat down in a window seat. As the airplane elevated from Birmingham's eastern side, he peered through the oval window. Below, he could see the fields, blasting furnaces, railroad tracks, and the Alley and the Court, which he was leaving behind, physically and psychologically. Panky's fiancée, who shared his hope of building a new life and a family, greeted him at the gate. They eventually married. Buffalo, not Birmingham, is where they felt they had a better chance at life. Even though they had left, they promised to send for their kinfolks who remained behind in Alabama.

A fugitive since 1969, Panky lived in Buffalo for years looking over his shoulders, knowing there was the possibility that he could be found and returned to Birmingham. Between 1970 and the early 1980s, Panky and his wife visited family members in Birmingham. They would drive during the middle of the night, popping in and out of town and never staying too long. While in Buffalo, Panky kept himself clean, trying his very best to obey the law and avoid the police. Panky and his wife also took steps to shield their four children (two daughters and two sons) from the life that Panky had witnessed in Birmingham. For more than a decade, Panky tried to live as a model citizen in Buffalo. But for him, freedom was lonely. Panky escaped from Birmingham by going northward, but he still thought about the family members he had left behind. He would send them care packages. Panky had gotten his youngest sister out of Birmingham, and he managed to get a younger brother up to Buffalo also. This brother, however, couldn't break Birmingham's hold. Not long after returning to Birmingham, this younger brother went back to prison for life.

Then one day they came: the police. And they were heavily armed and ready to shoot should Panky try anything. After living in Buffalo for more than a decade without any incident, the police had discovered that "Charlie Clency" and "Panky" were the same person. They had come to send him back to Birmingham to face charges. A SWAT team surrounded the house and demanded that Panky come out with his hands up, which he did, careful not to move too quickly. After Panky was apprehended, handcuffed, and then taken to jail, his wife immediately called a lawyer. Fortunately, they had been saving up for years to pay attorneys just in case this day ever arrived. The white judge in Buffalo agreed that Panky should not have received such a harsh sentence. He gave Panky credit for the time he served and dismissed the case.

Like many men coming of age in the United States, viable employment was also crucial for Black men like Panky to fulfill the role traditionally expected of men in U.S. society—that of breadwinner.[7] Viable jobs were important for their sense of dignity and self-esteem, and viable employment increased men's chances of getting and staying married.[8] Graduating high school and attaining employment helped to save

Panky's life. Exposure to a different world from the one he had grown up in and having steady employment allowed Panky and his wife to send their four children to college between the late 1980s and mid-1990s. Most of their family members still lived in Alabama, and they still wanted their children to know their kinfolks there. Therefore, they sent three of their children back to the South to attend college, specifically Alabama State University, Tuskegee University, and the University of Alabama.

Panky's northward flight to freedom and employment in Buffalo's steel mills allowed him to build a foundation for himself and his growing family. Like more than six million other Black migrants who left the U.S. South for lands in the North and West between 1920 and 1970, to either escape the South's oppressive structure or pursue their dreams in other lands, Panky left Birmingham and became a part of the Great Migration.[9] Buffalo was his promised land. In 1969, Panky took a risk, albeit a calculated one, to escape from Birmingham. He talked about wanting to model to his three younger brothers and two sisters that there was another way, but that "they had to break away from the hold that Birmingham and everything there had on them."

Panky is the eldest of all of my twelve siblings. I had no acknowledged sibling relationship with my Clency siblings until I was in high school. Before then, I had come to view the Clency family as my blood relatives, but I did not think of them as family members or kinfolks per se. I got to know Clara, one of Charlie Ray's daughters, during high school. Clara is twelve years older than I am. Once Clara became aware of my existence, she immediately took to me as her youngest brother. Clara had moved up to Buffalo, when she was a teenager, following her brother Panky. During the mid-1980s, she returned to Birmingham and moved into Central City, where we met during my senior year of high school.

I got to know Panky through his children, first his oldest daughter Treddia and then his oldest son Cleo. I first met Treddia in the mid-1990s when Mary and I visited the Sea Islands in South Carolina and Georgia. Treddia and her husband were stationed in Fort Benning, Georgia. Mary and I brought along one of my nieces, Santana, to teach her about the history of Black people in those regions, specifically the Gullah Geechee people who lived in Georgia, South Carolina, North Carolina, and Florida.[10] Treddia immediately welcomed me as a family member.

Cleo, Panky's oldest son, and I had first met in 2005 when he invited me to a family get-together at a restaurant in Birmingham. I was one year older than Cleo, who had heard about me from some family members and wanted to bring the Clency family together. I found this commendable and felt a sense of obligation to attend the dinner. My wife Mary and our two children, Amadi and Kamau, joined me. Once at the restaurant among the Clency family members, I felt awkward, not because I was the so-called outside child but because I had known and grown up with just about everyone in that room. Since childhood, we had been in each other's presence, whether around the Alley, the Court, or Central City or at school. I grew up as playmates and schoolmates to a nephew and two nieces, but we never talked about being related to one another until after Charlie Ray died when I was in high school.

During the summer of 2012, Cleo approached me about developing the Clency/Clancy family genealogy as part of the family's first reunion in Birmingham in 2013. I reluctantly assisted with the quest, unsure of where it would lead. My reluctance also emerged from not wanting to disrespect my mother and grandmother. I had not uncovered a thorough genealogical picture of my grandmother's early life and biological parents. I felt a sense of guilt at having more success in recovering genealogical information about Charlie Ray's family. Researching the Clency family was easier because few Black people with that name lived near Jefferson County. Like many African American people, I had hit a brick wall attempting to uncover information about my mother's side of the family. Whereas many of us experience this wall when it comes to locating information about our families during and after enslavement, the wall I encountered related to the time period in the early 1900s.[11] Numerous roadblocks halted the process of securing information about my maternal grandmother, such as my maternal grandmother's informal adoption and usage of multiple names. Her birth name was allegedly Alice Mae Hendrix, and she was purportedly born in Akron, Ohio. However, she revealed very little to her children about her past while she was alive.

I just rationalized the Clency family's history project as an academic exercise and something of value later on to my children if they ever wanted to know their genealogy. But this journey soon became more than an academic exercise once I became immersed in the quest to understand the experiences of Black people and families in Birmingham. I became intrigued while researching the family's history. The Clency/Clancy family's experiences told a story about more than just its mem-

Sankofa.
(Courtesy, jeff
carr.)

Sankofa Symbols

bers. It was also part of the larger story of Black people in the South and Black people in the United States. The Adinkra symbol Sankofa, which comes from the Twi language, spoken in Ghana (West Africa), provides one way to continue moving forward as a people and as a family.[12] Depicted as a bird with its head turned backward or a heart, Sankofa translates as follows: "It is not wrong to go back and fetch that which you have forgotten."[13]

CHAPTER 7   BLACK AND PROUD

Sometimes smells, sights, and encounters trigger memories. An encounter during a sunny but chilly Saturday morning in January 2014 would connect me to the past. It was a solemn day because I would say my final goodbye to a family friend nicknamed Pot, who had succumbed to kidney failure at fifty-six years of age. Before his passing, Pot had become a fixture in the Central City area, becoming known as the "hotdog man" for the countless hotdogs he sold and sometimes gave to customers. He also had a mean basketball game. I drove from Atlanta to Birmingham to pay my respects to Pot's family and support his mother, Mrs. Sarah Price. Throughout the city and state, people from all walks of life respected Mrs. Price for her tireless efforts to help the poor, feed the hungry, and clothe the naked. One of my mother's closest friends, Mrs. Price had once owned a house next to the Alley. Mrs. Price knew firsthand the forces aligned against Black girls and women, particularly young mothers raising children in poverty. She had raised her eight children alone after her husband's untimely death.

As a widow, Mrs. Price never took for granted how the Social Security check she received from her husband's sudden death sustained her and her children. After her children had become older, she volunteered with and eventually found employment with the Greater Birmingham Ministry (GBM), a multifaith organization. Formed in 1969 by Birmingham faith leaders from the United Methodist Church, the Episcopal Church, and the United Presbyterian Church, GBM emerged from the tumultuous events of 1968. The founders focused on helping the city to overcome its racist past and making Birmingham a more equitable city.[1] Before and during her employment with GBM, Mrs. Price had taken some college courses at Miles College—a historically Black college located in Fairfield, Alabama, a few miles west of Birmingham. She often substituted as a teacher at Powell Elementary School when my siblings and I attended the school.

Before her work with GBM, Mrs. Price taught mothers in Central City, the Alley, the Court, and beyond how to access social services to help them and their children. She demanded respect, demonstrated by her initiative in enrolling her children as part of the first wave of Black children to integrate the previously all-white Powell Elementary during the late 1960s. Mrs. Price insisted that her children attend Powell Elementary School, located only three blocks from their home, rather than the all-Black North Side Elementary, which was eight blocks away. According to Mrs. Price, there was no hassle getting her children enrolled into Powell: "The principal, although he was white, really did not believe in keeping Black people out."

On that January 2014 morning, I parked my car in the Ensley area of Birmingham (western side of the city). I walked up the stairs toward Bethel African Methodist Episcopal (AME) Church. Upon reaching the top of the church's stairs, I was immediately greeted by a man—somewhat aged but still kind of muscular—who called out my name: "Jerome, what's going on?" Automatically, I responded, "What's happening, man?" while simultaneously shaking his hand. All the while, I could not remember the name of this person speaking to me. I began talking to him in case something he said might trigger my recollection. "Jerome, you don't remember who I am, do you? You are the quarterback," he continued. After a second or two of looking closely at him, I realized that I was talking to Donovan, who had grown up with my uncles, aunts, and older brothers. Donovan was a close family friend, and I had not seen him in more than twenty-five years. He had also come out of the Alley. After our handshakes and hugs, we proceeded into the church. We sat in the back pews with my two oldest brothers, Ronnie and Richard Jr., as well as a host of other former residents of Central City, the Court, and the Alley.

A quick-witted man but known to take no mess from anyone, Donovan began to tell me of his earliest memories of Central City. He talked about when a "gang of white dudes" tried to run him out of Central City. He remembered one of the white males' names, Randy, who he said tried to "jump me over by the fence near the cake [a round gathering place in the center of a children's play area]. All of the other Black people ran because they were scared." Donovan proceeded to describe how

I, only about four years of age, reached down and gave him a stick that he used to defend himself against the white males.

Although I had remembered hearing the story before, I had little memory of this event. I thought it was just a family story that had become repeated over the years. Donovan confirmed what I had previously heard. In reflecting, I was glad that I was able to play some part in preventing Donovan from being attacked by a group of white males that day. Until the late 1960s, Black people could not walk through Central City to shop in downtown Birmingham. If caught, they would risk being beaten by white people, usually young males. To avoid confrontations and issues with the white police department who always sided with the white males, Black people from the Alley or Court areas had to walk down Twenty-Sixth Street toward the Terminal Railroad Station. From there, they would then walk down Fourth Avenue, which would lead them to the Black business district in the city. Things were supposed to be different in 1972. However, some of the remaining young white males in Central City were determined to create fear in Black people. They had heard of and did not like Black people like Donovan, who carried themselves without fear. "I was going to walk wherever I pleased," said Donovan as he recounted the story.

Donovan worked throughout his young adult years and afterward would hang around Central City, passing the time along. During the late 1980s, he got into an altercation with another Black man who had recently moved into Central City. Central City had been an almost all-Black community for about two decades by then. During the struggle Donovan shot and killed the man, who he said attempted first to shoot him. One of my brothers, Michael (aka "Big Meaty"), was with the two of them and witnessed firsthand the shooting in Central City. Donovan was acquitted of a first-degree murder charge after his lawyer successfully argued that he had killed the man in self-defense. Yet Donovan would later serve prison time after being convicted of murdering another man; his reputation preceded him.

Donovan and I spent about an hour reminiscing about life and how we had both come to call Central City home. We talked about how Black people had to constantly fight for respect and dignity and the right to be treated equally. "Ain't no man no better than me," said Donovan. We talked about Black folks having to fight to attend schools. We talked about when Rev. Fred Shuttlesworth and his wife Ruby tried enrolling Black children, including their daughter, into Phillips High School. "White folks didn't just let Black folks up in Phillips!" exclaimed Donovan in an excitedly teaching tone. "Although they didn't like the way he went about it, Shuttlesworth was all up in white folks' faces saying, 'you gonna have to deal with Black folks and treat us with respect.'"

Rev. Shuttlesworth pastored Bethel Baptist Church in Birmingham. He was also the membership chairman of the Alabama state chapter of the NAACP in 1956 when the state outlawed the organization. Rev. Shuttlesworth and Edward Gardner founded the Alabama Christian Movement for Human Rights to continue fighting for Black people's human and civil rights.[2] A fiery fighter for Black freedom, Rev. Shuttlesworth and Ruby led an often ignored attempt to break the shackles of legalized segregation by demanding educational equality for Black people in Birmingham.[3] The year was 1957. Within a few months the Shuttlesworths' efforts to integrate Phillips preceded the more well-known Little Rock Nine's integration of Central High School in Little Rock, Arkansas.

Phillips was arguably the most prized public high school in Alabama when Shuttlesworth attempted integration. Black people were increasingly moving into Birmingham from rural areas of the state, and A. H. Parker High School, the city's Black high school, could not accommodate the large numbers of Black migrants. In 1959, Birmingham's all-white city officials and board of education members built George Washington Carver High School on the north side of town to draw Black students and to discourage their parents from enrolling them at Phillips. They would build another Black high school, Carol W. Hayes, in 1960 on the city's east side.[4]

Many Black people demonstrated immense pride and affinity for schools such as Parker. They also knew that it was inherently wrong that white city officials did not provide equal educational resources to Black people. Consequently, some Black people fought to integrate white schools out of a deep commitment to equality and quality education as promised by the *Brown v. Board of Education* (1954) decision.[5] For Rev. Shuttlesworth, *Brown* would serve as inspiration in their efforts to integrate Phillips because it gave Black people "hope," like we "had gotten a new religion."[6]

The Birmingham Police Department allowed a mob of Klansmen to beat Rev. Shuttlesworth with chains, pipes, brass knuckles, and bats. Ruby was also beaten and stabbed, yet charges were dropped against the suspects. With a federal court–approved plan six years later, Black students began to attend all-white schools in Birmingham in August 1963.

A little more than a decade after enrolling the first Black students, Phillips's student population was predominantly Black. The school's rad-

White students protesting integration at Phillips High School.
(Copyright Alabama Department of Archives and History;
donated by the Alabama Media Group.)

ical transformation into an all-Black school mirrored patterns throughout the United States. Beginning in the 1970s, schools in many inner cities enrolled a significant percentage of Black and low-income students.
These patterns were not by chance. By the 1970s, millions of Black people
had left the rural South and migrated to northern and midwestern cities and southern urban areas. As equally a factor as Black migration patterns, white flight from urban areas began escalating around 1969 and
coincided with the enforcement of *Brown v. Board* through public school
desegregation. White Americans made their feelings clear, not only ver-
bally but also by moving to suburban and outlying communities.[7]

In many instances, white communities and realtors facilitated these
actions through racial steering and other means of deterring Black families from moving into predominantly white neighborhoods. These
practices and demographic shifts in the United States contributed im-
mensely to the existence of urban schools that enrolled significant numbers of low-income and minority children, many of whom were Black.[8]
With white people's departure from urban schools and communities, the
white business elite soon followed and withdrew their support. When
white people left the city, their money went with them.

Our conversation about Donovan's experiences growing up during
the Civil Rights Movement in Birmingham was helping me to see better

why he walked through life the way he did. As we stood in Bethel AME Church's parking lot, Donovan shared stories, not just about growing up in the Alley and Central City but also about his incarceration. As I listened, he talked about how young Black males, no matter if they are "in the hood, in corporate America, or the pen," have to stand up for what they believe. "You gotta carry yourself on the inside [in the penitentiary] the same way you carry yourself in the 'free world.'"

For too many Black males, prison becomes a way of life. According to a Pew Research Center analysis, Black men are "more than six times as likely as white men to be incarcerated in federal and local jails."9 Unfortunately, the dreams and futures of too many Black people, especially Black males, have been killed through their mass incarceration.10 Part of a dreadful industrial complex, prisons have cut off brilliant Black minds and souls from their families and communities, thereby leaving children and households fatherless, motherless, spouseless, and further impoverished.11 Prisons represent a multibillion-dollar industry, and their owners' profits dramatically increased through the criminalization and incarceration of Black people during the so-called war on drugs. Prisons might as well be a modern slave trade. The United States has the largest prison population on the planet, numbering 2.3 million people. And Black people, only 13 percent of the total U.S. population, constitute approximately 40 percent of the prison population.

Donovan and I also talked about how Central City, by the mid-1970s, had felt like it was now *our community*. Despite the harsh reality of Black people owning few of the businesses that we patronized, the services and markets in Central City were still accessible for us back then. In addition to the convenient proximity to downtown department stores and shops, we had access to a grocery store, convenience stores, an early childhood center, an elementary school, a high school, a community center, a boys club, a girls club, and a health clinic. But as Black residents began constituting a sizable share of the area, rumors circulated that the federal government, the city, and the housing authority were planning on tearing down Central City. One of the rumors was that white people in the southern suburbs of Homewood, Mountain Brook, and Vestavia— referred to as "over the mountain" due to their location on the other side of Red Mountain—wanted better access to the city. They did not want to drive past Central City anymore. Talk of such rumors went on for years without any action. And then, all of a sudden, these rumors became real.

In 1974, the Federal Highway Administration revealed plans to extend the Red Mountain Expressway by cutting through the mountain and eliminating Central City in the process. The Red Mountain Express-way was shaped by a geological cut into Red Mountain and was inte-gral in developing the city's suburbs. The Federal Highway Administra-tion and Birmingham's planners were accused of undermining families' efforts to foster community while buttressing the infrastructure and growth of nearby suburban communities. Business advocacy nonprofit organizations such as Operation New Birmingham zealously pursued the completion of the project.[12]

However, Central City's residents and neighbors did not sit idly by as their new community was threatened. Mrs. Sarah Price, along with Mrs. Lois Hines, another resident and the mother of five girls, could be seen walking throughout Central City and handing out flyers about an upcoming meeting. "Come on, Liz, Yvonne, and Joann. We're going to have to stop this because these folks are saying one thing, but we're find-ing out that they're planning to move y'all out!" The Central City area neighborhood president attended, along with Mrs. Hines, Mrs. Price, and some people from GBM.

Almost a hundred people from families with children and some el-derly white people attended the meeting. My mother attended because of what would happen to her and the other families and because of her loyalty to her friend, Mrs. Sarah Price. Mrs. Hines, another neighbor and community organizer, got up to the microphone, spoke, and left the audi-ence with the memorable phrase "Don't move us again!"

Whereas Central City's residents experienced roadblocks while seek-ing information regarding the plans to tear down Central City, the white people who worked with GBM were able to access the information. Mrs. Sarah Price had heard about how "the federal government had regula-tions regarding tearing down; that you couldn't tear down public hous-ing if you didn't make it better." The white people at GBM also informed her how some white people from Central City had gotten section 235 (under the Housing Act of 1968) that allowed them to purchase housing. Mrs. Price joined the fight because she had grown up with many of the Black mothers in Central City, including mine. Her house, located di-rectly across the street from Central City near Twenty-Sixth Avenue, was in the path of the proposed expressway.

Led by Mrs. Price and Paul Carruba—a white Italian man who had grown up in the area and whose family owned a grocery store—Central City's tenant organization marched to City Hall and attended the City Council meeting. Mrs. Price noted the plan included moving senior cit-izens into a high rise and dispersing families into other public housing communities throughout the city. However, some of the managers at the other public housing communities resisted accepting such large numbers of Black families. Their protest would eventually result in the city, housing authority, and federal officials changing their plans.

The Alabama Tenants Organization assisted Central City's residents in filing a federal lawsuit alleging the Federal Highway Administration violated residents' rights by planning the Red Mountain Expressway. The lawsuit named the Birmingham Housing Authority, U.S. Department of Housing and Urban Development, Alabama Highway Department, and Federal Highway Administration. After many back-and-forth contestations over several years, the governor of Alabama, George Wallace, signed an agreement. In his book, *The Most Segregated City in America: City Planning and Civil Rights in Birmingham, 1920–1980*, Charles Connerly described how the Central City community protest led to some sweeping changes around public housing throughout the United States, which included making sure that residents would serve on the committees that made final decisions about housing replacement. The final agreement had provided for "one-for-one replacement housing for the displaced tenants and provided tenants the right to influence decisions on the location and design of the replacement units." Six people would serve on a committee to determine the location of the new public housing complex and advise the architects. Of these six, two were Central City residents. Central City's residents felt victorious at having the opportunity to shape the new design and location of replacement housing. Consequently, they decided not to pursue any further litigation.[13]

The Federal Highway Administration had to develop another route for the highway. Instead of going through Central City, the Red Mountain Expressway would run alongside Twenty-Sixth Street near the former Terminal Station. But Mrs. Price's house stood in the way of that plan. She would eventually sell her house in 1984 and move onto Graymont Avenue in Birmingham. However, she stated that she never received sufficient money to purchase her next home without a mortgage. Renovations began in Central City in 1984, and the residents could return if they so desired. The new complex would be named Metropolitan Gardens. A Birmingham-based Black architectural firm, Owens and Woods, had secured the contract for the design.

During the renovations in the early 1980s, the Birmingham Housing Authority moved our family from one section of Central City to a temporary apartment located across the street from Powell Elementary

Renovation of Central City into Metropolitan Gardens, 1983.
(Source: Historic Images, https://outlet.historicimages.com
/products/abna21573.)

School. We stayed there for about a year. Afterward, we moved back into the same section we had left, but in a different apartment.

Central City's residents' efforts to protect what we considered home represented one way that Black community leaders resisted and became galvanized. Another galvanizing event was the 1979 murder of Bonita Carter, an unarmed Black woman, by a white Birmingham police officer. The shooting took place in the predominantly Black neighborhood of Kingston, on the city's eastern side. Bonita Carter was sitting in a car when a cop, George Sands, allegedly thinking that she had participated in an altercation with the store clerk who had been shot by another man, fired four shots at close range. Three bullets pierced Bonita's body and killed her. Protests erupted when Birmingham's mayor, a white man named David Vann, refused to dismiss Sands from the police force. Threats of a strike from the mostly white Fraternal Order of Police and pressure from the Ku Klux Klan influenced Mayor Vann's decision not to dismiss or punish Sands. Thousands of Black people took to the streets and marched to City Hall to protest the inaction. Approximately ten carloads of angry white people with the Ku Klux Klan drove through the Black Kingston community to support Sands. In response, armed Black men who had recently returned from Vietnam came to the defense of the Kingston community in case any white people attempted to drive back through the area.[14]

It seemed like every Black person in Birmingham was visibly upset at Bonita's killing and the nonprosecution of the police officer. We were upset and frustrated at how white law enforcers always got away with killing Black people. "Everybody was mad at the police. The police couldn't even go down Tenth Avenue without having bricks and rocks slung at them. It was like the Riots of LA, like the Watts Riots," said my brother Ronnie. Bonita's killing reignited Birmingham's Civil Rights Movement after lying dormant for about a decade. It politicized another generation of Black residents about police brutality and Black people's status in the city and the United States. Bonita's killing opened old wounds and memories of Black people's mistreatment by white people and white police officers. City leaders and officials had hoped to sweep this history under the rug with a cooling message of racial harmony and gradualism. The second Black member of the Birmingham City Council, Richard Arrington, seized upon the discontent among the grassroots. The time was ripe. Arrington capitalized on the Black masses' frustration and the fact that it was an election year to challenge David Vann and others for the mayoral position. In their strong show of protest for Vann's inaction, Black voters overwhelmingly went to the polls to elect Arrington as the city's first Black mayor. Arrington's most ardent supporters were the city's Black poor and working class.

A series of events and opportunities in 1979 propelled Arrington to the mayor's office. But his election as Birmingham's first Black mayor did not instantly change some white people's deeply held beliefs about Black people or radically alter our social conditions. We continued experiencing indignity and disrespect while shopping in Woolworth's department store downtown, the A&P grocery store near Eighth Avenue North, and convenience stores throughout the city; white store owners and employees still followed us when we shopped. Some people protested in the streets against this racial profiling. Others protested in nonpublic and lesser-known ways.

❏

My mother was one of the thousands of Black women domestic workers that had cleaned white people's houses since the city's founding.[15]

Birmingham's public bus system's administrators strategically situated routes so that Black domestic workers had reliable transportation to and from their cleaning jobs in the Mountain Brook, Vestavia, and Homewood areas. On her way from work, my mother would catch the bus that would drop her off near Willie's Super Market, a single-story tan brick building near the corner lot on Second Avenue and Twenty-Fifth Street, owned by Mr. Willie, an elderly Jewish man. Given his age, Mr. Willie mostly walked around the store ensuring things were in place. His identical twin adult sons managed the store's daily operations. Mr. Willie had also developed a reputation among Black people for watching and following Black customers to see if they were trying to steal. He had a dark complexion, while his two sons had a much lighter complexion and prominent European features. One of the twins was outgoing and interacted with the customers and knew just about every family that shopped there. The other twin displayed a businessman persona and a more reserved personality and always stayed behind the elevated counter, seemingly dealing with the store's business matters.

On one particular day my mother had had enough of Mr. Willie. He questioned her about whether she had placed an item from the store into her purse without paying. Mr. Willie attempted to search my mother's purse, and she vehemently refused, letting him know how she and her family had patronized the store for years. My mother was disturbed by his accusation. She let him know that she and her siblings had grown up with his children, that her mother had had an account and always paid on time, and that she had spent countless amounts of money in the store.

Immediately, one of Mr. Willie's sons intervened to defuse the situation by letting his father know he would take care of everything. My mother told us of how she "was never going to step back into the store until he offers an apology for insulting me and thinking that Black people want to steal his stuff." Leonard, a teenaged neighbor who bagged groceries at the store, overheard the conversation: "Man, y'all Mama told Mr. Willie about himself. But he always be following Black folks through the store. I just looked at Ms. Joann telling him about himself while I was bagging the groceries."

For the next five years, our mother refused to step foot inside Willie's Super Market. Occasionally, one of us would pick up items because there was no other grocery store within walking distance; the area was becoming deserted. Our families had little choice but to shop at Willie's Super Market. Mr. Willie and his family's lifestyle depended greatly on Black families; we relied on the food they would sell to us within the Black community.

About four years after the incident, I saw one of Mr. Willie's sons when I passed the store on my way to the Downtown Farmer's Market, where I worked during some summers. He asked, "How is your mother, Joann, doing? Let her know that we miss her around here." Our mother endured the inconvenience rather than suffer the indignity of stepping foot in a store owned by someone who distrusted and disrespected her.

Maybe our mother had become emboldened by the collective actions taken by Black people in Montgomery, Alabama, on December 5, 1955, when they refused to sit in the back of buses. Maybe she had heard of Claudette Colvin, a courageous fifteen-year-old Black girl in Montgomery arrested in 1955 for refusing to give up her seat in a "whites only" section of a bus. Months before Rosa Parks's well-known actions, Claudette's courageous refusal to move to the back of the bus ignited the talk of a mass boycott throughout Montgomery. Yet Black civil rights figures refused to use Claudette's case to challenge the repugnant segregation laws, partly because she was pregnant.[16]

My mother, in her own way and like many more unknown Black people, refused to allow Mr. Willie to dehumanize her. Maybe she also knew of the bravery of other Black women such as Mary Fair Burks, Jo Ann Robinson, Irene West, Thelma Glass, and Uretta Adair. They were members of the all-Black Women's Political Council (WPC), which initiated talk of a bus system boycott due to the mistreatment that Black people—many of whom were domestic workers—had endured in Montgomery.[17] Even before the Montgomery Improvement Association, led by Martin Luther King Jr. and E. D. Nixon, the WPC was at the forefront of politicizing, organizing, and supporting the broader efforts by Black people for freedom, dignity, and respect.[18] The WPC and other Black people knew they could gain a semblance of justice if they collectively withheld their money. Rather than ride the buses and continue to be treated as second-class citizens, Black people used their vehicles to transport one another instead. Likewise, rather than patronizing Willie's Super Market, my mother began shopping at a grocery store in the Mountain Brook area, where she said the people treated her with respect. Then again, maybe the lyrics from the Impressions' song "We're a Winner," "No more tears do we cry, and we have finally dried our eyes, and we're movin' on up," had inspired my mother, and many other Black people, to take a stand in her little corner of the universe.[19]

CHAPTER 8   FISTS, KNIVES, NECK BONES, AND COLLARD GREENS

Unexpectedly, loud echoes could be heard throughout our apartment, "boom, boom, boom!" My heart, like a rock thrown into a pond, skipped a beat as the banging sound intensified. Suddenly, a thunderous and demanding man's voice rang from the other side of the door. "Let me in, or I'll blow this goddamned door down!" Leaving the bedroom that she and our baby sister, Shelda, shared, our mother quickly ran into the other two bedrooms and stated in a stern but calm voice to the six of us boys, "Take Shelda (handing her over to Ronnie), and you all hide. Stay in the bedrooms and be quiet." She had been holding Shelda on her hip. I crouched, hiding with two of my brothers and Shelda. The other three brothers were in the other bedroom. My heart was pounding so hard I could hear it in my ears! I was scared about everything, afraid for my mother, and fearful of the booming voice behind the door. Where could we hide? Where could we run? There was nowhere to flee except through the front door. But he was there. We could hear our mother trying to convince the furious man that he had the wrong address. We then listened to the man's voice disappear and his footsteps loudly stomping down the metal staircase. Finally, it felt safe to come out.

Although we might have initially been afraid while growing up in Central City, we eventually had to learn never to show fear or to back down to anyone. Fighting was a ritual that just about every girl and boy in Central City experienced. Once two people earned respect, close friendships would usually form. Like most young Black boys growing up in low-income urban neighborhoods, I had to stand up to a couple of neighborhood boys, some of whom were much bigger and older than

I was. These altercations usually stemmed from verbal exchanges, initially playful, between one boy talking about the other's family, particularly the mother. The second boy often responded more mockingly than the first. We called this "playing the dozens." The object of this game is to jokingly and exaggeratedly mock the other person or his family members so that the other person gives in and ultimately quits the game. Amid the attacks, one must maintain his composure and avoid becoming visibly upset.[1] A crowd would usually judge and pick the winner after each contestant made comments such as the following: "Yo' mama so Black they marked her absent at night school." Playing the dozens, or what we also referred to as "cracking" on each other, was entertainment and a pastime. Generally, the jokes were untrue. If the joking became less about exaggerations and more about facts about someone's family, the line had been crossed, which almost always resulted in a fight.

But there were times when young people fought and the fights would become significant events in the neighborhood, such as when Damien, only nine years of age, sliced Jerald's arm with a razor blade. Jerald, twelve, was getting the best of Damien's older brother Donald. Consequently, Damien ran toward them while Jerald had Donald on the ground and swiped the blade across Jerald's forearm, marking a straight line that revealed flesh. Although almost any flaws in one's dress or physical features were subject to ridicule, now and then one had to be extremely careful about cracking jokes.

In Central City, and similar places elsewhere, respect was given to boys who demonstrated physical toughness and quick wit, excelled at football or basketball, and mastered smooth talking to girls. By the time a boy became a teenager, he had to have developed his unique way of distinguishing himself from others. One could distinguish oneself by wearing the latest fashions, walking with a particular strut or "pimp walk," or developing an impressive move on the football field or basketball court.[2] As young boys, we watched and copied styles from older Black males.

As early as ten years of age, I began to earn a reputation in Central City as a good football player and someone who could fight well. At home and in school I also received praise for my academic abilities. By my teenage years and in high school, I added a solid reputation as a nice dresser to my repertoire. These were other ways that we learned to be Black males in the Court, the Alley, Central City, Powell Elementary School, and Phillips High School. These ways, however, did not always capture Black boys who did not play sports, avoided fights, displayed gay or feminine behavior, and did not play the field when dating girls. They, too, were Black males navigating a society that too often imposed onto them narrow notions of what it meant to be Black and male.

Psychologist Richard Majors and sociologist Janet Mancini Billson, in *Cool Pose: The Dilemmas of Black Manhood in America*, noted how what we were displaying as Black boys in Central City represented a set of talking, gesturing, and mannerisms that ritualize masculinity.[3] Cool pose represents one effort by Black males—often but not exclusively from low-income and urban areas—to portray a sense of empowerment and maintain their dignity and pride amid racism, economic disadvantage, and discrimination. Whereas being cool allowed us to demonstrate uniqueness in style and show our toughness, it could also make it difficult to back down to someone who called you out of your name, talked about your family members, or hit you. From these numerous experiences, we transitioned from Black boyhood to Black manhood in Central City. Defending oneself in response to violence, no matter the risk, was important in maintaining one's dignity and reputation.

Generally, people living in some of the most depressed and destitute situations perpetrate violence against one another rather than people outside their immediate group. The violence is usually rooted in individuals' fears and insecurities about themselves. Whereas physical violence may come and go, psychological violence often remains. Before describing our experiences with violence in Central City, I situate violence within the historical and sociological context of the United States. Examining violence historically and societally provides insights for understanding violence among people residing in depressed economic and racial conditions like we were experiencing in Central City.

Acts of violence were at the core of the founding of the United States as a nation. In their efforts to gain control over the Americas, European settlers waged physical, psychological, cultural, and religious violence against the continent's first inhabitants (so-called Native Americans, whom we now recognize as Indigenous people).[4] The Bible, bullets, and disease served as ammunition during these genocidal acts. And violence against Black bodies and Black minds, in the form of enslavement, provided the economic foundation that would later sustain such warfare.

The barrage of violence against Indigenous people became embodied in the white American settlers' idea of Manifest Destiny and the notion that the Anglo-Saxon race was superior and had the God-given right to control the American continent.[5] This legacy of state-sanctioned violence continued throughout the enslavement of Black people and beyond and well into the twentieth century. For example, on August 6,

1945, the United States dropped the first of the two atomic bombs on Japan, arguably after it was clear that the Allies had already won the war. The U.S. military dropped the first bomb on Hiroshima and three days later a second bomb on Nagasaki. The first explosion killed eighty thousand people, with many more who would die from radiation exposure. The second bomb killed more than forty thousand people instantly. Violence, as H. Rap Brown, the former chairman of the Student Nonviolent Coordinating Committee and minister of justice for the Black Panther Party, said, "is a part of American culture. It is as American as cherry pie. America taught the Black people to be violent."[6] The following set of stories capture violence, between and among Black people in Central City, at the personal level.

⬛

During the year that One Stop Convenience Store opened, I got into a fistfight with Joey, who also lived in Central City. We fought inside the store, and the owners were not pleased. But first, I will describe what One Stop Convenience Store meant to us. In 1980, Mr. James and Ms. Leola, a Black couple in their mid-thirties who lived in the Norwood Community of Birmingham, opened One Stop a block away from Central City. The owners sold snacks and grocery items and allowed their store to serve as a sort of community center for many young people. They even allowed teenagers to work the cash register, sweep and mop the floors for a dollar or a meal, and restock the shelves with snacks. While raising their daughter, Dionne, Mr. James and Ms. Leola often found themselves having to counsel teenagers who came through not to buy snacks but to seek advice or encouragement. With a copy of the Bible and Dale Carnegie's book, *How to Win Friends and Influence People*, near the cash register, their encouragement could be in the form of posted quotes from the Bible or from famous people posted throughout the store. Sometimes all we needed was for someone to listen to us at the moment.[7]

Mr. James often used his store's platform and our attentive spirits to teach Black children who frequented the store about positive thinking: "If you tell a person that they are nothing, then that person will start believing that. The teachers need to be teaching this in schools!" Mr. James would exclaim. His critique of schooling for Black children in the United States was similar to Dr. Carter G. Woodson's assertion in his classic *Mis-education of the Negro*.[8] In essence, Mr. James was describing how U.S. society and its educational system had inflicted psychological violence by teaching Black people to believe that they were inferior and had contributed very little to world civilization. One Stop helped minimize the psychological violence in the community. But the store's presence could not always prevent the physical violence.

Joey and I were inside the store, and the altercation was over an arcade game. I was twelve years old with a stocky build. Joey, a muscularly built fifteen-year-old male, demanded that I allow him to play the pinball machine with the quarters that I had just inserted. Visibly upset that I would not let him play my game, Joey tilted the pinball machine. Furiously, I blared back and dared him, "Nigger, you better not do that again!" "Then what are you going to do about that, nigger?" responded Joey. And then Joey pushed me against the pinball machine. We said the word as if it was going out of style. Mostly, we used the word fondly and toward close friends. At other times, such as how Joey and I were using the word at this particular time, we said it with malicious intent. I took pride in not ever using profanity while growing up, something that my mother did daily. Instead, I used the word in anger, much like a curse word. At the time, we did not process its full meaning and how it is the most complicated and injurious word used against Black people.[9]

After Joey pushed me, I grabbed him and quickly wrestled him to the ground. Then, Mr. James rushed out from behind the counter while yelling, "Y'all get out of my store fighting. Don't be fighting in my store. You don't fight in the white man's store. Then why are y'all fighting in my store!?" Mr. James was right; such a fight would have rarely happened in the white people's stores down the street because we had been programmed never to try such a thing. Mr. James mustered enough energy to remove my arms from around Joey's neck. Mr. James then put both of us out of the store, allowing me to leave after Joey had gone. But Joey and I both lived in Central City, and it was inevitable that the fight would continue beyond the store.

After walking up the street away from One Stop and toward Central City, from a distance I noticed Joey with something in his hand. He was moving toward me. I could not quite tell what the object was. I had just about made it home, but Joey had intercepted my path. By now I had cooled off and just wanted everything to be over, but Joey was approaching with a vengeance, and then I realized that the object in his hand was a baseball bat. Quickly eyeing an iron pipe a few feet away, I rushed over to pick it up. Joey and I met up a few yards from where I lived. There was no way I was going to run upstairs! Instead, we both approached one another and began jousting around, threatening to hit the other. But I decided to throw the iron pipe to the ground, confident I could whup Joey without it. I felt good about my chances because I practiced tussling with my five older brothers.

Joey and I became more determined with a growing crowd egging us on. After flouncing about, all of a sudden I slipped. Then Joey, standing over me, raised the baseball bat above his head. He brought the bat down with all of his might across my back, producing a "cracking sound" and breaking the bat in two. The spectators gasped, equally surprised that the bat had broken across my back and that I seemed unfazed by the blow. Joey was also surprised. I sprang to my feet, quickly grabbed Joey, slammed him to the ground, and kept him penned until it was clear that he would surrender. "Jerome, are you okay?" asked my brother Michael after he had come over to see what was going on. "I bet Joey knows not to mess with you anymore." Michael then told Joey that he would have to deal with him if he tried anything again.

Although it placed me in grave danger to fight Joey with my bare hands, I felt that one hit with the iron pipe would have seriously hurt him. After feeling some reassurance, I took the chance that I would be okay. I had been protected before, when two men got into a fight in our grandmother's house in the Alley and one shot the other. I was a baby and sitting in the middle of the front room. If the fight between Joey and me had resulted in severe injury or death, local newspapers would have pounced on the story. The headlines would have read something like the following: "A young Black male in Central City bludgeons another Black male to death!" Although I knew I had a case to claim self-defense, without money to pay a lawyer, my family and I would have been at the mercy of the court system. And there is usually very little mercy for Black males in that system. While I escaped this potentially disastrous moment, too many Black people become victims of violence perpetrated by those closest to them. Some are unaware of the systemic and psychological violence against them daily, consequently denying them their childhood, dignity, livelihood, education, and adulthood.

In reflecting on the fight, neither of us was going to back down, no matter what. I later saw how important it was for Joey to feel as though he could control someone or something. I now think about how guns have replaced bats, pipes, and knives and that if one of us had had a gun at the time, death would have come quickly. Societal messages had told us to resolve our differences with our fists and weapons rather than words. I knew that if I had not done something, I would have been considered a chump and lost respect among my friends. Joey would have continued trying to punk me out—now referred to as bullying. Reflecting on that moment, I realize that Joey and I were only practicing what was modeled and preached to us in the community and within U.S. society. The U.S. government has historically handled and continues to handle domestic and international conflicts with violence.

⌐

Hunger, neglect, and poverty make people angry and sometimes violent. The temporary fullness that comes from eating a meal will not solve the fundamental issue of poverty. Although the hunger might subside, some of the anger persists. The free breakfast, school lunch, and summer lunch programs, sponsored by the federal government, kept us from becoming too angry. This anger would have definitely spilled beyond Central City. Like Bob Marley and the Wailers sang, "Them belly full but we hungry. A hungry mob is an angry mob."[10] The U.S. government's expansion of these food programs to urban and Black communities, as part of its War on Poverty program, occurred only after the Black Panther Party initiated a free breakfast program that served thousands of children living in poverty.[11] Almost all children in Central City and other public housing communities had to rely on these government programs to sustain us. They not only maintained us but also, in some ways, kept us calm and less angry.

Our mother used the money she received from cleaning white people's homes, along with the welfare check and food stamps, to buy food. Her demanding work schedule and parental duties left little time for her to prepare meals on a regular basis. Fortunately, Richard Jr., the second oldest, had developed some cooking skills. He mainly displayed these skills when he had to cook whenever our mother became ill from hypertension, even though she was only in her mid-thirties. Richard Jr. would take care of the place, including preparing meals, whenever our mother went to the hospital.

As the sole parent raising us, our mother got very little rest. Most nights after work she would stop by the grocery store to pick up lunch meat and white bread for dinner. My siblings and I ate most breakfasts and lunches at school during the school year. On Saturday mornings, we watched cartoons and ate cold cereal with milk. On weekends we received some home-cooked meals, usually something like pinto beans, greens, cornbread, and baked chicken. She topped it off with her home-made banana pudding and Orange Ade—a locally produced orange-flavored beverage. When school was not in session during the summer, we received food from the federal summer lunch program at the Phillips High School gymnasium. All seven of us, along with many of our friends, anxiously awaited the cold lunches delivered by the men driving the refrigerated trucks during the summertime. The lunch program got us and many other families through the summer months.

However, the worst times were the first week after school ended in late spring and the week before school began in late August or early September. Meals were not available because school was closed; consequently, there was no free breakfast or lunch. Moreover, the summer lunch program had not begun yet. Food scarcity didn't seem so prevalent within our household when I was younger. However, it became tougher once my brothers and I started becoming teenagers, one right after the other. This period brought about intense competition for everything, whether it be which bed one could sleep in or what food one ate.

Kenneth and Michael, the third- and fourth-born sons, were one year apart in age. They both stopped attending school during their late elementary years. After being suspended for cursing out the principal, Michael stopped in the seventh grade. Our mother never went back up to the school to re-enroll him. Kenneth stopped after completing eighth grade. He did not want to experience the embarrassment of being in special education courses while his older brothers, Ronnie and Richard Jr., were in the regular classes at Phillips. By the time Kenneth and Michael were teenagers, our mother had decided that it was best to choose which battles to fight with them. She did not force either to return to school. Our mother seemed at peace with Michael being at home during the daytime. In her mind, she no longer had to go down to the juvenile detention center to get him out. But Kenneth and Michael's presence at home all day would occasionally lead to confrontation, usually over food. After being away all day hustling for money through panhandling, Kenneth would return to the apartment, asking about the food he had left in the refrigerator.

"Who ate my hotdogs?" asked Kenneth. No one in the apartment responded, basically ignoring the question. "I know somebody ate my hotdogs because I left two of them in the refrigerator," continued Kenneth. "Man, didn't nobody eat your hot dogs!" countered Michael. "Your retarded ass ate them yourself," continued Michael in a negative tone. "Who your fat ass talking to?" responded Kenneth. "I'm talking to your dumb ass!" Kenneth approached Michael, standing in the kitchen, and said he had better not find out that Michael had eaten his food. If he did, he was going to "get his ass beaten." Michael then told Kenneth that he wasn't going to do anything. After a moment of silence, Kenneth threw a punch. Michael grabbed Kenneth and held him over the sink and started to hit him, cursing profusely in the process. Our mother intervened while shouting, "Let him up, Michael, and take that shit out of my house!"

Maurice and I grabbed Michael, but he was determined to let Kenneth know he was in charge. Then all of a sudden, Michael released Kenneth. "My eye, my eye!" shouted Michael. A gushing of blood oozed from what looked like Michael's right eye as he repeatedly screamed about his eye. Kenneth had reached over in the sink with his free hand, grabbed a fork, and plunged the tip into the area directly above Michael's eye. After being released, Kenneth stood there watching as Michael—panicking at the feeling of blood passing across the whiteness of his eye—hollered out in pain. "Call the ambulance, this crazy ass boy stabbed Michael in the eye!" yelled our mother. Our next-door neighbors called for help. Michael and Kenneth's fights were about more than food; both were trying to salvage their sense of pride and dignity. They had been pushed "close to the edge," as Grandmaster Flash and the Furious Five rapped, and "trying not to lose their heads."[12]

To keep the peace in the apartment and limit fights, our mother provided each of us with a monthly ration of food stamps. I started receiving mine when I was about twelve. After receiving the $300 worth of stamps for the month, our mother kept $100 for herself and Shelda, and then she would split the $200 among the five of us. Ronnie, the eldest, had his own money and could provide for himself. Thus, he accepted fewer than his ration of food stamps. However, the rest of us needed that allotment of $40 worth of food stamps, which rarely lasted the entire month.

Ronnie always seemed to keep money in his pocket. When Papa Slim, Ronnie's father, died during Ronnie's teenage years, our mother allowed Ronnie to receive the entire Social Security check due to his father's passing. He used the money to buy and trade comic books with friends. Ronnie sometimes would give money to our mother or purchase household items such as a television or a new dining room set. While in high school, Ronnie also bought himself a used white Cadillac. He became known to his friends as Boss Hogg, after the television character who drove around in a big white Cadillac on *The Dukes of Hazzard.* As his father, Papa Slim, had done before, Ronnie would flash wads of cash in front of family members and friends.

◗

Managing my $40 worth of food stamps required a careful balancing of the meals from school with the food I would purchase from the convenience or grocery store. I had to make the $40 last until the end of the month. For example, I would buy a loaf of bread and some lunch meat to eat for dinner throughout the week. I ate breakfast and lunch at school. If I needed a little extra cash, I could buy a nickel piece of candy and receive 95 cents in change from the $1 food stamp. By then, we could receive coins from the food stamps instead of those pink and blue paper "due bills." The federal government had changed this a few years earlier. Instead of receiving coins when the amount spent was less than a dollar, the cashier would write the amount—between 1 and 99 cents— that was due on a piece of paper, called a "due bill." People sometimes treated "due bills" like they were not actual money, as indicated by how you could sometimes find them strewn on the ground. But I did not; I collected these due bills whenever I found them.

To prevent the other brothers from eating our food, we would sometimes taint or keep track of our food. We spit inside soda and juice bottles, bought lunch meat with equal numbers of slices, and hid food in the bedroom. The hiding of food contributed to the roach problem in the apartment, alongside management rarely spraying pesticide. Although the competition for food sometimes tore us apart, there were other times when food brought the community and people together.

◗

"Let's see who gets first chance to bust the pack," said my brother Maurice to the circle of friends gathered around to watch the marble game. We made a line in the dirt, and everyone, including Maurice, DP, and I, shot our marbles toward the mark to see who got the chance to bust the pack. Most of us avoided Maurice in a game of marbles because he had a keen eye and could hit a marble from a great distance. Maurice would place the marble in his right hand, hold it toward his face, squint his left eye, and then use his thumb to propel the marble forward and toward its victim. "Clack" would go the marble. "Nigger, give me 'dem marbles! You're out!" shouted Maurice.

Maurice was the neighborhood marble champion. He went around to different sections of Central City to break people out of their marbles—often taking their most prized ones such as the cat's eye types. "Look at that cat eye; I got two of these bad mugs" was how Maurice would describe the new addition to his collection. After marbles we would play a "throw-up tackle" football game, which involved throwing a football into a crowd ranging from two to twenty boys. The brave soul—or fool, whichever way you want to look at it—who came away with the ball had the opportunity to get tackled or score a touchdown. Throw-up tackle was a football training ground for boys in the community.

During one particular football game in the summertime, we heard many people making their way toward some commotion while we were outside running around. Someone yelled, "RJ, go ahead and go home!" "RJ and James Jr. are out there fighting!" shouted a woman. A crowd quickly formed, seeming to agree that it was important that the two teenagers go ahead and settle whatever beef they had with the other. It seemed like everyone from our section of Central City, Sixth Terrace, was there.

"Who's fighting?!" asked DP excitedly. Immediately, we stopped our football game and ran off the field and toward the commotion, ensuring that we would serve as witnesses to someone getting their butt whupped. Maurice and DP ran straight toward the fight. Trailing behind, I remembered to keep a little distance, knowing that anything could happen. By this time, I had learned not to get too close to teenagers when they were fighting because the last time I did, a part of a metal skate cut the left side of my face, a faint mark of which remains. Big Willie (pronounced "Will-ee") had swung a skate at another boy, and it slipped out of his hand and cut me on the left side of my face.

Nevertheless, as all of us got closer to the fighting, the flailing hands appeared eerily familiar. "That's my mama," yelled DP. "That's my mama," said Maurice. Is it what we thought was happening? Were our mothers out there fighting? "Joann," said Maurice; "Mama," said DP. Our mother and Ms. Liz had attempted to stop two young males but ended up fighting themselves.

Immediately, our mother and Ms. Liz started to throw blows at each other until it was an all-out fight. After some neighbors rushed to break them up, each reluctantly returned to her apartment but continued to hurl every imaginable and insulting curse word she could muster. After retreating to her apartment, Ms. Liz got further upset and rushed up the steps to the apartment where we lived with a stick in her hand and determined to state her case. But our mother was through fighting and would not open the door. As soon as Ms. Liz retreated, the police arrived on the scene. Immediately, they placed her under arrest for going after our mother. "You wouldn't have gotten arrested if you had not gone back up there after her," said the police officer. "I'm just tired of having to deal with her shit!" said Ms. Liz. Maurice, DP, and I were embarrassed at what we, and all of our friends, had witnessed.

But none of our friends dared to say anything about our mothers' fight. If they did, we would fight them. DP, Maurice, and I never even talked about the fight. We continued to be friends, even though we were unsure how our mothers felt about one another at the time. Despite the fight, we resumed our game of throw-up football later that afternoon. Although our mothers seemed like they didn't like each other, this incident had no bearing on our relationship. We were still friends.

After getting dressed the following morning, our mother left her apartment. After getting downstairs to the first floor, she walked across the terrace and disappeared into the opposite stairways. Through each tiny window located between floors, one could see our mother heading up to the third floor of the adjacent building. After making it to the top of the steps, she knocked on a door. "Who is it at this time of the morning?" asked Ms. Liz. "Liz, it's me, Joann, and I want to talk to you about something," said our mother in a more mellow tone. "What do you want with me, Joann?" asked Ms. Liz. "Liz, I really want to talk to you if you could please open the door." Ms. Liz could hear the somber tone in our mother's voice and knew that something else must be going on and that our mother had no malicious intent.

Ms. Liz opened the door without worrying about our mother's intentions because the two of them had known each other since childhood in the Alley, where their families had lived. Moreover, one of our uncles was best friends with Ms. Liz's former husband. Ms. Liz and her former husband once lived with our Aunt Maxine and Uncle Monroe until they could get their place. But our mother and Ms. Liz had never been close friends. Ms. Liz was Aunt Maxine's friend.

Once inside Ms. Liz's apartment, our mother told her the real reason why she had come there. "I know we got into it yesterday, and I never thought that I would ever have to ask you this, but do you happen to have some food so I can feed my children?" asked our mother. Somewhat stunned by the request but understanding of the situation, Ms. Liz responded, "Yea Joann, I got some neck bones, some black-eyed peas, and some collard greens. You can have that if you want." Ms. Liz carefully placed the food into bowls, then put the bowls into a large brown paper bag, and said, "Take this. You can get the bowls back to me whenever y'all finish the food." Although the two women recognized their momentary lapse of civility the day before, Ms. Liz and our mother never apologized about the situation. They just walked away feeling as though they had achieved closure. Then our mother turned around and said, "He ain't no good for either one of us." "You so right, girl," said Ms. Liz. "I'm just so glad that God has provided me with enough food so that you can feed your children."

Our mother walked down the stairs, back across the terrace, back up some more stairs, and into our apartment. Then, she placed the food into the refrigerator. Later that day, our mother took the food out, grabbed a butcher's knife to cut up the neck bones as much as she could, and then placed the meat into the oven. She then put the collard greens and black-eyed peas into separate pots on the stove and heated the food for Sunday's dinner. While the food warmed, our mother made some hoecakes, which is fried bread made mostly of cornmeal, a little flour, baking powder, water, and salt. That Sunday afternoon we said grace, and the eight of us sat down and ate a pan of neck bones, collard greens, black-eyed peas, and those delicious hoecakes for dinner. We never knew where the food had come from that day.

Praise God.

CHAPTER 9   GOING TO SCHOOL

"Honey, I always told Joann that she could have been doing something else besides jus' cleaning white folks' houses. But she had to make some money to take care of y'all." These were Aunt Sandra's words. Aunt Sandra was one of my mother's younger sisters and was also our babysitter. Whenever she came over to keep us, Aunt Sandra especially made sure the apartment was pristine. Her obsession with keeping everything clean showed how she didn't want to be, as she described, "one of those nice-nasty people. You know, folks who like to look good when they hang out with their friends but keep a nasty house." In addition to protecting us against germs and becoming sick, Aunt Sandra also cleaned so that "the white folks living in Central City didn't think nothing about us. You know, saying 'Black folks don't clean up after themselves.'"

Aunt Sandra would keep us when our mother began cleaning white people's houses over the mountain. She was around fourteen years old. In the mid-1960s, when she was around eleven, Aunt Sandra had stopped going to elementary school because she struggled to learn school-related information. When Aunt Sandra was a child, her parents—Mama and William Collins—took her to the Birmingham Board of Education to be assessed. But Aunt Sandra said that "Mama and Daddy became frustrated [with the process] and eventually just pulled me out of school." She was not alone. There were other situations of friends and family members who described how the Birmingham public school system would go for years without following up on whether a child was in school, possibly because of the existence of only one enrollment director for the "Negro schools" in the city as late as the mid-1960s. Like other children the schooling system had left behind, Aunt

Sandra relied on "mother wit" to guide her through life. Her sound advice and wisdom—knowledge she shared with just about everyone who sought her out—showed us that intelligence, as the late poet Maya Angelou and others often reminded people, was about more than just going to school.[1]

My earliest recollection of school involved our mother cooking oatmeal in a small pot for me and my brother Maurice. She then spooned the oatmeal into glass cereal bowls. Our mother combined milk, butter, and sugar to sweeten the oatmeal, which formed a syrupy mixture. After Maurice and I had eaten our breakfast, our mother dressed us, combed my hair with a small comb, and styled Maurice's hair, which was longer and much thicker than mine, with an Afro pick. Then she placed our raincoats on us. "Get your bags and let's go," she demanded. Our four older brothers had already left for school. As our mother held each of our hands, Maurice and I stomped down the brick and metal encased stairs from our second-floor apartment to the first floor.

Once at the bottom of the stairs, our mother pushed open the heavy metal hallway door and we walked around the corner. The drenching rain began to beat down on us, only to be deflected by the yellow raincoats and matching hats with paint peeling from the fabric, rerun clothing she had purchased from the Goodwill Store on Twenty-Sixth Street. A rain scarf protected her head. We made our way around the corner and found shelter inside a hallway of another apartment building. People were going up and down the stairs, opening their umbrellas or placing brown paper bags over their heads as we stepped aside. Our mother kept the door open, and we reluctantly walked back into the rain. Peeking out the door, our mother had seen the white station wagon turn the corner. "Come on!" she shouted. We briskly walked toward the vehicle as I jumped over a small puddle to avoid getting any wetter on this sloppy day.

"Good morning. Have them to get into the back seat," said the driver, a dark-skinned, middle-aged, heavyset Black woman. After a quick goodbye hug from our mother, Maurice and I climbed inside the station wagon, and we both faced the rear window, joining the other five children. Towels on the car's floor absorbed the water and mud from our shoes. As we settled in the station wagon, Maurice and I joined the chorus of children singing "Jesus Loves Me."

Shortly after entering the warehouse-looking building in a residential area of Birmingham called Collegeville, all of us—the children—sat down and said a morning prayer at the Christian-based daycare. Everything was there in one large room: picnic tables where all of us ate lunch, learned, and played. On sunny days we played outside and sat on the logs that served as benches for eating our sandwiches. The dog at the house next door watched us children with curiosity behind an enclosed fence.

Then we stopped having to ride in the white station wagon. "I finally got ya'll into the Nursery!" exclaimed our mother as soon as she entered the apartment one day. The Nursery was in Central City and one block from where we lived. Unlike the Christian-based daycare where our mother had to pay a small fee, there were no costs for us to attend the Nursery and we no longer needed to ride in the white station wagon. On my first day at the Nursery, I walked into the building with my mother, but I did not want to stay. "I wanna go home!" I cried, not used to being left alone with strangers. I did not want to leave the comforts of 2508 Apartment C, Sixth Terrace North in Central City. Maurice attended the Nursery also, but he was in another room with the older children. I was no longer by my mother's side or with Aunt Sandra, which had always been the case for the first three to four years of my life.

But being with someone other than my mother, or Aunt Sandra, was very different. "Jerome, it's going to be alright; I'll be back to get you soon. I promise," our mother reassured me. The women at the Nursery, Black and white, comforted me by telling me that I would be fine. Located in the Central City rent office's basement area, the Nursery had a front office for the director and secretary, a set of classrooms, a small kitchen, and an enclosed patio area where children went outside to play. There was no dining area; the teachers brought breakfast and lunch to us in the classroom, and we ate our meals in a family-like setting. Two of my favorite activities included listening to the teachers read stories and riding tricycles with classmates.

One particular teacher at the Nursery, Ms. Shay, eased my transition from home to daycare. Ms. Shay was a recent graduate of Spelman College, a historically Black women's college in Atlanta. During an interview with her years later, I learned that she had also been studying to become certified in the Montessori method, which relied on children taking the initiative in their learning.[2] Ms. Shay had been one of the first teachers in Birmingham to be trained using the Montessori approach.

"What would you like to do today?" Ms. Shay often asked our class. I enjoyed playing games and making snacks such as roasted pumpkin seeds and oatmeal and coconut cookies. I loved going to the Nursery, where we snacked on vanilla wafers, banana slices, grapes, and crackers. After becoming used to the routine and going there daily, I was not ready to leave the Nursery when one of my brothers, Ronnie, Richard Jr., Kenneth, or Michael, would come to pick me up. And every day upon returning home, our mother would ask, "Jerome, what did you do in school today?" She would become tickled when she would tell her friends of my response. "I ate five times is what Jerome would tell me!" According to my mother, the opportunity to eat encapsulated my first experience of going to school.

⌨

Ronnie and Richard Jr., the two oldest, served as academic and social role models for us in the household; they were smart at school and also popular in Central City. A loquacious person, Ronnie enjoyed combining words as part of his rap game, at first when trying to impress his peers and teachers, and later to impress the girls at school. Although Ronnie rarely earned top academic grades, he had an uncanny talent for stringing together disparate words into a cogent sentence and thought and enjoyed engaging in word battles with students and teachers. Ronnie was also an avid comic book collector. He shared his comic books with all of us, whether from DC Comics, Marvel, *Richie Rich*, or *Archie*. Not only did the comic book stories provide entertainment in the absence of a television and telephone in our apartment, but they also inspired our fascination with drawing the characters. Comic books served as some of the first books in our household because they encouraged and allowed the rest of us the opportunity to become readers.[3] Even our mother read comic books.

Richard Jr., the second oldest, academically and musically talented, earned top grades throughout elementary school. His teacher even skipped him from sixth to eighth grade. Richard Jr. served on the Safety Patrol at our elementary school, and I felt proud when I saw him standing outside making sure that my friends, siblings, and I crossed the street carefully. Both he and Ronnie received awards and other recognition for their artistic talents at Powell Elementary School. As Richard Jr. matured into adolescence, he would spend considerably more time

Richard Lee Morris Jr. (with the afro and dark pants) and friends in Central City. (Courtesy, Richard Lee Morris Jr.)

looking at his image in the mirror and enjoying the attention he received from girls. By the time he got to high school, however, he had transitioned from a top student to a "ladies' man." Like many Black males, then and now, seeking ways to validate their manhood, Richard Jr. aspired to become a playboy like some of the older guys he watched while growing up, particularly males like Slick. He liked the way they dressed, talked, and "played the girls." As a lanky, stylish, and well-groomed teenager, Richard Jr. also relied on his soulful singing voice as an instrument to win the admiration of the girls in school.

Ronnie and Richard Jr. first enrolled in Powell Elementary School in 1967. At the time, the teachers and students were overwhelmingly white. Originally called the Free School, Powell's history dates back to 1874, and the present building was constructed in 1888. The city of Birmingham initially built the school for white children. According to some observers, Powell was "the most modern and the best equipped elementary school in the South."[4] By 1972, most white families with school-age children had moved out of Central City and abandoned Powell. Some of the white teachers, however, were still there when I began attending Powell during the fall of 1973. By the time I would leave Powell for high school in 1982, almost all of the teachers at the school were Black women.

My kindergarten teacher was Ms. Green, a Black woman with sandy-colored hair. Maurice, two years older than me, was in first grade, Michael in third, Kenneth in fourth at another school, Richard Jr. in sixth, and Ronnie in eighth. Our sister Shelda was still a baby, not even one year of age. Our mother was at home with Shelda for the first year. When she resumed working, she would ride the bus to take Shelda to Mama's apartment at the Harris Homes (nicknamed High Chaparral or the Chap) housing project in an area of the city called Woodlawn.

My first grade teacher was a white woman, my second grade teacher was a Black woman. Second grade was memorable—when I was referred to the school's speech pathologist, a Black woman named Ms. Summer. Like many Black people speaking in a southern Black vernacular, particularly those from lower- and working-class backgrounds, I often said "da" for the "th" sound. Ms. Summer, a brown-skinned woman with an Afro and large glasses, showed patience when working with me:

> MS. SUMMER: Put your tongue between your teeth like this [showing me how she placed her teeth]. Do this while blowing air out of your mouth. See [making the "th" sound over and over]. Now you try it Jerome.
> ME: "Da." It's kinna hard to do.
> MS. SUMMER: Keep trying, it takes a little practice.

Ms. Summer interjected when I asked whether I should go "wif" her to her office instead of "with" her. Like many Black people in Birmingham, we spoke using the pronunciation and grammatical rules of what linguists now refer to as African American English or African American Vernacular English (AAVE).[5] Rather than correct our speech, Ms. Summer would say, "That is how you would probably say the word at home or around your friends in Central City. But here is how we say it at school."

While working on my PhD almost twenty years after I had first stepped into a school, I began reading books and articles about how Black children's speaking styles had become a contentious educational debate in the United States. During the 1990s, the Oakland, California, school board had passed a resolution acknowledging AAVE, commonly referred to as "Ebonics," as the primary or "home" language spoken by most Black students in the district. Board members asserted that white educators should consider Black students' home language when teaching them standard English.[6] Years before the Oakland Ebonics debate, however, a judge in Ann Arbor, Michigan, ordered teachers to incorporate Black English when teaching Black children living in poverty "standard" American English.[7] Occasionally, I reflected on my experiences learning from Ms. Summer at Powell while learning about AAVE in graduate school.

Whereas six of us had attended Powell, one of our brothers did not. Instead, Kenneth, the third oldest, caught the bus to Lincoln Elementary School near the Smithfield community to attend special education classes. Lincoln was about two miles west of Central City. Our mother did not contest Kenneth's assessment and placement into special education. She knew he learned differently from the rest of us and did not know how best to meet his learning needs. Kenneth began attending Lincoln in 1970, while in the fourth grade, but he did not like attending a different school from the rest of us. He "shot hookie" as much as he could. By seventh grade, Kenneth returned to Powell and attended regular classes through eighth grade. Years later, as an adult, Kenneth recounted to me a possible reason for his delayed learning.

Kenneth informed me that he could barely hear the teacher or some of us at home when we would call his name. We all knew that Kenneth had had an ear infection when he was much younger that caused him to place cotton balls in one of his ears. Pus would ooze from his ear, something that I later learned was the sign of an infection. As an adult some years later, Kenneth described the ear infection and how it affected his learning: "Man, that ear infection affected my hearing, and I just didn't want anybody to know or to tell the teacher. I still can't hear too well out of that ear. It sounds kind of hollow." I asked Kenneth if he remembered his brothers jokingly nicknaming him "Pus Ear." He said that he had forgotten about our jokes toward him. I was relieved to know that he did not feel that we had been abusive or malicious by giving him such a negative nickname.

Kenneth attended school up to the eighth grade, but he refused to go to high school because he would have been placed in JV classes, another name for special education classes. He said that he "wasn't going to go to no high school and be in no special education classes like I'm retarded or something." Kenneth had excelled in some of his classes, even those when he attended Powell, and often earned 90 or 100 percent on his spelling tests. Kenneth knew he was not slow; he just struggled with some subjects, something that is not unusual when we now think about how children can be strong in some academic disciplines and struggle in others. A friend of his who was concerned about how he was feeling back then, and who wanted Kenneth to join him in high school, encouraged him to just go up to Phillips High School and register for the regular classes because nobody was going to question him once he signed up for the classes. Although encouraged by his friend, Kenneth never registered. "Maybe I should have done that," he told me.

I often reminded Kenneth that when he attended school that he did not have enough people advocating for him. Kenneth's refusal to attend high school represented one way he could preserve his sense of self-dignity, especially since his older brothers Ronnie and Richard Jr. were viewed as bright students throughout school and had achieved some popularity at Phillips. People were always going to compare Kenneth to Ronnie and Richard Jr., and he knew that.

Once he reached his early thirties, Kenneth began moving back and forth between living in Central City with our mother, staying with relatives, and living on the streets of Birmingham. He resents Birmingham to this day because he associates it with the poverty we experienced while growing up, his struggles in school, and his homelessness as a young man. In 2001, Kenneth purchased a one-way bus ticket and left Birmingham for good. He now lives in a city in the southern part of Alabama. While there, he met several people who helped him to get disability support.

❏

Silence. Nobody, nothing moved. Our brothers had forewarned us to mind our manners in Mrs. Gede's classroom. "She ain't nuthin' to play with," is what they told us. They had prepared me and Maurice on how to enter, where to sit, how to behave, and when to talk. They told us to always raise our hands and say "yes ma'am" and "no ma'am" to her. I sat on one side of the room, Maurice on the other. Maurice always seemed shy about having me around him and a little embarrassed at the two of us in the same sixth grade classroom.

There she sat, high on her throne, behind a desk. She called roll in alphabetical order, first getting to my name and then Maurice's. "Now I expected one of you to be here this year because it seems like I always have a Morris in my classroom. But two, what did I do to bring that on me?" asked Mrs. Gede while smiling and chuckling simultaneously. "Which of you is the oldest?" she asked. "I am," said Maurice. Maurice was our mother's fifth son at Powell, and I was the sixth. She then asked us about our older brothers, jokingly reminding us to "tell Big Meaty," our brother whose actual name is Michael, that she had asked about him.

Mrs. Gede's smooth brown skin, jet-black hair, and pleasant face greatly contrasted with the military-like stories that we had heard. The long dress, pumps, and constant attention to her watch were exactly as our older brothers had said. Even those of us who thought we were tough dared not move. "Form a line up front, by row," she ordered us.

One by one and row by row, we filed into a single line, all twenty-five of us. A bottle of rubbing alcohol and a stack of those wood-looking, coarse-feeling paper towels sat on her desk. She poured rubbing alcohol into her hands and wiped them clean with the paper towel. "Proceed with the procedure," she commanded, making sure we walked in a single-file line out of the classroom, past another classroom, and into the library. "I'll be back to pick you up in thirty minutes" was all she said. "Whew, she doesn't play," I said to myself.

"Class, Mrs. Gede sent you to the library so that I can go over how to use the card catalog for your reports later this year," stated Ms. Watt, a white woman who served as the school's librarian. She was the kind of teacher who would scare students with stories of what would happen if the Russians were to take over the United States, let alone the world. According to her, "People in Russia don't have any choice in which schools they can attend, where they live, and where they work. You should be thankful that you are free in America."

It was still the first week of school, and I was beginning to wonder whether my experience in Mrs. Gede's class was going to be a dream or a nightmare. Everybody seemed to like her, even though on the first day of class she reminded me of those dictators in communist Russia whom Ms. Watt had told us to fear. By the first week of school, all of us sixth graders had adjusted to Mrs. Gede's classroom routine. By January, we would become immersed in U.S. history, from learning about the U.S. Constitution to writing social studies reports on significant Black people such as P. B. S. Pinchback, who served as the first Black governor of Louisiana.[8] Class was more than reading textbooks. On some days, Mrs. Gede would just put an album on the record player of the Fisk Jubilee

Singers' rendition of the African American spiritual "The Gospel Train." We listened and then began singing along:

> The gospel train's a comin'
> I hear it close at hand
> I hear the car wheels rumblin'
> And rollin' through the land
> Get on board, little children
> Get on board, little children
> Get on board, little children
> There's room for many a more . . .[9]

In Mrs. Gede's classroom, we learned how the Jubilee Singers from Fisk University, a historically Black university in Nashville, would travel throughout the world during the 1800s to raise money for their university. One day, Mrs. Gede stood before us and recited "The Creation" by James Weldon Johnson and then told us we had to memorize it by the beginning of February, only two months away. We also learned "In the Mornin'" by Paul Laurence Dunbar and "The Negro Speaks of Rivers" by Langston Hughes—all before "Negro History Month" in February.

The time was mid-January. Mrs. Gede called me to the front of the class. "Jerome, let me hear you recite 'The Creation.'" I stepped up toward the front of the class and began, but not a word emerged from my lips. I knew how to recite the poem because my mother told me how well I had done it at home. Still, I was silent. "Jerome, go ahead and recite it," said Mrs. Gede. I wanted to, but I also did not want anyone to mock me when they saw that a brown spot had formed on one of my front teeth. It had become rotten; it was like a vice grip forcing me to keep my mouth shut. "Are you shy, Jerome?" "No ma'am," I said. "Then go ahead and speak up. You said it to me at my desk; go ahead and say it in front of the class," she demanded but in an encouraging way. I wanted to speak up, but I couldn't. Speaking in front of the class was very different from doing so in front of the teacher or my family.

Mrs. Gede had corrected me earlier when I stood before her, seemingly not noticing the brown spot on my tooth. She kept telling me to "bring it out." But if I had opened my mouth in front of my classmates, they would have taken whatever flaw I had and run me into the ground. "Yuk Mouth" and "Cavity Creep" were a couple of the nicknames that Central City playmates gave children who had tooth decay. One childhood playmate, who quarterbacked for our peewee football team, joked about how I scored multiple touchdowns while playing running back in a football game only because I had imagined a toothbrush was running after me!

The time was early February. Mrs. Gede eventually chose ML, a classmate, to recite "The Creation" during the Negro History Month program. ML had been born a few days after Dr. Martin Luther King Jr.'s assassination in 1968 and seemed to inherit King's oratorical style. While standing on stage before the crowd during Powell's Negro History Month program, ML began to recite:

> And God stepped out on space
> And he looked around and said
> I'm lonely.
> I'll make me a world!
>
> And far as the eye of God could see
> Darkness covered everything
> Blacker than a hundred midnights
> Down in a cypress swamp.
>
> Then God smiled
> And the light broke
> And the darkness rolled up on one side
> And the light stood shining on the other
> And God said, "That's good!"[10]

By the end of Johnson's poem, which he had written in the tradition of a Negro sermon, ML had convinced the audience members (parents, teachers, staff, and students) that he was actually God when he concluded the poem with the words, "Then into it he blew the breath of life. And Man became a living soul. Amen. Amen."

After ML's beautiful speech, another classmate, Barbara, walked boldly to the center of the room, all dressed in a tattered dress and a multicolored head wrap:

> 'Lias! 'Lias! Bless de Lawd!
> Don' you know de day's erbroad?
> Ef you don' git up, you scamp,
> Dey'll be trouble in dis camp.

Barbara synchronized her arm movements, feet stomping, and head gestures with her voice's highs, lows, intonations, and cadences. The audience sat enthralled by this little girl's ability to transform into a Black woman from a hundred years earlier:

> Ma'ch yo'se'f an' wash yo' face,
> Don' you splattah all de place'
> I got somep'n else to do,
> 'Sides jes' cleanin' aftah you.
>
> Tek dat comb ah' fix yo' haid
> Looks jes' lak a feddah baid.
> Look hyeah, boy, I let you see
> You sha'n't roll yo' eyes at me.

Laughter erupted when Barbara chastised Lias for rolling his eyes! Barbara came from a large and very religious family. Her folks were sanctified Black people. Barbara spoke effortlessly when she embraced Paul Laurence Dunbar's characters from his 1913 poem "In the Mornin."[11]

For Mrs. Gede, it was important to teach us Black children about our people and history in dignifying and nondegrading ways. Mrs. Gede's commitment to teaching our history, our poetry, and our spirituals emerged from her personal and professional lived experiences. These experiences were deeply grounded in her working-class Black roots and shaped by the racial stratification within the city and the class stratification she witnessed among Black people, even within all-Black educational and community spaces. Mrs. Gede was a 1950 graduate of Parker High School in Birmingham, at the time the largest high school for Black people in the United States. She graduated from Miles College, the historically Black college in Fairfield, Alabama—a little town that borders Birmingham. Years later, she would earn a master's degree in education from a local predominantly white university.

At the time that she attended Parker, the school was excessively overcrowded and there were about five hundred students in her graduating class. She recalled how ninth graders at that time were placed in a group of small houses located on what they called Parker Annex. Indicative of the great inequity between Black and white education, white people could send their children to a number of white high schools, including Banks, Woodlawn, West End, Ensley, Ramsay, and Phillips. Black people's children first could attend only Parker High, and later Ullman High School. As she noted, "Parker had the task of giving education to just about the whole Black population in Birmingham." Amid this inequity, however, Mrs. Gede was careful to note how the Black principal and teachers "did the best they could with what they were working with." She felt the school could not adequately teach everyone, so she learned how to teach herself the material.

At Parker High, Mrs. Gede fondly recalled one particular teacher who assigned *Up from Slavery* by Booker T. Washington as a class reading. She said she always "wanted to know why anyone didn't have a book about the contributions of Black people." Mrs. Gede, fortunately, had an aunt who embraced her love for Black history and bought her some of Carter G. Woodson's books and readings on Negro history.[12] She even informed me that the Birmingham public school system would later adopt some of Woodson's books for the Black schools. "I learned a lot of history about Black people from that book. I developed a love for Black history, a love for civics, and a love for things about history." Mrs. Gede's deep love for history and especially Black history would encourage her to read on her own, without the teacher's prompting.

Mrs. Gede's precociousness as a student, however, was not readily visible to or acknowledged by some of the teachers at Parker High School, partly because the school was overcrowded and also because she was not the kind of child the teachers expected would achieve. Mrs. Gede's parents were not the middle-class Black parents, such as doctors and lawyers, who could minimize the racial and educational inequities that their children experienced. Nor could her parents provide her with the social class advantages that some Black children experienced in an all-Black educational and community context. She particularly recalled a time when the Black teachers overlooked her for a history scholar's bowl team. She had taken a statewide test over history and placed seventh in the state. The teachers and administrators at Parker were impressed by this achievement but did not know how she was able to score so high. Mrs. Gede informed them that she had studied the material herself. After she had scored so well, the principal and teachers wanted to place her in a scholar's bowl. "The doctors' and lawyers' children," she emphasized, "had been handpicked for the scholar's bowl and the school was preparing them for competition." Still, none of those coached students scored anywhere near her level. Mrs. Gede noted that she "came from Ensley by way of a bus. What Parker [school officials] would do is get the children from the Smithfield area [middle-class Black area at the time] who walked to school and zeroed in on them. I was from the wrong side of the tracks, do you know what I mean?"

During the spring of 1982, a fellow eighth grader at Powell who also lived in Central City and I were extended the opportunity to enroll in one of two academically enriched high schools, Ramsay Alternative Magnet School and Huffman Magnet School. Both schools had a substantial population of white teachers and students. Due to white people's resistance to busing, district leaders throughout the United States began using magnet schools in the late 1970s and early 1980s as a way to attract white students to city schools, to promote school choice, and to voluntarily desegregate the schools.[13] Like many urban public school systems in the 1980s, the Birmingham public school system embraced the magnet strategy to desegregate, but especially to retain white students in the district.

A few of the Black families from Central City had decided to send their children to Ramsay and Huffman, hoping for a good education. Not just in Central City, Black families from impoverished communities throughout the city faced a dilemma when seeking what they felt was a quality education for their children. Like others, they were concerned about the lack of resources and derelict facilities that too often accompanied the predominantly Black schools where we were zoned. Many Black families were excited to get their academically motivated children into a magnet school—which had more resources than regular city schools.

One of our teachers at Powell, Mrs. Turrentine, pointed to my classmate and me one day in class and said that she wanted to speak with the two of us about our choice of high school. Mrs. Turrentine, the most senior teacher among an almost all-Black teaching staff at Powell at the time, sat us down and encouraged us to "consider Phillips High School because many of the 'white' schools only want to take the best and the brightest Black students from the 'Black' schools. You can get a good education in the Black schools." Mrs. Turrentine, a graduate of the historically Black Miles College near Birmingham, was disturbed by the way the white schools siphoned off talented Black students, ultimately leaving the Black schools with the most challenging students to teach. She wanted people to see that "good students also can come out of the Black schools."

That conversation with Mrs. Turrentine encouraged us to attend Phillips instead of Ramsay. We had heeded her advice. Although Phillips was once a white school up to the early 1960s, by the 1980s it was almost all

Black. Mrs. Turrentine helped us to understand the problem of following white people when they run away from Black people. Like thousands of Black educators before her, and like some today, Mrs. Turrentine's advice politicized us about desegregation and the dynamics of educating low-income Black students across the United States.[14] Similar to critical race theory (CRT) scholars today, she talked about how the city's magnet school process was really set up in the interest of white students, teachers, and schools.[15] Mrs. Turrentine's perspective, like that of many Black educators before and since the 1954 *Brown v. Board of Education* ruling, challenged conventional narratives about Black people's views of public school desegregation.[16] She encouraged us to attend Phillips with a vengeance, despite how many outsiders had negative views of this now predominantly Black school.

Some of our Powell classmates who attended the magnet high schools talked about how they felt that some of the white teachers and students in the city's magnet schools expected less of them. Catching the buses early in the morning and arriving back later in the evening also meant that some Black students had little time to engage with the rest of us from Central City. Black students who once attended these schools noted how attending schools outside of their Birmingham neighborhoods had created a wedge between friends and former schoolmates. Some felt disconnected from their communities, their friends, and the neighborhood schools.[17]

❏

"Jerome, are you going to the prom?" asked one of my teachers, an African American woman who taught government and economics.

"I'll wait until my senior year," I answered.

"No honey! You're the student government president and you have got to be there this year," she asserted.

"I'm the president-elect," I responded. "Besides, I hadn't planned on going to the prom this year, and I would have to get a tuxedo, a date, and a ride."

"Now, you know it's not a big thing for me to just swing over to Central City and pick you up as I finish organizing the setup for the prom. I just got to get there early if you're going to ride with me," she said encouragingly.

"I appreciate the ride. I'm just not ready to fork out some money for a tuxedo," I responded.

"Honey, you know you are one of my children. I've got this. Don't you worry about it!"

"Thanks!" I said.

"The owner of the tuxedo shop and I went to high school together. She helped to put on a fashion show at our school, and I can call her to see about getting you a tuxedo," said my teacher.

I later went to the tuxedo shop to be measured. The cost to rent the tuxedo had already been paid by my teacher, who understood the dire economic situation that my family and I were experiencing.

On prom evening, my teacher, who also coordinated the prom, pulled up in her white Cadillac, and all eyes in Central City fixated on her and her car. I got into the car wearing my tuxedo, and we drove over to Birmingham's South Side where the prom was taking place. After the prom, I had to make my way back home. My teacher had a cleanup crew, but they had to load up many of the party items and transport them back in her car. Fortunately, a friend on the football team had driven to the prom with his date. He gave me a ride back to Central City.

The following Monday in our world history class a classmate and a teammate on the football team began cracking jokes on me: "Fellas, after the prom was over, I saw Jerome on the side of the highway, all dressed up in a tuxedo, with his thumb all up in the air and shit! The nigger was hitchhiking!" Laughter erupted from most of the students in the classroom. His joke was a little too close to the truth for me to handle. A girl whom I liked sat in front of me in the classroom. She also heard the joke and seemed to have laughed a bit. It was okay to crack jokes about what one had or did not possess in front of a group of guys, but it was off limits when such talking took place around a girl. I had lost my composure. I pointed my finger at the student's face, telling him to stop lying. He swung at me, and I swung back. We began tussling. Our teacher—a burly Black man who doubled as the world history teacher and the football team's assistant coach—had left the room momentarily. The teacher quickly returned after hearing the commotion. He broke up the scuffle. After class had ended, the teacher just sat us down and told us not to try that again. He also reminded us that we were football teammates and should not be fighting in class. No one called the principal or the police on us, as is too often the case for so many Black boys and girls attending schools today.[18] No suspensions or expulsions were issued. Little was made of what had happened. The incident was over. We both went to class and then on to lunch, where he of course continued to tell his version of the fight.

After escaping that incident, I realized that I needed to keep my cool. Everyone was watching and had high expectations of me. I thought back to the time when another teacher at Phillips, also a Black male, pulled me aside during my freshman year and reprimanded me for running through the hallways. I was with a classmate of mine when I should have been in class. After running me down—he must have run track in high school or college—the teacher (who taught electronics classes) began scolding me: "Morris [some of the teachers referred to me by my last name], I've heard some good things about you from the other teachers. You've got too much potential to be acting like a fool around here! You need to tighten up and act like you've got some sense!" This teacher pulled me aside and reminded me why it was imperative that I focused academically. He was not the only one.

Another Black male teacher, who taught chemistry, reminded me and my fellow eleventh grade classmates during one class session about the sacredness of teaching. During this particular session, tears literally came to this teacher's eyes when he saw how some of us were not taking seriously the unit on stoichiometry that he was teaching in his chemistry class. After witnessing this act of love and commitment to us, we felt embarrassed and collectively apologized to him. As a sixteen-year-old Black male, this was my first time ever seeing a man, let alone a Black man, cry. Our chemistry teacher enjoyed teaching, loved teaching us chemistry, and loved us as students. That profound moment by the chemistry teacher—as well as the generosity by the history teacher to pay for my tuxedo to attend the prom—illustrated to me, in the words of Brazilian educator and philosopher Paulo Freire, that "it is impossible to teach without the courage of love, without the courage to try a thousand times before giving up."[19] Granted, there were some teachers who would make us wonder about their reasons for teaching, but most of the teachers at Powell and Phillips cared deeply about us, not just academically but as people. These educators wanted us to do well in life, and they focused on developing what researchers are now calling "the whole black child."[20]

❏

Going to school in Central City was close to home, familiar, intergenerational, and culturally affirming. This was especially the case with Powell Elementary School. Like the roles that many schools historically served in Black communities, Powell, though not intended for us Black students at first, had become a pillar of strength for the families and students in Central City and nearby communities.[21] Children who attended the school from the mid-1970s through the 1990s benefited from an amazing principal named Eva Hardy Jones. A Black woman, Mrs. Jones assumed Powell's principalship in 1976, during my fourth grade year. She was tall, regal, dark skinned, and stern. Mrs. Jones represented the antithesis of the previous principal, a chubby white man. As a Black woman from Birmingham, Mrs. Jones demanded that students respect teachers, parents, and themselves and insisted on high academics, but she also knew that we needed additional resources given our families' circumstances.

Like Black principals throughout the South, Mrs. Jones would petition the district and the local business community for resources for our school.[22] Her approach to the principalship, as I reflect on it in terms of my historical understanding of Black schooling, is reminiscent of the approach of Booker T. Washington, the famous founder of Tuskegee University. Mrs. Jones reached out to families in Central City, provided resources to the families there, and bridged Powell with key businesspeople throughout the city. During her time there, Powell became registered as a historical landmark. Moreover, she convinced the school board to purchase the nearby and vacant Trailways bus station so that the students could have a gymnasium.[23] I was honored when Mrs. Jones welcomed me back as a substitute teacher after I had graduated college and regularly invited me to speak to students during my graduate school days.

Almost all of my teachers at Powell were Black women. In addition to my kindergarten and second grade teachers, I also had Black teachers in the third, fourth, fifth, sixth, and eighth grades and throughout high school. Each teacher left an indelible imprint on me and shaped what I would imagine a teacher to be for Black children. Most had graduated from nearby Miles College, Alabama State University, Tuskegee University, or Alabama A&M University—historically Black colleges and universities in Alabama. The relationships between Powell's educators and our families and the centrality of the school in our lives had shown to me the power of such schools and educators in low-income Black children's lives. These experiences modeled to us how a school can serve Black children, families, and communities in poverty. Not until I attended graduate school would I begin to connect the Black teachers with a tradition of Black education that had been so common in the South and in the history of Black schooling.

In my research for my dissertation about twenty years after I first stepped into Powell, I captured similar relationships among Black educators and schools that I was researching in St. Louis and then Atlanta. I published some of this research in 2004 in an academic article titled "Can Anything Good Come from Nazareth?"[24] In the article, and later in a book titled *Troubling the Waters: Fulfilling the Promise of Quality Public Schooling for Black Children*, I pleaded for serious study of contemporary Black schools, and the educators in them, that worked for the betterment of Black children, families, and communities. Moreover, I put forth the Communally-Bonded Schooling Model (CBSM). CBSM is a framework that views the relationships among schools, families, students, and communities, as well as a sense of history and culture, as integral to Black students' academic success.[25] This model recognizes the strengths that existed within Black schools and communities, while taking into account how racism still shapes Black people's experiences throughout U.S. society.[26] Key aspects of CBSM include (1) intergenerational trust and cultural bonding between educators and Black students; (2) critical presence of Black educators in the schools; (3) educators who reach out to Black families; (4) principals who bridge schools and communities; and (5) schools that serve as pillars in Black communities. The CBSM should be seen as part of a larger effort that connects schooling to housing and economic policies that enable and sustain Black students' educational success when they go to school.[27]

As I have shown above, going to school is not just about a physical place; it is also about the relationships that children have with educators and the curricula they are being taught. For Black children to go to school and excel there we must ensure that their educational ecosystem (the child, the family, the school, the community) is fully supported for the optimal development of their educational and social success.

CHAPTER 10   THE SUGAR JETS

The sun beat down as sweat poured from the glistening faces, arms, and legs. The fruit juice or Kool-Aid frozen in a cup—which we referred to as freeze cups or bebops—barely cooled us from the blistering sun and heat. The street barriers were up, and the adults cooked hamburgers, chicken wings, hot dogs, and spare ribs on the grill. "One Nation Under a Groove" by Funkadelic blasted over the speakers while we danced. Adults played card games, and all of us on the Sugar Jets football team sported new jerseys—we had saved up enough money through fundraisers to buy our football uniforms. Happiness was in the air, and we were now on the move.

In the middle of Twenty-Fifth Street, with his shirt off, stood Chicken George. He was not the enslaved Black man who raised chickens for cockfighting, as seen on Alex Haley's *Roots*.[1] Our Chicken George was the neighborhood hype man who danced, sang, and philosophized about life—especially after drinking a little alcohol.

"What's the matter with my team?!" Chicken George shouted. Immediately, a chorus of ten-, eleven-, and twelve-year-old boys—fully decked out in our football uniforms—responded together: "Oh, your team's alright!" Chicken George repeated the call but with a sense of questioning whether we were truly ready to go out and compete on the football field: "Y'all don't hear me! I said, what's the matter with my team?" Bravely, and with all eyes on us, we responded, "Oh, your team's alright!!"

The bus sat near the curb, like a white, red, and gray fortress on wheels! We had earned, begged, and saved enough money. Our football team's bus, a once old and yellow school bus, had been transformed. Before raising money to purchase the bus, our team members would ride in the back of pickup trucks and station wagons to our football games. We later nicknamed our bus the Double Dutch Bus, after Frankie Smith's 1981 hit song.

◖

At the block party, others joining Chicken George included his singing partner Slim, a lanky brown-skinned man with a smooth basketball game, a soulful voice, and a receding hairline. Slim had grown up in the Alley, where everyone used to call him Sonny Boy. People in Central City now knew him as Slim. Slim sang Sam Cooke's "Summertime," Chicken George danced the "Mashed Potato," Brenda, Toni, and Chelsey—in unison—danced the "Bus Stop." Brother Jones played African drums called the djembe, and a group of young boys formed the Central City Poppers (CCP). I was a dancer in that first CCP group, but I did not stay with the group for long. Other CCP dancers came from not only Central City but also the Norwood Community. Inspired by the hip-hop cultures emerging from New York and California, CCP, the Electric Poppers, and similar dance groups in other Birmingham housing projects made money dancing at house parties, at block parties, and during halftime at high school basketball games.[2] Hip-hop was everywhere, not just on the East Coast and West Coast. As scholars have begun to chronicle, and what we were experiencing back then in Central City, hip-hop had made its way to the South.[3]

Another group of males at the block party sparred with nunchucks. Almost every young male thought he knew kung fu or karate, just because many of us had seen Bruce Lee's *Fist of Fury* or *Enter the Dragon* at the Melba or Empire theaters downtown. The Carver Theatre, located on Fourth Avenue in Birmingham's once-thriving Black business district, was no longer showing featured movies.[4] My older brothers, Richard Jr. and Ronnie, would take Kenneth, Michael, Maurice, and me to the theaters. After watching the movies, we often pretended to be Lee, the martial artist icon with lightning feet and hands, or Jim Kelly, the soul brother and karate expert who wore a perfectly shaped Afro and sideburns. We danced and sparred when the deejay played Carl Douglas's 1974 hit song "Kung-Fu Fighting."

On the basketball court in the park, teenage males with nicknames like Amp, Monkey Man, Steele (my brother Ronnie), Trickwood, Boone, and Wolf would run back and forth shooting hoops. While one set of players was competing on the court, another stood on the sideline talking jive while waiting for their chance to show off their ball skills. "My up," shouted one player on the sideline. These block parties would go off every year without a hitch, except for this particular day when the deejay stopped "One Nation Under a Groove" in the middle of the song after two teenage males began fighting. One male stabbed the other one. "Damn, man, Black folks can't have a good time without some crazy shit going on!" said the deejay while packing up his albums and turntables.

⌐

Our neighborhood had two football teams: the Central City Vikings (Central City Community Center's football team) and the Sugar Jets, which Sugar Man had started. The Community Center's football team was sponsored by and received funding from the Birmingham Housing Authority. The Sugar Jets, on the other hand, relied primarily on fund-raisers and donations. Mainly consisting of boys from Central City, the Sugar Jets' players also came from other public housing communities and neighborhoods such as Hooper City, ACIPCO, Collegeville, Fountain Heights, Druid Hills, and Norwood.

I began playing football when I was seven years old, starting with the Community Center because the Sugar Jets did not exist at the time. My play cousin Pee Wee, who lived in the Druid Hills / Fountain Heights area, was the Community Center's star player. We considered him and his brothers and sisters "play cousins" because our families were very close and had grown up together in the Alley and the Court. Cuz (a version of the word "cousin") was one way to describe the depth of the relationship with folks we might not have had a blood connection with, but our parents had grown up together.[5]

During the first official football game I ever played in for the Community Center, I caught a ball intended for an opponent—an interception. After I caught the ball, I ran as fast as I could. I looked right and left and saw that many people on the sidelines were pointing and shouting something at me. But the noise seemed like an echo in my ears, rendering me unable to figure out what they were saying. It finally became clearer when Pee Wee caught up with me: "Cuz, you're going the wrong way!" Pee Wee grabbed me and turned me around. I ran full speed in the other direction, eluding tacklers, determined not to go down. All I knew about football then was to run hard and run fast, and that's what I did. I scored a touchdown after starting in the wrong direction! Propelling us to victory that day was Pee Wee, who scored three touchdowns.

Around nine years of age, I became a member of the Sugar Jets. I was about ninety pounds and had just completed the fourth grade. Sugar Man gave me jersey number 45, and I played on defense. I also wore jersey number 46 sometimes. Sugar Man, recently released from prison, had moved into Central City with his girlfriend, Ms. Liz. He would often tell us years later that he started the football team to "give back to the community. Coaching the Sugar Jets helped me about as much as it helped you all. It helped me to stay focused and out of trouble."

"Call Backyard Special Number One!" hollered Sugar Man. We had three plays on offense: Backyard Special Number One, Backyard Special Number Two, and Backyard Special Number Three. For Number One, Petro, the star of our team, caught the pitch from the quarterback. With his left arm, Petro threw off the opposing defender, who had pierced deeply into the backfield. He pivoted and reversed the field to the left side, passing by all of us, his teammates, and outrunning Ensley's players for the touchdown. Petro scored his sixth touchdown of the day, leading us to victory! Petro was unstoppable, and not just that day. He went on to excel as running back at Phillips, even though the team struggled throughout his career. I became the next player from the Sugar Jets and Central City to excel on the Phillips football team. Like Petro, I took the Sugar Jets' spirit with me to Phillips.

October 1984: I was a high school junior, and we were in Huntsville, Alabama, playing against J. O. Johnson, one of the state's top football programs. After I had played multiple positions, including cornerback, linebacker, and quarterback, the coaches decided to place me exclusively at quarterback my sophomore year. We were an all-Black high school team playing an integrated football team in J. O. Johnson. I had thrown a couple of touchdowns earlier in the game, but I had also tossed an interception.

As I made my way to the sideline following the interception, Coach Kelly, our head coach, jerked me by the jersey and screamed, "Jerome, why did you throw that goddamned football across the middle and got it intercepted? Didn't I tell you about that?"

"Coach, I was trying to go to the open receiver," I countered.

Fuming, Coach shouted, "I told you about throwing the ball across the middle! You must think that you're the Messiah or some shit; ain't but one Messiah, and his name is Jesus Christ!" Then all of a sudden,

Coach's body contorted and he squeezed out the words, "You gonna give me an ulcer!"

Without warning Coach Kelly pulled back, and all I could see was his large fist coming toward me! It plunged into my stomach with a mighty smack. He almost knocked the wind out of me. Instinctively I responded. I had already mentally rehearsed how I would react if a coach ever hit me again because of the way Coach Kelly slapped players across their helmets after committing mistakes. I also thought about the time that the B team coach paddled me during my ninth grade year because of interceptions I had thrown during a game. This time, I vowed, I would not let coaches get away without retaliation.

I immediately swung at Coach Kelly, barely missing the side of his face. He was paying the price for hitting me and other players and for the hits that other coaches had dished out over the years! Fortunately for Coach Kelly, some of my teammates intervened and slowed my blow by partially restraining me. Off guard, Coach Kelly stepped back and shouted, "Oh shit! Y'all let him go! Let him go! If he tries to hit me, I'm going to make his ass walk back across the Tennessee River to get to Birmingham! You won't be getting back on my bus if you hit me! What kind of shit is that? This nigger done lost his goddamned mind!"

Not really. I thought that Coach Kelly had lost his mind or that he thought it was acceptable to hit players. But by the fall of 1985, the beginning of my senior year, I had fully earned the coaches' respect, and Coach Kelly turned the offense over to me, allowing me to call plays on the field. Although I did not land that punch in Huntsville, my willingness to fight back had stopped Coach Kelly from ever trying to hit me again and made him think about physical contact with other players that year. There were consequences for his actions. I had learned this lesson while growing up as a little boy in Central City. Phillips High School, from my perspective, would be no different. In Central City, if others knew that you would fight back, they were less likely to mess with you. I would take this lesson to Phillips and beyond.

It was fall 1985 and the beginning of the football season. We had just won our first game, beating Wenonah by a score of 12–9 the week before. The next game would be a showdown featuring two offensive powerhouses—Parker and Phillips, both located on Eighth Avenue and just two miles apart. Some people nicknamed this game the Battle of Eighth

Author's high school football photo. (Courtesy, *Birmingham News*, original photo by Bernard Troncale.)

Avenue, but there truly was no rivalry because Parker had beaten us at least ten years running. As the first Black high school in Birmingham, A. H. Parker (originally named Negro High and then Industrial High) was the grandfather of Black high schools in the city and state. The school had a storied academic and athletic history. It seemed as though every Black person in Birmingham had some connection to Parker. My grandmother and mother had attended Parker, which was once the largest Black high school in the United States, enrolling approximately three thousand students in the late 1920s and early 1930s.[6]

For me, the game between Phillips and Parker was meaningful in so many ways. First, few could remember the last time Phillips had beaten Parker; some of my high school friends, specifically those in band and Key Club, waged bets that we could not beat Parker. One even dared to say, "Look, Jerome, I know you are the quarterback and everything, but Phillips can't beat Parker; those dudes are too big for y'all!" I looked at him and said, "Man, you are saying that to my face?" "Yeah, Jerome, I don't see y'all doing it." Another friend said, "I bet you ten dollars y'all won't win. Man, Parker has that bad quarterback; plus, Phillips hadn't done nothing in years."

Second, at the time Phillips suffered from a lack of school spirit caused by a negative reputation. A recent dismal football history further compounded this feeling of dread. Thus, as Black people in a once all-white school that the white business community and alumni immediately abandoned after the school had become predominantly Black, we were trying to build new traditions at Phillips, to become a proud and new Black high school. The only problem was that we were not "the Black high school"—Parker owned that title.

Third, I had grown up in Central City with Parker's quarterback and one of their starting receivers. Their families had moved out, one to the Smithfield public housing community and the other to their grandmother's house in Fountain Heights. We were also classmates at Powell Elementary, played together for the Community Center and Sugar Jets, and always competed against each other, whether academically or athletically. Bragging rights were at stake!

Finally, I still had not gotten over how Parker had beaten our team during my junior year. That year Parker's defense sacked me multiple times, partly because of our struggling offensive line and partly due to my inability to elude tacklers. By my sophomore and junior years, I had developed into a good passer—thanks to the countless hours I invested working out with former players from Phillips and Carver who had gone on to play college football. But my understanding of the quarterback position, of when to scramble to extend plays, was still developing. I blamed myself for some of the losses my junior year and vowed that teams would never sack me the way Parker's defense had the previous years.

During the spring and summer months leading up to my senior year, I trained in the weight room every day and wore ankle weights to increase my foot speed and quickness. Derrick, nicknamed DC, was my workout partner. DC, a receiver, and I committed ourselves that year to becoming better football players, students, and people and changing Phillips's football trajectory. Every day after school, DC and I would meet on the practice football field with our cleats, a football, and jugs of water. We trained without coaches' supervision. After working out, DC and I regularly stopped by the One Stop Convenience Store. Mr. James, the owner, always provided us with an inspiring message. As DC and I would enter the store, Mr. James would shout, "Here they come—the greatest quarterback and receiver in the state of Alabama! Give these young men whatever they want! Man, Parker better watch out when y'all play them!" Mr. James, a Parker alumnus, counterbalanced the negative societal and school messages. Unfortunately, sometimes these messages would come from some of the people in the school and the community.

❏

My mother was determined to attend the 1985 Phillips versus Parker football game. She hoped to catch a ride with Sugar Man, who would transport folks to see some of his former players compete. But unable to get to the game, my mother began walking the three-mile journey along Eighth Avenue North from Central City to Legion Field in Smithfield. She always wore a long dress and tennis shoes and kept a purse across her shoulder.

Phillips's band, riding in a couple of yellow Blue Bird school buses, hadn't gotten too far down Eighth Avenue North when one of the band members shouted, "Hey, that's Ms. Joann, Jerome's mom, walking to the football game!" "Stop the bus!" called out the band director. After the bus stopped, the director, in a very polite and mild manner, asked, "Mrs. Morris, where are you going?" When she responded that she was headed to the game, he replied, "You come on and get up in here. You can ride to the football game and back with us."

I didn't know how my mother had gotten to the game. During warm-up drills, I just looked up and saw her sitting with DC's mother in the stand. They were drinking and enjoying themselves. After seeing all of the people from Central City in the stands at Legion Field, our coach walked over to me and said, "Goddamned Jerome, you've got a moth-erfucking fan club!" I felt I had already won with my mother, the Sugar Jets, and Central City behind me. It mattered not whom I competed against or had to fight.

Our team entered the stadium and the game fired up! We had to pri-marily rely on the passing game because our running backs had played sparingly. Two of my cousins, Devon and Reginald, were on our offen-sive and defensive lines.

Errors marred the first and second quarters of the game. By halftime, we were losing 20–0. Back in the locker room, however, Coach offered a few words of encouragement and refrained from the animated antics he would typically display on the sidelines. He just looked at us and said in a very calm manner, "Fellas, we have got to do something." I nodded in agreement. On our way out of the locker room and while running back onto the field, DC caught up with me and said, "Rome, you hadn't really thrown to me at all in the first half."

"Yeah, man, you're right. We have been training too hard to lose this one. I'm finna come to you, okay?" I responded.

DC was encouraged: "A'ight man, I'm ready, Rome! Let's do this thang!"

At the beginning of the third quarter DC ran an out-and-up route on one of the first plays from scrimmage, and I launched a 65-yard pass. Touchdown! The score was now 20–6. Everyone got hyped, and our school's band began to play "I'm So Glad":

> I'm so glad I go to Phillips High,
> I'm so glad I go to Phillips High,
> I'm so-so glad I-I go to Phillips High,
> Singing glory Hallelujah! (Whooh!)
> I'm so glad!

Our band director had brought to Phillips "I'm So Glad," originally based on the African American spiritual "I'm So Glad Jesus Lifted Me," when he arrived in the 1970s after graduating from Tennessee State University, whose band had popularized the song. The song would be played by many historically Black colleges and universities and almost all of the predominantly Black high school bands in Birmingham.[7]

With our band playing in the background, I kicked off the football to the opposing team and then tackled the returner. But Parker immediately scored another touchdown to increase their lead, 26–6. Afterward, Parker kicked off to us, and my play-cousin, Lil D, a freshman, returned the ball to around the 20 yard line. Looking back, many of us involved in that game were relatives or close friends. In addition to my two cousins on the football team, two of my nieces (on the Clency side of my family) were part of Phillips's band; one was a majorette, and the other played a band instrument. Parker's quarterback and one of his receivers had grown up with me in Central City, and we had all once played for Central City and the Sugar Jets.

After receiving the snap in the shotgun formation, I rolled to the right and launched a deep pass in DC's direction. The defender tipped the ball and changed its path. Anticipating the tip, DC honed in on the ball's trajectory, caught it, and raced to the end zone, untouched, for a 72-yard touchdown. We were now trailing 26–12. Our stingy defense, led by players with nicknames such as Skull, Big Walk, and Bulldog, stopped Parker. After we got the ball back on offense, I delivered a pass across the middle to the slot receiver, Valentine, who had also been my next-door neighbor since age four, on fourth down with 10 yards to go. He had made one of the most clutch catches of the game. The next play I scrambled to the right, moved to the left, attempted to run, and then I immediately saw a receiver streaking toward the goal line. Instead of running, I launched the football approximately 50 yards and toward the right side of the field to Skull for a touchdown! He spiked the football, to the coaches' disappointment. Although our team had been penalized 15 yards, Skull had fired us up! We still trailed 26–18.

Our defense became even stingier and forced a fumble, giving the ball back to our offense. From the shotgun formation I received the ball from the center, stepped forward as though I would run, and then threw the ball to LC, another slot receiver, who was open in the end zone: 26–24! We decided to attempt a two-point conversion. DC faked as though he was running to the sideline and into the flat, then peeled back inside the defense, just behind the linebacker, where I delivered the ball. Good! We had tied the score at 26 at the end of regulation.

We received the opening kickoff in overtime. On our first play I didn't even have to look over at DC, but the entire stadium knew that I would throw to him and that there was nothing anyone could do. Lined up to my right, DC ran a square-in route, and I hit him for a touchdown. We led for the first time in the game, 32–26! For the two-point try DC switched over to the left side of the field. Parker blanketed him with their two best cornerbacks, both of whom would eventually play at the University of Alabama. I then went back to DC on a "Z in and Z out" route for a successful conversion, giving us a 34–26 lead! Parker also scored a touchdown in overtime, but our defense, bending but not breaking, denied them on the two-point conversion! We had finally beaten Parker after more than ten years of futility. Our team, coaches, and fans joined the band, belting out, "I'm so glad I go to Phillips High!"

The following morning, Parker's quarterback walked almost three miles from his family's apartment at Smithfield Court to Central City to offer his congratulations. Although Parker had beaten Phillips ten years in a row, the fall of 1985 was a different story. Parker's quarterback had thrown four touchdowns, but I had eclipsed him with five! But nobody should have lost that well-played game. He and I gave each other big high fives and exchanged hugs. That game was our final competition, and we both understood that.

The victory over Parker was not just a football victory; it was a triumph over deeply embedded self-doubt that too many of us had internalized. It was a victory for a group of Black students taught to believe that they were nothing and did not have a rich tradition to embrace. There were few prominent Black family names, little academic or athletic pride, and no community clout to inspire us. Our triumph was a transcending moment for the school, the students, the coaches, my teammates, and myself. For those of us from Central City, this victory was a testament that we could shine when many before had doubted us.

Later that season, DC and I earned Alabama all-state honors. After that game and the season, I realized that many younger males growing up in Central City, Fountain Heights, and Norwood were looking up to DC and me. Several Phillips football players would be selected to the all-state team in later years, including three from Central City between 1990 and 1993.[8]

Almost thirty years after that game, during the summer of 2013, a few of Coach Kelly's former players organized a luncheon for him. Coach did not have much longer to live. I took Amadi and Kamau, my children, because I wanted them to meet the coach I had told them so many stories about. I also wanted Coach Kelly to meet them. About fifteen former players gathered at a restaurant outside the city, and Coach Kelly was so happy to see all of us. We all greeted each other with hugs. Coach Kelly stood to make a speech midway through the luncheon, thanking all of us for showing up. He talked about how he felt so blessed to be there because he did not think that he would live to see another year. In an apologetic tone, Coach Kelly described why he was so tough on us, that he had learned how to be that way from his upbringing. While pointing directly at me, he also noted that he had learned he could not hit everyone because some players were more sensitive than others. I interpreted this to mean that he knew some players would not let him hit them and would fight back. With tears in his eyes Coach shared, "I don't have to live another day because you fellas have made my day and my year! I just want to thank you!"

As a Black child coming of age in the 1940s and 1950s in rural Bessemer, Alabama, Coach Kelly had experienced the deep depths of poverty and racism. He wore every emotion on his sleeve. Coach Kelly earned a scholarship to play college football at Alabama State University, from which he graduated. He also worked while in college, using part of his salary to send money back home to care for his mother and siblings. He shared, "I had to be the man of the house, and I was responsible for helping to take care of my Mama. When any of my brothers or sisters acted up, I had to set them straight. As they say, spare the rod, spoil the child." Coach Kelly would take this grinding attitude about life and his belief in corporal punishment right into his profession as a teacher and high school football coach.

Coach Kelly passed away in June 2014. As I made my way into the church to attend the funeral, Blue, a teammate from high school, jokingly said, "Yeah, Jerome, I remember that time you and Coach Kelly got into it." Blue sang in the church's choir, and he and Coach Kelly had stayed in touch for years. Also present was Big Walk, who had gone on to play professional football in the NFL.

The pastor who delivered the eulogy compared Coach Kelly's life to a football game and reminded many of us in attendance that we too were in the fourth quarter of our lives. However, "there might not be any overtime." As he preached, I read through the obituary and noticed that Coach had moved away from football and had no longer been known only as Coach Kelly. He had become Deacon Kelly. With a new name and a new title, he had thrown off that old life and gotten himself "ready for the Lord." Blue, other members of the choir, and the whole church began to sing,

> I've moved from my old house,
> And I've moved from my old friends,
> And I've moved from my old way of strife.
> Thank God I've moved out to a brand new life.[9]

CHAPTER 11 FIRST IMPRESSIONS

Growing up in Central City, my brothers, friends, and I had to look good! And we had to have money to get that fresh haircut from the barbershops downtown, either Etheridge Brothers or New Breeze. When we didn't have enough money to go there, we could still get a fresh cut from the neighborhood barber in Central City who was so precise that he used a razor blade to edge our hair. He charged us only two dollars for a haircut.

As young people, we were brand loyal. Just about everybody wanted fashionable clothes or shoes. We purchased Levi's jeans and Jordache tennis shoes from Jean's Glory downtown. The pressure was on to look good. With parents only scraping by financially, many of us did without or just accepted that our mothers could not purchase fashionable clothing for us. Some young people resorted to stealing clothes, jewelry, and even money whenever the opportunity presented itself.

Fortunately, some of us got summer jobs at the Downtown Farmers Market, about five blocks away from Central City at Twenty-Sixth Street and Second Avenue North. Market days were long, hot, and tiresome. Frank, the farmer I worked for, was a country-looking white man who wore cowboy boots, blue jeans, a cowboy hat, and a scruffy beard. He sold purple-hull peas, black-eyed peas, sweet corn, watermelons, and homegrown tomatoes. Frank was from Chilton County—just an hour south of Birmingham. Peaches were his specialty.

Like just about everything else, my brother Maurice, my friends, and I competed to see who could earn the most money by becoming the "top tip earner" for the day. Although the base pay was around twelve dollars a day, we could make tips by taking customers' purchases to their cars and providing pleasant customer service. Tip amounts ranged from a quarter to a dollar. While the pay was good for young males who were barely teenagers, we still had to adapt to being around the white farmers, whose attitudes toward Black people ranged from genuine niceness from some to subtle racism from others. But one of our peers who worked for the Freemans, the only Black farmers at the market—earned more than all of us. The Freemans fed him breakfast and lunch daily. He also made fifteen dollars a day without tips!

One day Frank, the farmer I worked for, sent me to purchase some grocery bags from Willie's Super Market. The market was only one block away. On my way there, a large white man stopped me. "Young man, I can sure use your help pushing this car into the shop," he said, with one arm inside the left side of a Mercedes-Benz while his body was out of the car, simultaneously trying to push and steer. He stopped and stood, and I could see that he was about six feet two inches and weighed more than three hundred pounds.

"Yeah, I can help, but how much are you going to pay me?" in my trying-to-sound-like-I-knew-how-to-make-money voice. "Besides, this was a white man, and I should do all that I could to get as much from pushing the car as possible," I thought to myself. As Black children, we had seen some of the things that white people possessed, but mostly from magazines and television because we rarely got a chance to see how they actually lived. One day our mother took Maurice, Shelda, and me to one of the houses of the white family whom she cleaned for regularly. They were out of town that day, so we never got a chance to see or spend time with their children. We saw only the inside of their house.

"Sure, I'll give you something," said the white man. "Just push from the back of the car so that we can get it up this slight hump here. Now, on the count of three, I want you to push. One, two, three, push!" I pushed with all of my might as if I had superhero strength. We got the car into the dusty, gray, and paint- and chemical-smelling building. Mission accomplished! We began talking.

"Do you work at the market?"

"Yeah, I do."

"How is it?"

"It's a'ight."

"My name is Preston," he said while reaching out to shake my hand. I placed my midsized hand into Preston's large hand, and we shook hands. "What's your name?" he asked.

"Jerome." I continued, "I always pass by here and smell car paint and see cars out and everything. Do y'all just be painting them cars and everything in here?"

"We paint, we do bodywork, a little of everything. I am the world's greatest auto repairman!"

We both laughed.

"Bodywork? What is that?" I asked.

"You know, like removing dents out of cars and repairing cars that have been in wrecks."

"Oh, that's what that means?" I said and asked simultaneously.

There was a sign outside the shop reading "Preston's Foreign Car Body Shop" in neat letters. I had seen it numerous times while at Willie's Super Market across the street. But when I read the words "body shop," although I could smell paint fumes every time I passed the building, I thought of someone who worked in a mortuary or something like that. Back in Central City, we would lump this description into one category, "fixin' cars."

After realizing that Farmer Frank would be looking for me to return soon to the market with the grocery bags, I abruptly ended my conversation with Preston: "I've gotta get right back. Talk to you later." I then hurried across the street.

Back at the market later that day, I had just finished bagging some peaches, plums, and peas for a customer when Preston approached me. "You forgot to get paid after helping me to push the car into the shop," said Preston. "Oh, yeah, I did," I said after finally remembering that I left without getting paid. "Here, take this." It was a ten-dollar bill. "Hey, thanks for that. I appreciate it! I just like talking to folks."

"Do you know anything about working on cars?" Preston asked. "Uhn uhn, but I've got an older brother named Michael who knows a heap about cars," I said. Preston then asked: "Well, do you fix up bicycles? You know. When I was a young boy like you, we always rode around and would fix our bikes whenever they would break down." "I don't got no bike; I sometimes ride my brothers' bikes, but I never got into fixing up bikes." Preston seemed shocked at my response. "Well, I can teach you some things about fixing bikes and working on cars. I want to offer you a job to work in the shop with me." "You would? What would you want me to do?" knowing that I had very little interest in learning how to fix cars.

"Maybe you can help me organize my tools, run errands, and clean up the place a little bit." "Oh, I can do that!" I exclaimed. "How much do you make here at the market?" asked Preston. "Twelve dollars a day." "What time do you get to work?" "Seven in the morning, and we stop at five."

"Well, I can pay you fifteen dollars a day, and you can come in from nine in the morning until four in the afternoon. I also cover lunch for you," he said. "When do you need me to start?" I excitedly asked. This white man seemed nice, I thought to myself.

Once I began working for Preston the following week, he made sure I had a hearty breakfast and barbecue and steak lunches from some of the best places in Birmingham, including Fife's Restaurant at Fourth Avenue and Twenty-Third Street, Milo's Hamburgers, and Niki's on Finley Avenue. Preston loved to talk and eat, and I enjoyed talking and eating with him. But Preston also understood that I, like many of the other young males at the Farmers' Market, was in survival mode at times. We had learned to portray a facade of street smartness and toughness as a way to protect ourselves. Preston began asking me questions about life and what I wanted to do when I grew up. He revealed to me a little about his childhood, his relationship with his "tough" father, how a lot of people had helped him in life, and how he had once attended Phillips High School for a few months in 1960—back when it was an all-white high school that refused to admit Black people.

⌨

"Hello, and how are you doing? Could you please tell me where I need to go to get to the school's library?" asked the visitor as she stepped inside the front entrance to Phillips High School. "Just go down the hall, up the stairs to the second floor, and then take a right. The library will be on your left-hand side," I informed the visitor, a white woman who appeared to be in her mid- to late forties. Sensing her unfamiliarity with the expansive school, I continued, "Don't worry, I'll take you there." As I proceeded, she followed, walking alongside me and up the stairs to the library. "How is the school here?" "I really like it a lot," I said, never knowing that she was querying me about the school and had latitude on whether to use the information as part of her evaluation of the school. She continued asking me a series of questions, including what grade I was in and my name. She then informed me that she had come to Phillips to attend the meeting of the Southern Association of Colleges and Schools, commonly referred to as SACS. Phillips's beautiful library provided an excellent forum for official school system meetings. "Oh, by the way, my name is Ruth."

A few months after that encounter, a letter arrived in the mail inviting me for an interview that would eventually determine whether I would be selected for a summer study program to Hitachi City, Japan, Birmingham's new sister city, for which I had applied a few months before. The program's leaders planned to select four students from the pool of applicants interviewed. The interview was scheduled for a spring Saturday morning and would occur at Birmingham's Central Library, three blocks from our apartment. The night before, I rehearsed the essay I had written as part of the application process. I also ironed my black slacks and white buttoned-down shirt, set out my penny loafers, and then smoothed out the sport coat I had purchased earlier that week from the Jimmie Hale Mission's Thrift Store on Twenty-Fourth Street and Third Avenue. For years, my family occasionally stopped by the Mission to find excellent deals on clothes and household items. The Mission partly contributed to my high school attire and some of our family's furnishings.[1]

I arrived at Birmingham's Central Library and made my way to its main conference room. The Birmingham and Hitachi Sister City Commission coordinator, a representative from the mayor's office, and a third person, the lady I had met in the Phillips High School hallway and who had asked me for directions to the library, all greeted me. "Hi Jerome, it is nice to see you again," said Ruth. I was shocked and ecstatic that the lady I had previously met was now interviewing me for an opportunity to travel to Japan. Before the formal interview began, she expressed how much she appreciated how I took the time to talk to her and walk her to the library when she couldn't find it. After the interview, I felt confident about my chances. The committee members informed me that I would receive notification in the mail.

A month passed, and I had not received anything. I became nervous and checked the mailbox every day, to no avail. Then one day a Black male in his mid-twenties, whom I had seen in Central City only about a few months or so earlier, brought a stack of mail to me. "Are you Jerome Morris," he asked. "Yeah, that's me. What's up man?" I asked cautiously. "Oh man, I just moved around here with my old lady. Your mail has been coming to her address; I guess y'all got the same address but on a different street." "That must have been why it took so long. Thanks for bringing my mail around; I appreciate it," I said to him. "Where you from?" "Oh, my folks 'nem from Tuxedo Court, you know, the Brickyard." "What brings you over on this side of town?" I asked. "Oh, just got on downtown at this little place. It's cool and all, but I need a little more." "Wishing you the best," I said. "Appreciate it." "What's your name, man?" I asked. "Johnathan, most folks call me JJ."

As soon as JJ handed me the mail, I quickly skipped past the few letters from different colleges inquiring about football and noticed a piece of mail with Birmingham's Sister City Commission stamped in the left-hand corner. I tore open the envelope with exhilaration, unfolded the letter anxiously, and began to read, "Dear Jerome Morris: On behalf of the Sister City Commission, Birmingham Public Schools, and the Mayor's Office, we are pleased to announce that you have been selected as one of four 'Youth Ambassadors' to represent the City of Birmingham in Hitachi City, Japan." It went on, "If you are not able to make all of the meetings and participate in the orientation, then we will select an alternate in your place."

They didn't have to worry about whether I would make all of the meetings, I thought to myself. It was also possible that I might have missed out on confirming my selection for the Japan trip had it not been for JJ, who delivered the mail to me. Our family did not own a telephone, so it was challenging to receive messages. But our next-door neighbors were great and gracious about allowing me to give their telephone number out and then relaying messages. I didn't want to wear out their generosity. They were terrific neighbors!

JJ's delivery was crucial; otherwise, the alternate student would have traveled in my place. My life could have taken a different direction. Fortunately, I got a chance to thank JJ a few months after returning from Japan. I ran into him during the fall of 1985 at a city government building where he served food in the cafeteria. As one of the Student Government Association presidents from the city's high schools, I was required to attend a citywide meeting at this particular building. "What's happening, man?" I asked JJ once I had recognized him. "It's a'ight, trying to hold it down. You know how things can be." Both of us nodded in agreement. "Thanks again for getting me those letters. I could have missed on that opportunity to go to Japan had you not gotten that mail to me," I said to him. I placed my order: "Man, please give me some of that barbecue chicken, collard greens, macaroni and cheese, and roll. Also, let me have some sweet tea and banana pudding." After coming up from staring at the food, I then asked JJ, "How long have you been working here?" "Nah, man, I don't work here. I am *in here*."

I immediately became embarrassed at the naïveté of my question because I could not see anything JJ could have done that would have landed him in the city jail, where the meeting was held. I continued, "You mean to say that you are in here, like in being locked up?" "Yeah," said JJ. Was my first impression of him incorrect? After eating my food and completing the meeting, I thought about Black men like JJ. I guess law enforcers saw JJ differently than I had. They must have treated him differently. I could not wrap my head around why the Birmingham public school system had its student leaders tour the city's jail. Were we meeting there because of a lack of meeting space or because of the good food? I was not sure.

⌐

The big day had arrived. It was a Saturday morning, and we were flying to Japan. We traveled via the now-defunct Eastern Airlines with short layovers in Atlanta and Los Angeles en route to Tokyo. In preparation for my trip, the Vulcan Kiwanis Club, which sponsored our high school Key Club, ensured that I, who served as the Key Club's vice-president, had a couple of new sport coats, slacks, and ties. The Vulcan Kiwanis Club's members transported me to the department stores to purchase new clothing. This all-Black Kiwanis Club was committed to ensuring that I represented the city of Birmingham, the Key Club, and especially Black people well in Japan. Moreover, with its professionally dressed members and regular conversations about Black entrepreneurship and civic engagement, the organization had introduced me to professional attire and "middle-class Black culture."

The trip to Japan was the first time I had traveled on an airplane. It was also my very first time traveling outside Alabama. Two white women, one whose husband worked at a local college and a teacher at a local high school, served as chaperones. The plane landed at Narita International Airport in Tokyo. We deboarded and made our way by minibus to Keio Plaza, a luxurious hotel with beautiful rooms in downtown Tokyo. I shared a bedroom with two high school males, one white and the other African American, also selected for the trip. The female student chosen for the trip, who was white, shared a room with the two adult chaperones. All of us, the four students, attended different high schools in the city. This trip became my first glimpse of how the rest of the world viewed people from the United States. One instance, in particular, comes to mind.

On our first day in Tokyo, the chaperones allowed us (the three high school males) to walk around downtown Tokyo to do some shopping since Tokyo was a relatively safe city, even though it was home to over eight million people. As we walked, several individuals spoke to us and seemed amazed at these three teenagers who looked every bit "American" in our mannerisms and dress. A young Japanese woman, appearing to be in her early twenties, caught our attention, or we caught hers. Her name was Yuzuki, and we saw her while passing by a department store.

"Hello," she said in English. "Konichiwa," we responded in Japanese. The three of us proceeded to speak Japanese to her while Yuzuki wanted to practice her English. We soon seemed to be speaking in a common language, a combination of Japanese and English. Yuzuki asked us where we were staying, and we informed her that we were at the Keio Plaza. Did Yuzuki perceive us as wealthy since we were staying there? Maybe so because she then said she wanted to get to know us better and asked whether she could come and visit us at the hotel. Knowing by looking at one another that we should have said "no" to her request, our pride as young males said it wouldn't hurt anything if she were to come over to our room. We were going to talk and learn more about each other, which is how we rationalized agreeing to let her visit us. We all walked cautiously back to the hotel, careful not to make it appear as though we were hiding something.

We nervously caught the elevator and proceeded to our hotel room. "Please sit down," I said to Yuzuki. Before we could get into a good conversation, we heard a knock at the door. Was it the hotel staff arriving to clean the room? No, it could not be because they had cleaned the room earlier in the day. "Open the door. It is us," said one of the chaperones. "Which one of us would open the door and get caught?" I asked myself. Quickly, we told Yuzuki to hide somewhere. "The bathroom; put her in the bathroom," one of us said. We finally answered the door, keeping the chain on the door, as we talked to our chaperones while the door was ajar. "Why are you peeking through the door?" asked the other chaperone. They had caught us in our deception.

"Open the door!" she insisted. We unlatched the chain on the door and allowed them in. While inside, our chaperones could still tell something was amiss. They smelled the room and noticed an aromatic smell. "Why did Yuzuki have to wear perfume?" I asked myself. "Are you hiding something? What is that smell?" asked one of the chaperones. "No ma'am," I said. "But there is someone who wanted to get to know us. Come out, Yuzuki," I said. Yuzuki emerged from the bathroom. The look of disappointment immediately swept across the chaperones' faces.

They scolded us for allowing Yuzuki up to our room and for hiding her in the bathroom. "You all are supposed to be leaders, and we expected you all to set the example for Birmingham's young people," said one of the chaperones. The word "leader" was attached to us. Carrying ourselves as leaders is what they expected of us; it was our responsibility

Taking a photo in 1985 with my Japanese host family in Hitachi City, Japan. (Source: Author's collection.)

to uphold that standard and expectation. Our chaperones reminded us of our roles as city representatives and that we should bring only honor to Birmingham when traveling abroad. They noted that they would tell Mayor Richard Arrington and the school board if something like this occurred again. The threats and embarrassment were enough to keep us focused throughout the trip. It was a learning experience for us, namely how we as young males did not know how easily a situation could degenerate and be misinterpreted. Throughout the remainder of the trip, the three of us were on our very best behavior.

CHAPTER 12   INNER-CITY CHURCH JOYS AND PAINS

No one in our apartment regularly attended church. There was an occasional baptism or joining a church by my brothers when they became teenagers. However, that was about the extent of it. They would join a church, get baptized, attend for a little while, and then stop going. As a child, I viewed church as where funerals occurred and where I could wear our new clothes for Easter Sunday. Instead of attending services, my brother Maurice and I religiously played football every Sunday morning with other boys our age in Central City.

But somehow, we managed to absorb the spirit of the Black church through our daily living. For example, our mother listened to church music every Sunday morning on the city's Black radio station, WJLD 1400 AM. She sang along with Mahalia Jackson about Jesus meeting the woman at the well, and she enjoyed the way Sam Cooke and the Soul Stirrers sang "Jesus Gave Me Water." While we were not a churchgoing family, there were some in Central City. A few of these families were what we called sanctified folks, people we saw as overly religious. They seemed to go to church throughout the week, always quoted scriptures from Revelation about how the world was in its final days, and said that women and girls should wear only dresses and should not serve from the pulpit.[1]

Every now and then, however, our mother had the urge to take us to church. This urge usually appeared when some major issue was going on in her life, such as the time our brother Michael went to the juvenile detention center or the times when she would fight other women over a man. When I was about six years old, our mother dressed up Maurice, our sister Shelda, and me and took us to Beulah Baptist Church. Maurice and I both wore black slacks and white dress shirts. Our mother dressed Shelda in a floral-print light-colored dress. While our mother held Shelda in her arms, Maurice and I walked alongside our mother, nine blocks from Central City to Beulah Baptist. Nine blocks seemed like a great distance back then, especially on this summer day. We had left early enough to avoid entering the church sweating. Beulah Baptist Church was located in a rectangular-shaped brick building on Eighth Avenue North near downtown Birmingham.

Upon entering the small building, we were greeted by a group of Black women, all uniformly in white dresses. They escorted us into the sanctuary and directed us to a long and dark bench. The people, children included, were decked out with their suits and dresses. On stage sat three Black men dressed in black and dark brown suits. Behind them sat choir members, all outfitted in matching robes. After a brief prayer by one of the men, the choir stood and sang an opening song. Afterward, a man who sat on the largest chair in the center of the stage rose from his seat. He was tall. Rev., the name they called the man, began speaking slowly.

Midway through the sermon, Rev.'s cadence quickened. Our mother started to shout, scream, and cry. We barely ever went to church, but that did not stop our mother from shouting more than anyone in that place. She was "happy" was how the grown folks in the church described the moment. There was nothing that I could do. I felt confused at what was going on and looked at Maurice, who seemed tickled by what had happened. It also seemed as though Rev. enjoyed seeing everyone become excited.

After Rev. sat down for a few minutes, the organist began to play. The sounds emerging from the organ caused the lead singer, a woman, to sing more forcefully, and our mother to shout even more. The woman sang,

> Jesus met the woman at the well
> Jesus met the woman at the well, Lord
> And He told her everything she'd done. . . .
> He said, woman, woman, where is your husband?
> He said, woman, woman, where is your husband?
> He said, woman, woman, where is your husband?
> And she said oh oh, oh oh Lord, I have none!
> He said, woman, woman, you have five husbands
> Well He said, woman, woman, you have five husbands
> Oh! He said, woman, woman, you have five husbands
> But the one you have now, he is not yours![2]

Whereas Rev.'s preaching had stirred our mother to shouting, the woman's singing and the church music had her throwing her hands in the air, contorting her body, and screaming "Hallelujah" and "Thank you, Lord." She also had tears in her eyes. The only thing I wanted everyone to do at that time was to be quiet. "Shut up!" I thought to myself. But that was not going to happen because a woman in the back of the church, in between Rev.'s pauses and the singer's singing, egged them on: "Take your time, take your time," she said encouragingly.

Finally it ended! Everything had settled down, but our mother continued to whisper, "Thank you Jesus, thank you Jesus, thank you Jesus." After the service, our mother talked to a group of women who said they would pray for her. While there was moaning and hollering just an hour earlier, everybody was happy and smiling by the end. We then began our long walk back home. Our mother carried Shelda, and she began to sing with a gentle and sacred soulfulness about how Jesus had met the woman at the well.

In reflecting on that day in church, I realize that I didn't understand that Rev.'s preaching, the woman's singing, and the spirituals at Beulah Baptist were not the sole causes of my mother's shouting. She was releasing her pain—the stress, sorrow, and regrets she was feeling at the time.[3]

When I was about ten years old, a church would come to us in Central City, traveling inside a school bus converted into the "Joy Bus." They were from the Church of Christ. The Joy Bus leaders gave us snacks and prizes. I was proud of myself when they handed me a new white Bible as a prize for memorizing the titles of the twenty-seven books of the New Testament. The Joy Bus's leaders had names like Johnny, Susan, and Cowboy Donald, the most colorful of them all. Wearing boot-cut blue jeans, a cowboy hat, and cowboy boots, Cowboy Donald, along with his fellow Christians, would ride up into Central City in the Joy Bus singing loudly, "I've got the joy, joy, joy, joy down in my heart."

As a child back then, I did not think much about why the people on the Joy Bus had come to Central City. I was just excited at the opportunity to learn about church stuff due to my fear of going to hell. I am almost certain that I associated their race as white people with the common depictions of Jesus, and God's pointing hand as that of a white man. But that was how I felt as a child back then.

As an adult, I would learn that the Joy Bus was part of a national movement known as Joy Bus Evangelism. This movement involved hundreds of predominantly white congregations throughout the South and consisted mainly of missionary-minded white people who called themselves "brothers" and "sisters" in Christ. Like in other cities, they traveled throughout Birmingham's different public housing projects to save so-called inner-city souls.[4] In many ways, these twentieth-century missionaries continued the actions of earlier white missionaries who had traveled the world to spread their version of Christianity. They presented themselves as color-blind white people, something that I did not think much about then. In reflection, I realize that they said nothing about the city's and country's racist past toward Indigenous people or Black people. They said their mission focused on glorifying God and that Jesus loved us as children, whether "red and yellow, Black and white."[5] The Joy Bus leaders appeared to be filled with happiness when they came through Central City. But their expressions, so joyful and cheerful, were different from what our mother displayed when she had the Spirit.

The Spirit made our mother happy sometimes but sad other times. The saddest time was at our grandmother's funeral in the spring of 1981. Our grandmother, whom we called Mama, was our mother's best friend in the entire world. She understood everything our mother was going through because she had experienced many of the tribulations herself. Mama too had felt the pain of losing six children during childbirth before my mother—the seventh child—was born. At the age of sixty-five, Mama died in her sleep in her apartment in Birmingham's Harris Homes housing project (commonly known as High Chaparral or the Shep). Mama prayed for our mother daily. Like Mama, our mother would pray daily for her seven children. I had never seen my mother wail the way she did at Mama's funeral; she sang with a mixture of joy and pain.

A few years later, while in high school, some classmates would occasionally ask me whether I was "saved," which meant that I had been baptized. I told them that I was not. Churchgoing people could make you feel like the most sinful person in the world if you had not "gotten right with the Lord." Birmingham is in the Bible Belt, and seemingly every respectable Black person had a church home. For many people attending church and accepting the Lord into their life was sufficient. It did not matter what they had done or were doing, nor did it matter if they were "good people." If they had not been saved, they were going to hell.

During my senior year of high school, I began to feel tremendous pressure to go to church from peers and adults, and I caved. Seventeen years old at the time, I was a little past Birmingham's standard in terms of "giving my life over to the Lord." Nevertheless, I joined a church and got saved in March 1986 at Greater New Antioch Baptist Church near Finley Avenue. A classmate from Phillips who was a member of the church invited me to attend one Sunday. Three people joined me to witness my baptism: my mother, one of my high school teachers, and a high school girlfriend.

After we had been seated for some time, I was called up to the front by Rev., the pastor, to get baptized. In unison, the church's choir and parishioners sang,

> Take me to the water,
> Take me to the water,
> Take me to the water,
> To be baptized.

During the singing, Rev. said, "In the name of the Father, In the name of the Son, and in the name of the Holy Ghost, let the church say Amen"; he then dunked me into a round vessel of water placed near the pulpit.

At the time of my baptism, I did not know the full sacredness of the water in our people's experiences. The African American spiritual hymn "Take Me to the Water" was our people's song about baptism. But water had many more meanings. It was also used as a secret mode of communication, such as in the song "Wade in the Water." Black people sang that song to warn others to change course by wading through the waters. Traveling through the waters was about not only changing one's life but also fleeing captors during enslavement. Though the water could be troubled, it represented a necessary step toward freedom.[6] On that day, I was on that path, a path that would continue beyond church.

Although I attended Greater New Antioch Baptist Church for a couple of years, my experiences were memorable and supportive. A fellow church member and Phillips classmate showed me church through his actions. He knew that I could not get to church regularly because I had no transportation. So just about every Sunday morning he drove five miles from his parents' home to pick me up and drop me off. Moreover, the church family provided scholarships to young people, including me, who went off to college.

My ideas around religion began to broaden when I traveled to Jordan the summer after graduating from high school. I received a scholarship from an organization and program focused on educating young people about the Arab world. "Are you Muslim, Jerome?" Jordanian Muslims posed that question several times throughout that trip. When I answered that I was not, *Insha'Allah* (which means "if it is God's will") would almost always be their response. On this trip I was challenged to think more critically about how one's place of birth and upbringing are critical in shaping one's values and religious beliefs. I told people that I was a "Christian," although I had not become fully immersed in the religion's doctrines while growing up. That was all I knew to say due to the social pressures from people in Birmingham. I began to understand that if I had been born in another country, I most likely would have embraced the predominant beliefs and religious system there. But I had grown up in Birmingham.

As Black folks, most of what we received over the past three hundred years was the Christianity white people imposed on us. Although this Western model of Christianity had become a tool of oppression against Black and other people worldwide, in our creative way we took the religion and shaped it into a liberating and transformative force for human rights and consciousness.[7] For me, any religious or spiritual approach worth anything had to say something meaningful about and for the experiences of Black people, no matter where we were. Dr. Musa W. Dube, a biblical scholar from Botswana who befriended me and Mary (my wife) when we lived in Nashville, reminded us to critically examine the Bible and demonstrated how to read it in decolonizing and liberating ways for women and Black people.[8] This meant that Black people living in the Central City housing project represented those who once lived in the biblical town of Nazareth, where Jesus lived. Just like Nazareth then, good could also come from Central City.[9]

Throughout college and into adulthood, I made efforts to seek out religious and spiritual spaces that addressed Black people's social conditions. These spaces might involve joining a Black book club, creating a mentoring program for Black adolescent males in a Nashville middle school, or attending the Million Man March in Washington, D.C., in October 1996. Moreover, I regularly attended several churches along the way, more so for the cultural affirmation and community than for the religiosity. One such place was Metropolitan Interdenominational Church in Nashville, pastored by Rev. Edwin C. Sanders. After leaving Nashville and moving to Georgia in the late 1990s, Mary and I regularly attended and then joined First Afrikan Presbyterian Church in metro Atlanta. Led by Rev. Dr. Mark Lomax and grounded in Black liberation theology, First Afrikan provided cultural sustenance and community for me, my wife Mary, and our two children, Amadi and Kamau.

Outside of church as an institution, two people further reminded me of how the Black church is not a physical place but a spiritual space. Rev. Dr. Alton B. Pollard, a Black church studies scholar and leader, and rev. jeff carr, an interspiritual faith leader and cofounder of Infinity Fellowship in Nashville, teach us that the Spirit resides within. Still, I never became a "church person," and I am still not one today. However, whenever I go to church, I primarily go to hear the spirituals, which capture our people's stories. Those stories represent the sacred texts that we as Black people must continue to write—far beyond any religious book or doctrine.[10]

CHAPTER 13   APRIL FOOLS' DAY

Shelda was the youngest of the seven of us and the only girl. I still remember her birth in 1972, when I was four years old. Our mother finally got that baby girl she so desired! When Shelda arrived from the hospital, we all took turns holding and kissing her. Although she was the youngest sibling, Shelda did just about everything that we did. However, I would find out later that she would experience the world differently from her six older brothers.

On one particular day, when I was seventeen years old, Shelda and I packed our dirty clothes into a large black plastic bag, and I heaved the bag over my shoulder. While I toted the bag of clothes, Shelda, who was thirteen at the time, carried the laundry detergent and bleach in a brown grocery bag. Every other Sunday morning, we would take our clothes to the laundromat. For the previous three years, Maurice and I had made this trip to wash our clothes, but he was now in Jacksonville, Florida, in the Job Corps program, which is a federal program that provides vocational training to low-income young men and women ages sixteen to twenty-four.[1] Maurice and one of our homeboys from Central City went to Job Corps together on a buddy plan. They both took up brick masonry as a trade.

Shelda and I left Central City and began to walk the six blocks to the laundromat. Halfway there, I challenged her to a race to the top of a hill. Shelda, a good runner, immediately took off. With the large bag over my shoulder, I still tried to catch her. Although she was ahead of me, I noticed that she moved a bit slower than usual this time because of the weight she had picked up. The oversized blouses she now wore could no longer hide her chest area, nor could the jeans conceal the extra weight gain.

Nevertheless, Shelda and I made it to the top of the hill, turned left, and stopped to go into Church's Chicken restaurant. We spoke to the assistant manager who had once lived in Central City with her husband and four sons. She gave each of us a couple of pieces of free chicken. "Tell Joann hello for me," she reminded us. We walked a couple of more blocks and entered the laundromat managed by a slender and brown-skinned woman whose children and grandchildren attended Phillips High School. Shelda and I had brought some quarters and dimes with us, making sure we budgeted the right amount of money to squeeze as much time as we could out of the dryers. After finishing our washing and drying, we retraced our steps back to Central City.

A few weeks after noticing Shelda's drastic weight gain, our mother asked me to come into her bedroom, where Shelda was sitting on the bed. "I have something to tell you," she said. Our mother's eyes began to well up, and I knew that something was seriously wrong. "You know how you are always mentioning how Shelda looks like she is picking up weight?" "Yea" I responded, waiting for her to get to the heart of the matter. "Shelda . . . Shelda. . . ." The pauses were too long to bear. "Shelda is pregnant." "What are you saying?" I asked. "Jerome, Shelda is going to have a baby," she continued. The words "Shelda" and "baby" simultaneously coming out of our mother's mouth pierced my ears. I could better imagine my five older brothers, or even me, becoming a parent. I could not imagine Shelda becoming a parent so early.

Shelda was thirteen and was being thrust into parenthood prematurely. Her pregnancy became a mirror for my brother and me and how we viewed and treated girls and women. Too often, a young man would impregnate a young woman, but after hearing the news he would leave the young woman to parent alone while he did his own thing, sometimes making more babies. Now and then, an impregnated and academically promising young girl would leave high school before graduating, never to return.

After attempting to run everything through my head, I then asked our mother, "Are y'all for real?" "Yes, Jerome, it's real," sobbed our mother. She raised Shelda's blouse and showed me her swollen belly. Shelda was also crying, partly from embarrassment at having to face family and partly because our mother was crying. "I didn't want to tell anybody because I couldn't believe that this had happened to my baby!" our mother sobbed. "Had Shelda, only thirteen years old and completing the seventh grade, even grasped the seriousness of the situation?" I asked myself. Whereas the future was uncertain for all of us growing up in Central City, I was terrified of what the future held for Shelda.

"Now it all made sense," I thought to myself. That explained why Shelda had begun wearing baggy shirts and blue jeans, and even dresses, which she rarely wore. That explained the increased weight she had put on, something I initially thought happened because she was entering puberty. That explained why Shelda would miss school when she felt sick. Part of the reason for my obliviousness is that I had been in my closed world. I was finishing my senior year of high school, preoccupied with which college I would attend and play football for. I was also preparing for a summer study abroad trip. I had developed a myopic way of approaching the world, determined not to let anything or anyone distract me at that time. Our five older brothers were also oblivious to what was going on. They seemed to know even less than I did about Shelda's predicament.

Later that night, I relayed the news to Kenneth and Michael. Our mother had not mentioned anything to them. I lay awake in bed, running a script through my head of our sister's life and thinking of whom to blame for her pregnancy. Was it our fault as her brothers or our mother's fault? Was Slick to blame for not being involved in Shelda's life as her biological father? I tossed and turned during the night and became angry. Then I thought about the joy that Shelda had once brought into our household when she had first arrived as a baby. Shelda was growing up fast, too fast!

The following morning I stopped to use the telephone booth in Central City. Before dialing, I checked the change return section to see if a quarter had dropped. Realizing that nothing was there, I inserted a quarter into the slot and quickly dialed Ronnie's telephone number. He lived with his girlfriend in Collegeville—a public housing project located in the city's northern section. Ronnie's girlfriend—whom he later married—picked up the telephone. I said hello and then asked to speak with my brother. She must have known that something was wrong by the way I was talking. She told Ronnie that I needed to talk with him about "something important."

"Hello?" asked Ronnie. "Hey, Ronnie," I said. "Hey, Jerome, why you calling me so early in the morning?" "Man, I called to tell you that I talked to our mother last night, and she told me that Shelda was pregnant!" "What did you say, Jerome?" as though he must not have heard me correctly. "I said that Shelda is pregnant." "Jerome, man, don't be calling me with no April Fools' Day joke! Don't play with me like that man!" exclaimed Ronnie.

The date was April 1, 1986, April Fools' Day, which I hadn't even noticed. My brothers and I were notorious for playing pranks on each other, even if it wasn't April Fools' Day. But this was no joke. At the time, I had only wished that it had been because our sister's pregnancy and the decision to have the baby would be the most life-changing moments for Shelda and one of the most important decisions our mother would have to make as a parent.

But we all soon realized that our mother had already decided months ago that Shelda would go through with the pregnancy. Our sister was already six months pregnant at the time we found out, and we believed our mother intentionally hid Shelda's pregnancy from us. Although our mother was very liberal about many things, she held strong convictions about pregnancy. An unplanned pregnancy, a male's refusal to acknowledge his child, and a child being born into dire social and economic circumstances were not going to sway her decision. Our mother believed that no birth was an accident. She had witnessed numerous unintended births and other Black mothers' steadfastness in taking care of their babies. She knew the stories of her own mother's six lost deliveries—a combination of miscarriages and premature deaths—before successfully birthing our mother, the seventh child. "God gives you no more than you can bear," she often said.

Like other Black women living in poverty and growing up in intergenerational households in which the cultural expectation was that the grandmother would play a significant role in their grandchildren's raising, our mother had already decided that she was going to take care of the baby once Shelda delivered.[2] Mama (our mother's mother) had done this for our mother and two of her younger sisters (Aunt Sandra and Aunt Brenda) when they became pregnant as teenagers. So our mother figured she would do the same for her daughter. She would not be the first nor the last Black mother in Central City taking care of her teenage daughter's children. Several mothers in Central City, some in their late thirties and early forties, became grandmothers when their teenage daughters—and teenage sons—had children.

I interrupted Ronnie during the telephone conversation to let him know that my telephone call to him about Shelda's pregnancy "ain't no

April Fools' joke." I told Ronnie that our mother called me into her room last night, and she and Shelda were sitting on the bed. They both began to cry. I asked, "Why are y'all crying?" She couldn't get the words out of her mouth. She said, "It ain't none of my fault. I tried my best to tell her about things!"

Ronnie was at a loss for words. He paused and then said, "Man, I don't believe you. Shelda is too young to be pregnant." "Yeah, she is too young, but she is!" I said. "She is showing."

"Who got her pregnant?" asked Ronnie, with a sense of wanting to exact retribution for the crime committed against his little sister. "Our mother and Shelda said that it was Trickwood's and Bean Belly's 'nem little brother who got Shelda pregnant." "You mean the one with the big gaps in his mouth?" asked Ronnie. "Yeah, that's who Shelda said she been messing with," I said. "He is only thirteen or fourteen himself." "Let me get off this phone, man, and call Richard Jr. and Maxine and Sandra 'nem. I can't believe it. Imma come over there this morning."

Ronnie and I hung up. I then made my way across the street to Phillips High School and did my very best not to let the news from the previous evening consume my day. The school year would end in late May, with me graduating as the salutatorian of my graduating class. In addition to signing an athletic scholarship offer to attend Austin Peay, I had received several academic scholarships from local civic organizations, most notably the all-Black Vulcan Kiwanis Club and the Birmingham Emancipation Proclamation Association, a local organization committed to civil rights and voter registration. The association's president presented me with a check during watchnight service at a local church to bring in the new year and celebrate our people's emancipation from slavery. Moreover, my fellow church members at Greater New Antioch Baptist Church raised money and gave me a cash gift to offset the expenses for the Jordan trip. Black organizations such as the Kiwanis Club, Emancipation Proclamation Association, and Greater New Antioch provided me with additional resources to offset my educational and travel experiences.

During the summer of 1986, I traveled to Amman, Jordan, on a scholarship given by the National Council on U.S.-Arab Relations. During the middle of my stay in Jordan, I received a memorable letter from my mother. She had written letters every week to make sure everything was okay since there was so much negative publicity in the media about the Arab world. In writing her back, I continued to reassure her of my safety.

I told her how Jordan was a very stable country with strong diplomatic relations with the United States. But this particular letter in mid-July was different from the previous ones:

> July 6, 1986: Hi Son (Jerome). How are you doing? I am writing you to let you know that Shelda had a baby girl who was born on July 1, 1986. The baby's name is Santana, and she weighs seven pounds and six ounces. She and Santana are fine. We look forward to seeing you when you return from Jordan. Be careful over there.
>
> With Love,
> Your Mom

That baby girl's birth washed away the initial disappointment that we all experienced. Joy had replaced pain. Love had replaced anger, and life had been renewed and given new meaning.

CHAPTER 14   PLAYER NO MORE

Shortly after returning to the United States from Jordan in July 1986, I left Birmingham again—for summer camp for enrolling freshman football players at Austin Peay State University. I had stayed home in Birmingham to see my family for only three weeks before I would catch a Southwest Airlines flight to Nashville. The one-way airline ticket was on sale for twenty-nine dollars. The coach who recruited me to attend Austin Peay was a young Black male, about twenty-five years old. I refer to him as Coach C. He was short, stocky, and brown skinned. He coached linebackers and aspired to become a head football coach. Coach C. picked me up from Nashville's airport, and we drove the forty-five minutes to Austin Peay's campus, located in Clarksville, Tennessee. During the ride, we talked about the football possibilities at the university. I had never heard of Austin Peay until Coach C. came to Birmingham and recruited me. He and another young Black male coach had come to my school to meet with my high school coaches and me. They also met with my mother and me in our Central City apartment.

Coach C. told me that my performance against J. O. Johnson High School, out of Huntsville, Alabama, had impressed them. I had thrown for more than three hundred yards and three touchdowns that game. J. O. Johnson was a powerhouse in Alabama at the time and had just beaten Moehler High of Cincinnati, which was the second ranked high school football team in the United States. As a football player, I modeled my game after Walter Lewis, the University of Alabama's first Black starting quarterback. Like Lewis, I could gain extra time to throw by scrambling around. Although I was selected as the city of Birmingham's 1985 Offensive Player of the Year and earned second-team all-state football honors in Alabama's Class 6A football division, I received no major college offers to play quarterback. Alabama State University and Austin Peay were the only two schools that offered me football scholarships. Did it have something to do with my height? I was five feet, ten inches and weighed 165 pounds. Did I not receive enough exposure because of the high school I had attended? Or was the lack of significant university recruitment related to the fact that I was Black?

My high school coach, who had played football at Alabama State University, felt that it was very important that I go away to school and get away from Central City. After visiting Alabama State and Austin Peay, I decided to sign with Austin Peay, a predominantly white public university with a student population of about seven thousand undergraduate and graduate students combined. Honestly, as a Black male coming from a housing project in Birmingham, I was impressed by Austin Peay's athletic, dormitory, and dining facilities in comparison to Alabama State's, which all affected my decision. I would go to Austin Peay intending to put the university on the map in college football.

After the forty-five-minute drive on Interstate 24 from Nashville, we finally reached Clarksville, a small city compared to Nashville and Birmingham. I felt an eerie silence when we arrived at Rawlings Hall, a three-story all-brick building that served as the university's football dorm. After climbing the steps to the second floor with the blue suitcases and carry-on bags that my Aunt Maxine and Uncle Monroe had bought me for my trip to Japan a year before, I took out the key given to me by the coach. I opened the door. The dorm room was frigid!

I dropped off my bags in the room and then walked to a department store about a couple of miles away. I bought a set of sheets, pillows, and a blanket. Shortly after making my way back to the dorm, a young Black woman, around twenty-one and driving a red car, offered me a ride. She must have felt sorry for me as I was struggling to carry the bags back to my dorm. I told her that I had just arrived in town and would be a member of Austin Peay's football team. She graciously gave me a ride and told me that she was dating a member of the team.

The next day, Coach C. stopped by the dorm to check on me. He asked if I wanted to ride with him to pick up another freshman football player. I rode with him to the tiny Greyhound bus station where we picked up Tony, an Italian American male who had ridden a bus from Pennsylvania. Tony wore blue jeans and a white T-shirt and had his hair shaved closely. Instead of suitcases, he carried two duffle bags and a plastic bag filled with his personal belongings.

Later that week, the other freshman football players arrived on campus with their families—with all of their belongings packed in cars, vans, and station wagons. I thought about my situation and Tony's and how we had arrived to campus by ourselves. Whereas I owned suitcases and flew, albeit via a twenty-nine-dollar one-way ticket, Tony had arrived with duffle bags after traveling for more than twelve hours on a Greyhound bus.

Playing college football was still on my mind and in my system. I had gone to Austin Peay partly with the hope of continuing my and my community's goal of playing quarterback. Everyone in Central City expected so much of me athletically and academically; many believed that I would at a minimum play for Auburn University or even make the NFL. And I had begun to embrace the narrative of using sports as a way of getting my family out of poverty. In addition to football scholarships I received academic offers, one of which was a four-year engineering scholarship to attend Tennessee State University (TSU), a historically Black university in Nashville. The person who delivered the news was an older homeboy from Central City who had graduated from TSU and had gone on to work with Alabama Power Company as an engineer. I turned down the scholarship to TSU because I also wanted play college football. I had not been recruited by nor received any offer to play football at TSU, and out of pride I was certainly not going to be a walk-on there. I would make these life-changing decisions with little input from my mother or the rest of my family. Like numerous Black males who play sports at predominantly white universities, I would be forced to negotiate multiple identities at the white university (student, football player, and Black male). Whereas I had been a high-achieving student, a leader, and an athlete at my Black high school in Birmingham, different kinds of experiences and new identities would emerge in the predominantly white state university.

During the second academic quarter of my freshman year at Austin Peay, a group of us (Black male students who played football) jointly enrolled in a literature course in the university's English department. A month into the course, and after comparing our graded papers, we all noticed that we were making Cs, Ds, and Fs on just about every written assignment. We concluded that the professor, a white male, must have thought that all of us were just Black male "athletes" who didn't care much about school. Seemingly without ever looking closely at our papers, the professor gave all of us nearly identical failing or almost failing grades. After becoming disturbed by what was happening, I mustered enough courage to question the professor about his grading pattern. He informed me that I had not correctly interpreted the poem "Ode on a Grecian Urn" by John Keats. I then informed the professor that although I played football I knew something about writing and interpreting poems. I told him that I had won poetry competitions in high school, so I was confident in my interpretation of the poem. I later began receiving As and Bs on my English assignments. The encounter with this professor, and similar others at Austin Peay, would become pivotal in shaping my racial identity and broader understanding of prejudice, discrimination, white educators' perceptions of Black students' abilities, and the dynamics of racism and whiteness in schooling and society.[1]

I had entered the predominantly white state university with a general belief in "educational and academic meritocracy" and that professors would judge me based on my classroom performance and not necessarily my race. For the most part, the Black teachers at the predominantly Black public schools in Birmingham did not bring students' race into the issue of academic performance. However, social class issues have always been present in schools. Until college, my interpretation of schooling was that my effort and ability, not necessarily my race, would determine my academic performance.[2] I was not clueless about race or racial hostility; I knew something about institutional racism from reading, hearing family stories, and learning from some of my homeboys who participated in Black-centered reading groups in Birmingham. They helped elevate my consciousness about Black people's worldwide struggles. Although I had read about racism, I still had few interpersonal interactions with white people, especially in educational settings. Most of my teachers at Powell and Phillips were Black. Thus, I was initially somewhat judgmental of some of my Black Austin Peay football teammates when I felt they should have been studying more if they wanted to earn better grades. I hadn't fully factored white professors' low expectations of Black students into Black students' academic experiences in predominantly white schools.[3]

There were several high-achieving Black male students who played on the football team and would go on to have careers beyond sports.[4] But many students who played football or basketball thought about their grades only when it involved their academic eligibility. Young people, particularly Black males, too often learn this way of thinking from adults, including community members and high school and college coaches. These students would play the sport for a year or two but then return to their hometown without a college degree. I felt bad for those who had to leave Austin Peay without completing their degree requirements. Moreover, my naïveté regarding educators' racism and bias had become challenged in that English professor's class and other settings. I was now prepared for such racist encounters should they arise again, and I would commit to ensuring that other Black students did not have similar negative and inequitable educational experiences.[5]

◗

One fall afternoon during my freshman year of college, and while walking to the two o'clock football team meetings and film study, I passed a dark-brown and petite young woman. Little did I know that she would offer a different way of seeing life, especially my understanding of white educators' racism and bias. I had previously noticed her on campus and liked the way she carried herself. But she seemed not to have noticed me at all. After passing by her one Tuesday afternoon around one forty-five, I made sure to walk the same path to bump into her on the way from her Thursday class. Upon seeing her, I said hello and she responded—but that was it. We did not strike up a conversation. She carried her books in both hands, close to her chest, and wore a burgundy Members Only jacket. Although I did not muster up a conversation, I would get the opportunity to see her again at a homecoming party a few weeks later.

On October 24, 1986, after our homecoming football game, I went to the homecoming party of Alpha Phi Alpha—a Black fraternity—at a local Clarksville nightclub. While there I saw this young woman again and introduced myself, but she attempted to throw me off by using an alias. However, a mutual friend had already told me her actual name, Mary. After some small talk, Mary eventually acknowledged that she had shared a false name. Sharon was not her real name! I wanted to know Mary even more, but she told me she had come to college for education, not dating. She too was a freshman.

After football practices I would go to Mary's dorm and sit and talk to her in the lobby. We eventually exchanged telephone numbers before leaving school for Christmas break. I reluctantly provided Mary with a telephone number, telling her that I preferred to write letters instead.

During the first few days of the 1986 Christmas break, I stayed with Aunt Maxine and Uncle Monroe, who lived in a house on the outskirts of Birmingham in a small town called Tarrant. I stayed there primarily to use their telephone and speak with Mary over break. But I couldn't stay too long; I still needed to spend time in Central City with my mother, my brothers, and my sister and her new baby girl. They were missing me, and I was missing them. But I was also really interested in Mary.

"Jerome, some girl named Mary called you," relayed Aunt Sandra, who lived with Aunt Maxine and Uncle Monroe. "Good, she called as promised in the letter." Later that evening, Mary called back, and I was there to answer.

"Why are you never at home?" asked Mary. "I just be out and about but was trying to get back," I responded. "Well, your aunt said you weren't over there yet. What did she mean? Do you even live there?" Mary had honed in on my lie. A couple of times before I had called Mary from the payphone inside the Trailways bus station near Central City. That had become expensive, and I needed to talk from a regular telephone. I gave Aunt Maxine and Uncle Monroe's telephone number to Mary. But a couple of times I could not get over to their house to receive the call from Mary. I confessed.

"I don't live here. This is my aunt and uncle's house. We don't have a telephone where I live," I said. "Why did you have to lie to me?" Mary asked. "Well, I didn't know what you would think. I guess I was embarrassed." "There was no need to be embarrassed about something like that. Let's just write letters and talk when we are able," said Mary in a very mature, loving, and reassuring way. I realized then that Mary was a thoughtful young woman and the person I knew I would want to play a part in my life and me in hers. But Mary and I would have to learn more about each other's backgrounds.

Mary and I had different upbringings and educational experiences. She and her two younger brothers were raised by their mother and father in Henderson, a rural town in West Tennessee. They were working-class Black folks, surrounded by an extended network of family members. The Black people lived in one section of Henderson, the white people in another. Mary and her brothers had to attend the town's schools, which were predominantly white. But Mary's parents and those in their generation and before had attended Black schools. They graduated from Chester County Training School, which later became Vincent High School in 1963. By the time Mary enrolled in first grade in 1974, however, the town's Black elementary and high schools had been closed due to public school desegregation.[6]

Nearly all of Mary's teachers, from kindergarten through high school, were white due to the firing and demotion of Black educators during desegregation. While she did what she could to survive those schools and make it to college, Mary always asserted that the white teachers had very low expectations of her and other Black students. Whereas I had always loved going to school and felt supported by my Black teachers in Birmingham, for Mary and many more Black children like her, schooling was a site of suffering.[7] Unlike me at the time, Mary was acutely aware of white educators' low expectations of Black children because this was her and her Black peers' experiences.[8] Consequently, Mary was not surprised when I told her how the white English professor at Austin Peay had prejudged Black male students who played sports. She noted how white teachers often overlooked some of the academically talented Black students from her high school.[9] Such students would be placed into low-level courses.[10] "Jerome, you are naïve if you think that these white folks don't just give Black students bad grades!" Mary was right; I experienced this prejudgment with an English course and also a well-known math professor at Austin Peay who showed little mercy to Black students. Both were white males.

During our freshman year of college, Mary and I spent a lot of time talking and walking around the campus. Then, seemingly all of a sudden, I decided that I wanted to pledge Alpha Phi Alpha, the oldest undergraduate Black fraternity in the United States. After attending Alpha's interest meeting known as the smoker and learning of the organization's history and reputation for achievement and activism, I aspired to join the organization that included Black luminaries who changed the world—W. E. B. Du Bois, Paul Robeson, Thurgood Marshall, and Dr. Martin Luther King Jr. Alpha Phi Alpha was founded on the campus of Cornell University in 1906 as a study group for Black male students. Amid extreme racism and discrimination during the early 1900s, Black male students at Cornell decided to come together and support one another academically and socially.[11] Initially brought together by a Black staff member at Cornell by the name of C. C. Poindexter, this group of Black male students understood the power of unifying to ensure they not only survived but thrived at a white university and in a society where they and their peers experienced overt racism and discrimination.[12] Like those Black male Cornell students, I wanted to be a difference maker more than eighty years after the fraternity's founding.

I had a close relationship with my five older brothers in Central City and felt a sense of brotherhood with football teammates from elementary school through high school and college. But joining a Black male organization in which its members professed "manly deeds, scholarship, and love for all mankind" was inspiring. Members from Austin Peay's chapter of Alpha Phi Alpha (Theta Pi) had been trailblazers themselves; they were instrumental in founding Austin Peay's first Black student association, then called STOMP (Society to Organize Minority Persons). I began pledging, referred to as "going online," for the Alphas in March 1987, the beginning of the spring quarter of my freshman year. Going online would entail emotional, academic, financial, and romantic sacrifices, as my time with Mary would be limited. She did not like my sudden decision, mainly after I had spent the previous four months courting her and convincing her that I was worth her time. Mary wanted to be sure before she put her heart out there.

Although I didn't have the money to foot the bill, fortunately I had what people often refer to as a full-ride scholarship. But I later learned that an athletic scholarship, especially for low-income students like me, was a package that included several resources, including Pell Grant funds. Unlike a loan, the Pell Grant is a subsidy provided to low-income students to offset the costs of attending college.[13] It was a significant sacrifice to pay the three hundred dollars to pledge Alpha, partly because I regularly sent some of the refund money from the Pell Grant and the Key Club scholarship that I received back to my mother to assist her with the bills in Central City. Because I always kept some pocket money, my mother thought that I got paid to attend college until I told her that it was the other way around. "College is not free," I would say to her. She thought this way because two of my older brothers, Ronnie and Richard Jr., had gone to local junior colleges and received refund checks after the Pell Grant funds had paid for their books and tuition. Ronnie took some courses at Jefferson State Community College in Birmingham. Richard Jr. attended and completed an associate degree in business from Booker T. Washington Business College located in downtown Birmingham.

I called Preston, the white man I had worked for at the automotive body shop when I was growing up. I explained to him the process of pledging a college fraternity and how I wanted to become an Alpha member. Preston sent me a hundred fifty dollars in the mail to offset my cost to pledge. After paying the three-hundred-dollar fee, I went through the pledging process.

Pledging entailed innumerable physical exercises, study hall, and staying awake with my line brother, a running back on the football team, throughout the night. We were in excellent shape as football players and saw pledging as another workout, although the mental part was very demanding. We started as a pledge line of four, but a couple of pledges "dropped line" before completing the process, leaving us as the only two pledges. Besides the physical and mental challenges, one particular Alpha member was determined to make me quit for another reason.

Whack! "Number Two!" referring to me by my line number, "I don't like your motherfucking ass anyway!" said one of the Alphas. Without provocation, this particular fraternity member had hit me across the head with a baseball glove. When the glove landed on the back of my head, I immediately turned around and hit him in the face with my fist, knocking him to the ground.

Before the confrontation, my line brother and I had been standing in line, one behind the other, in the front room of the Alpha house near campus, reciting, in unison, "Invictus" by William Ernest Henley. The lines from the poem, "Out of the night that covers me, black as a pit from pole to pole, I thank whatever gods may be for my unconquerable soul" had become ingrained in my memory and would propel me to action. Although the pain from the lick was not as poignant as the reason why he hit me, the stinging feeling had sent fury throughout my body.

"Ohhh, shit! Bruhs, did you see that. Number Two done hit a bruh!" shouted one of the fraternity members. "Break line," commanded one of the brothers. The dean of pledgees (DP)—who was responsible for monitoring and ensuring that fraternity members followed the pledging rules—had stepped away for a few minutes. The DP was also responsible for ensuring we truly learned what it meant to be an Alpha man. So another brother intervened to resolve the matter. "Y'all motherfuckers going to fight this one out," said one of the brothers. A week before this particular incident, I had informed the Alphas that another fraternity member—I will call him Big Brother Steve—had been harassing Mary, my girlfriend. I told him how another male student informed me that he had to walk Mary from the library to her dorm because Big Brother Steve had pulled Mary's arm and demanded that she go with him. The male student said that Mary was terrified. Big Brother Steve's dislike for me was evident, which is why the Alphas decided to pull me from the pledge process and demanded that we "fight it out like men."

"Number Two, take off your Sphinx [a wooden black-and-gold carving in the shape of a sphinx placed around my neck to indicate an initial phase of the pledge process] and go to the back of the house," said one of the brothers. Before crossing over and becoming fully fledged members of Alpha Phi Alpha, the brothers of Alpha referred to the pledges as Sphinx Men. I did as commanded and proceeded to the back of the Alpha house, where I waited, and waited, and waited. "Man, he's taking too long to come out; they must be up to something, or he must be getting something," I said to Number One.

Then the Alphas, seven of them, all came out to witness what was about to go down. Big Brother Steve was the last one out, and he stood near his seven brothers, but about five feet from me as though he was ready to fight. He began to speak in a raised voice: "What you're going to . . . ?" Before he could finish his thought with the word "do," I snatched all of the 160 pounds of Big Brother Steve, lifted him above my head, slammed him into the side of the Alpha house, and began beating and kicking him. He curled up into a ball to protect his head and body from the blows. Although the incident had to have lasted no more than fifteen seconds, it felt like I had landed at least fifty blows, a combination of punches and kicks.

"Let's go, Number Two!" shouted my line brother. As line brothers and Sphinx Men, Number One and I shared linked fates. He knew that he would have to pay for my rebellion if he stayed around at the Alpha house. As if we were eluding tacklers or slave catchers, Number One and I dashed from the back of the Alpha house, hurdled sticks and rocks through the woody area that separated the fraternity house from the university's main campus, and ran to Number One's room in Rawlings Hall, the football dorm. His roommate, who was also our football teammate, opened the door for us. "Goddamn Man, I'm glad you whupped his crazy ass for trying to mess with your lady!" said Number One. I stayed in their dorm room for the night because my roommate was also a Big Brother in Alpha Phi Alpha. Number One and I were officially runaway pledges.

The next afternoon during football practice, three of the chapter brothers, who were also football teammates, approached me to tell me that the other Big Brothers needed to meet with Number One and me. The chapter brothers had discussed the matter among themselves. As we stood in the front room of the Alpha house on Marion Avenue, the DP began to speak: "Number Two, as we have said before, we are men before we are Alphas. You showed us that you are a man. One of the aims of Alpha Phi Alpha fraternity is 'Manly Deeds.' Big Brother Steve can't have any more contact with your line. If he tries to, you let me and the other brothers know."

A slight smile came across my face, and that day I became even more determined to join that group of brothers. During the late spring of 1987,

I would cross over as a Theta Pi chapter member of Alpha Phi Alpha. The brothers and I agreed that my line name would be "Malcolm X II."

⌐

As far as football, I had limited success as a quarterback at Austin Peay. I played in some games as a quarterback, kickoff returner, and punt returner but started as a quarterback only once over two years. However, I felt as though I did not achieve what I was capable of during that time. My athletic underachievement, I believed, was linked to several factors—my increasingly deep interest in issues facing Black students on the predominantly white campus and the coaches not preparing me well and placing me in a style of offense that could maximize my talents. A couple of events would foretell the end of my football days at the university.

During football camp in the spring of 1988, the new coaching staff had decided to switch me from quarterback to cornerback. I did not learn of this move until I returned from a student leadership conference that I had attended in Atlanta. The switch from quarterback to another position was an all-too-familiar fate for Black males who starred as quarterbacks in high school, especially if they enrolled at predominantly white colleges and universities later. Hall of Fame quarterback Warren Moon, who would go on to become one of the most prolific passers in professional football, was encouraged to change positions coming out of college if he wanted to play professional football.[14] I knew about Moon's journey at the time. The usual rationale, which my coaches presented to me, was that the Black quarterback was athletically talented enough to play another position. Coaches across the sport give many Black males who dream of playing quarterback a similar message.[15] Black quarterbacks are punished for being athletic.

I was disappointed with what I viewed as a demotion. At the time, I believed the move was related to more than my athletic ability to play other positions. I was also an active member of the university's African American Student Association (AASA). This engagement with Black student organizations would foster tension and unease between the coaches and me; tension between the head coach and the quarterback rarely bodes well for the quarterback. The head coach, a white man, once told me to "be careful of groups that will try to use your leadership for the wrong purposes." My strained relationship with coaches would become exacerbated by another encounter, with Austin Peay's famous basketball coach.

The encounter occurred when a few other Black students who played sports and I were playing a pickup basketball game in the university's gym.[16] I deliberately refer to us as "Black students who played sports" instead of the often-used "student-athletes" because of the way that term is used to commodify and commercialize Black male students for the economic benefit of schools, from elementary to college.[17] While we were playing basketball, a middle-aged white male ran onto the court. He began to question us: "Who told you to come out here and shoot with them? They are working on some things!" shouted Austin Peay's basketball coach. It appeared as though the coach was talking to me by the way he was moving toward me. I politely asked, "Are you talking to me?" "Yes, I am talking to you!" he continued shouting. I asked him why we could not play basketball in the gym. Looking at one of my Black football teammates to contradict me, the basketball coach continued stating his point. Stepping off the court and taking himself out of the matter, my football teammate told the coach that he had "nothing to do with it." I also made my point, letting the coach know that it was springtime, not basketball season, and that we were "just having fun." I stepped off the court but not until I let the coach know that students, and not just basketball players who he insisted attend "unsupervised" practices, should also be able to use the courts at that time. The coach went back upstairs to his office.

After eating dinner in the school's cafeteria that evening and then arriving in my dorm room, I received an unexpected call from a newly hired assistant football coach, who was a young Black male. "Jerome, this is Coach. I want you to know that the head basketball coach told me what happened today. He asked you to get off the basketball court where his players were practicing, but you refused. Now, we have to have good relations with the basketball program. So, I'm going to need you to go over to the Dunn Center and apologize to him for what you did." "Coach," I responded, "we were out there shooting for fun, playing a friendly game of basketball. It's springtime, and any student should be able to use the Dunn Center's court during this time of year. The basketball players had no problem with me out there. I don't know why I owe him an apology." "You are going to have to apologize, Jerome. He has them out there getting ready for next year," said the coach. "I'm sorry, Coach, but I don't feel I should do that," I said. We both ended the conversation.

A few months after the incident with the basketball coach, I needed surgery for a hernia I had suffered during weight lifting. The operation occurred in June 1988. Mary, who had gone home for the summer, had her mother bring her up to Austin Peay to join me as I went under the knife. Dawn, our close friend, picked Mary and me up and drove us to the hospital. The surgery was successful, and afterward the doctor told me to take six weeks to recover and limit my physical activity, including football. None of the coaches visited the hospital during the surgery or stopped by the Alpha house where I lived during my recovery that summer. Mary stayed on campus for a few days and checked in on me.

"We need you back by the start of football camp in August, Jerome," said the young Black coach who had previously demanded that I apologize to the head basketball coach. I reported to summer football camp on time, but I would have to practice lightly during the first few weeks. Those were the doctor's orders. But against these orders, the coaches pressed me to get in full practice gear as soon as summer practices began. One moment during the summer stood out. While backpedaling during one of the cornerback drills, a coach—the same one who asked me to apologize to the basketball coach—said to me, "Pick it up, Jerome. Stop that half-stepping. You got a bad attitude son!" I was taken aback by his description. I had never heard a coach or anyone in such a role say this about me. I had developed a reputation for always going all out. "Where did he get this view of me?" I was a little winded after taking off a few weeks in the summer due to recuperating from the hernia surgery. But I was giving it my all. "Oh, I remember!" I thought to myself. I believe the coach's comment had something to do with my refusal to apologize to the basketball coach. This incident shaped the way he viewed me as a person and as a player. It also affected the way I viewed him.

I was disturbed by the comment because it conveyed that the coach was interested only in my ability to play football. One of the fastest ways for a player to lose favor among coaches is to become labeled as having a bad attitude. Unfortunately, this is the unfair label often applied to so many Black people who participate in athletics, at the high school, college, and professional levels. I was further disappointed at how no one from the coaching staff checked in on me while I was in the hospital; their only concern was whether I would be back in time to start the next season. And only during summer camp did they ensure I was ready to play. I was especially disappointed at the young Black coach for asking me to apologize.

Several thoughts went through my mind during the remainder of the summer regarding my football future. Should I accept the demotion to cornerback, along with the mistreatment that I felt? The Saturday evening after the first week of school in the fall semester of 1988, and after football practice had ended earlier that day, I told Mary that I was leaving the team. "What took you so long, especially after the coaches didn't care anything about you or come to see how you were doing after your surgery? But they are now ready for you to get on that football field and play for them, even though you haven't fully healed!" I made a long-distance telephone call to our next-door neighbors in Birmingham and asked them to bring my mother to the telephone. When she got to the phone, I told my mother that I was no longer playing football because of what had happened. She just said, "Jerome, do what you feel is important. I know everything will be fine." She and I did not talk about how I would fund my education. Ever since childhood my mother had always trusted that I would make the right decisions in life.

After not showing up at Sunday night's practice—six days before the first game, against Kentucky State University—I met with the head football coach the following Monday afternoon. He asked why I had not attended practice the previous evening. I informed him that I did not want to play football anymore for the school. "But Jerome, you are a great athlete. If anyone could move to cornerback and contribute right away, it would be you. It seemed like a natural fit for you." The coach said they were depending on me to play. I then talked about not being interested in playing cornerback and how nobody consulted me about switching from quarterback. "Jerome, we had to move you because of the new offensive coordinator's scheme," said the coach. "Why did you move the other three Black quarterbacks too?" I asked. He could tell where I was going and didn't offer a response.

"Well, what are you going to do about the scholarship you just signed this year? Don't you think you should pay back the scholarship?" the coach asked. I informed him that he could "have the scholarship back." "Well, are you leaving school and going back to Birmingham?" "No," I said emphatically. "I am going to graduate over the next two years, even if I have to take out a loan to pay for my schooling." (I did not tell him about the Key Club scholarship I received, which came to me in a check at the beginning of each semester.) Since I had signed the scholarship papers during the previous spring, the university was obligated to cover my fall semester of classes. I would later pay the out-of-state tuition rate for the second semester of my junior year and my entire senior year. I said bye to the head football coach and walked out of the office and over to the registrar's office to increase my course enrollments from fifteen to twenty-one semester hours as we were still in the drop-add period. That evening, a couple of football graduate assistants came over to my dorm room. At the orders of the head coach, they moved my belongings out of the football dorm and into a general dorm.

A commonly held belief is that college athletic scholarships are for four years. In reality, schools offer and honor only year-to-year athletic scholarships. If the coaches are not satisfied with their athletic performance, they can reduce or revoke scholarships. I witnessed this at Austin Peay. At the beginning of summer camp during my sophomore year, coaches reduced one player's scholarship because he had arrived at summer football camp a few pounds overweight. They eliminated his meal plan. Many of the players were disturbed at what had happened but reluctant to comment. I thought about this and the business of sports. I decided not to become overly concerned about how my leaving at the beginning of the season made the coaches feel. Football was no longer enjoyable like when I played for Central City, the Sugar Jets, and Phillips High.

I still loved playing football, but not for Austin Peay's coaches. At that time in my life, I felt the need to fully become all that I was capable of becoming, which was more than a football player. During my junior and senior years, I even shunned my athletic identity. No doubt, there was withdrawal from not playing a sport that had pervaded my entire life; it was painful to terminate my football life so abruptly. The way I felt that semester of my junior year must have been how people addicted to alcohol and drugs feel when they stop cold turkey. The pangs were immediate. For example, during the first Saturday evening after leaving the team, I sat alone in my dorm room, tuned into the radio station, and listened actively as the commentator colorfully described the first game of the 1988 season, against Kentucky State University. Only six days earlier I was on the football field practicing for the season opener. It was a home game, and while listening to the radio broadcast I envisioned where I would be on every play. I was sad, but I was also happy that people whose primary purpose was athletics were not dictating my schedule and life.

Over the next couple of years, and to deal with the withdrawal, I took advantage of my time away from college football. Intramural football sufficed. It mattered not that I had to relinquish my role as Austin Peay's starting left cornerback, starting punt returner, and starting kickoff returner or that I would have to take out student loans to fund the remainder of my schooling. I would miss playing with my teammates, but I felt that playing football was not fulfilling for me anymore. I felt remorseful and vindicated when Austin Peay's football team won only three out of eleven games that year and went winless the following year. The program entered a downward spiral that lasted most of the next decade.

During the remainder of the fall 1988 semester, I focused on being a student and soaking up the overall college experience. In addition to serving as the president of the African American Student Association, I fully engaged with Austin Peay's Student Government Association as a senator, immersed myself into Alpha Phi Alpha fraternity, and interned at the National Council on U.S.-Arab Relations in Washington, D.C., during the summer of 1989. The internship allowed me to reengage, beyond the university campus, with the kinds of political and social-justice-related issues I felt passionate about addressing. While there in D.C., I spent time with the council's executive director, who regularly reminded us interns of our obligation to serve. During one of these sessions, I met the widow of Dr. Malcolm H. Kerr, the former president of the American University in Beirut, who had been assassinated. The Kerr Scholarship that I received after high school to travel to Jordan was named in honor of Dr. Kerr. Mrs. Kerr and I talked about the politics of the Arab world, but I mostly remembered her speaking proudly of her son. Mrs. Kerr's son had been an All-American basketball player at the University of Arizona; he had gotten drafted the year before to play professional basketball for the Portland Trailblazers. His name was Steve Kerr, who would later play and win championships with the Chicago Bulls before leading the Golden State Warriors to multiple NBA championships as head coach.

By the fall of 1989, I poured my energy into creating something that would serve Black students for generations to come—a Black cultural center. Mary and I served as the vice-president and president, respectively, of Austin Peay State University's African American Student Association (AASA). In these roles, we rallied the students behind creating a Black cultural center on the campus. Other key AASA leaders and members instrumental in petitioning for the cultural center included Shawn Pruitt, Vinton Fleming, Kathleen Payne, Stephanie Steele, and Carter Smith. Dr. James Mock, a political science professor at Austin Peay, educated us about the politics of race on campus and in society; he also introduced us to the purpose and benefits of a cultural center for Black students. As students, we used our own funds to travel to Nashville, where we received the blueprint for a Black cultural center from Dr. Raymond Winbush, the director of Vanderbilt University's Black Cultural Center at the time. Our strategy for bringing the cultural center into existence entailed (1) meeting with Austin Peay's president, (2) organizing student rallies and marches, (3) writing newspaper articles, and (4) building alliances with student organizations at nearby institutions such as Tennessee State University (TSU). TSU's campus was about fifty miles south in Nashville.

In the fall of 1989 and spring of 1990, Black students at TSU would lay bare almost a century of neglect of the historically Black university by the state of Tennessee. Led by their visionary and charismatic Student Government Association president jeff carr, TSU's students staged a protest, including a hunger strike for better housing accommodations and campus food.[18] jeff, also a member of TSU's chapter of Alpha Phi Alpha (Beta Omicron), galvanized students across fraternities, sororities, and athletics. Those of us from AASA at Austin Peay made frequent drives to Nashville to show solidarity with the TSU protesters.[19] The TSU students' hunger strike was successful, and the state's political leaders relented to their demands. Although less known than many other sit-ins, these actions would lead to Governor Ned McWherter making sure TSU would become the recipient of about $127 million in campus improvements. Tennessee's white leaders had neglected the Black students and the historically Black university for far too long.

Back at Austin Peay, we felt victorious in knowing that the university's administrators had agreed to create a Black cultural center on the campus. I graduated from Austin Peay in May 1990. Mary transferred to TSU during the summer of 1990 and graduated from there in 1992. In the fall of 1992, two years after Mary and I had left, Austin Peay State University would formally dedicate the Black cultural center. As AASA's leaders, we proposed the center's formal name as the El-Hajj Malik El-Shabazz African Center of Cultural Study—named after Malcolm X. But Mary and I were gone in 1992, and the fight was now in the hands of AASA's current members and student leaders. Instead of naming the cultural center after Malcolm X, the university's administrators, in consultation with the newly hired director and a couple of professors, decided to name the cultural center after the first Black student to graduate from the university, Rev. Wilbur N. Daniel.

Black students' collective actions and solidarity at TSU and Austin Peay demonstrated that we could work across campuses to change our respective universities. Historians and other scholars must place these protests within the broader context of the Black freedom struggle. TSU's students were especially part of a rich tradition of Black student protest emanating from Nashville. Thirty years earlier, Black student leaders from Fisk University (Diane Nash), American Baptist College (John Lewis, C. T. Vivian, James Bevel), and Vanderbilt University (James Lawson) led sit-ins to protest a white supremacy structure that dehumanized Black people. Fortuitously, some of the most iconic figures from this earlier period, such as Nash, Vivian, Bevel, Lawson, and Dr. Bernard Lafayette, were in Nashville celebrating the thirtieth anniversary of that city's sit-in movement. TSU's Black students had picked up the baton and carried on a noble tradition of protesting for human rights and equality. Some of the earlier movement's veterans met with the TSU student protesters in 1990 during their hunger strike.

After Mary and I had completed our undergraduate studies, me at Austin Peay and she at TSU, we were at a crossroads, deciding our next steps in life, including our relationship and careers. Mary and I had worked well together as fellow students bringing about changes on university campuses. We knew each other's temperament, families, and leadership styles. We loved and enjoyed being around one another but had not yet decided what our long-term plans would be in terms of our relationship. Honestly, I was at an impasse and needed to reground myself on what I wanted to do in life.

So, in 1990, after graduating college, I went back to Birmingham for a year to reconnect with my family in Central City. I missed them a great deal due to my being away every summer during college, whether training for football or participating in internships in the United States and internationally. When I went back to Birmingham that year, I felt unsure of how I saw myself. I was living in Central City in Birmingham, but I was no longer a football player and no longer a student. While back home during the fall of 1990 and spring of 1991, I worked in the downtown branch of Birmingham's public library and as a substitute teacher at Powell Elementary and Phillips High. Between working and spending time with my family, I studied for the law school entrance exam. I applied to law schools but was not accepted to those I wanted to attend. Fortunately, a program at a university in St. Louis provided opportunities for potential law students. I completed an application and was selected for the summer prelaw program. However, I could not enroll in law school there because I did not fare well in that summer program. I left St. Louis and joined Mary in Nashville. Although I was still trying to

Jerome and Mary in college and later, on their wedding day in 1992. (Source: Author's collection.)

gauge my next steps in life, I knew that I was not going back to Birmingham, and law school was not of interest anymore. So I stayed in Nashville with Mary, which eventually led to my moving in with her that year. Mary and I lived together for one year in a one-bedroom apartment. During our second year together (1992), I enrolled in a master's program in education at Peabody College of Vanderbilt University.

We were happy that our families, who had met on a few occasions, liked each other. After doing what folks called "shacking up" for one year, Mary and I decided it was time to follow the advice of soul singer Al Green: "Let's Get Married." We began planning a large wedding. Out of the blue during one sunny but crisp fall evening in late September 1992, Mary and I decided to visit the Nashville-Davidson County Courthouse to get our marriage papers. Not wanting to leave our families out of this significant milestone, we called everyone but gave them only a week's advance notice. They suspected something else had prompted us to marry, but we reassured them there was no baby on the way! One week later, Saturday morning, October 3, 1992, Mary and I jumped the broom at Centennial Park in Nashville. In addition to our immediate family members and some of Mary's close friends, classmates from my graduate program at Peabody, former professors from Austin Peay, and a few of my fraternity brothers attended the wedding.

CHAPTER 15   THE JOYS AND PAINS OF CENTRAL CITY

I made sure that I went to bed no later than ten o'clock to be ready for the early morning telephone call requesting me to come in and substitute teach. I taught only at Powell Elementary or Phillips High. Both were one block from our apartment and I had no car. I purchased a telephone for our apartment to not miss any opportunities to earn the fifty dollars per day. The phone was the first one we had had in about ten years. When I was around twelve years old we had a telephone in the apartment, but the telephone company disconnected the line after about four months due to our failure to pay the bill.

My regular sleep routine and preparation for work the next day would become interrupted on that late evening in February 1991 in a way that I could not have imagined. I was asleep in bed. Then all of a sudden, around midnight, I heard a loud banging on the front door. This abrupt disturbance was eerily reminiscent of when a man had stood outside the apartment door banging and threatening to "blow it down" with a shotgun. But this time I was twenty-two, not five. While my sister and her now four-year-old daughter slept undisturbed in their bedroom, I walked down the narrow hallway to the front door. Hearing my footsteps and the banging on the door, my mother awakened, got out of bed, and followed behind me. As I made my way past my mother's bedroom, she asked, "Jerome, who is that at the door this damned time of night?"

A loud voice behind the door then began shouting: "This is the police! If Maurice is in there, tell him he had better surrender, now!" My mother then went to the door to tell the police Maurice did not live there. The officer then asked, "Are you related to him?" "I am his mother," responded my mother. The officer then told her to open the door, which she gently did. With the door barely ajar, eight police officers busted through the opening with drawn guns, almost knocking my mother to the ground. Upon seeing me, they instantly pointed the guns at my face, chest, and abdomen, everywhere! One of the officers then ran to the back door and opened it to have an additional backup of about five more police officers join in the raid. Another officer began shouting violently, "Put your arms over your head and turn around. Now! And don't move!" all the while nervously pointing the gun at me. I quickly prayed that he would not pull the trigger, given how his hands were trembling at the time. I knew how easily police officers tensed up when they saw Black males. I was aware that a slight movement could immediately result in the officers blasting me with their guns. There were too many stories of police officers—whose only defense was that they had mistaken an object such as a wallet or a pen for a weapon—shooting and killing Black men. With what seemed like an arsenal of weapons pointing at me, another officer took handcuffs from the side of his belt and moved toward me, while two more checked my sister's bedroom and demanded that she remain there with her daughter. It all seemed like a dream or a movie. Flickering flashlights provided the only illumination to the apartment's dimly lit front room.

All I could make out from the commotion were lots of metal rods and lights. A few police officers then pushed me up against a wall and placed the gripping handcuffs on my wrists. With multiple shotguns pointed at me, one of them shouted, "Maurice, don't you dare move!" Puzzled, and now with my hands cuffed behind my back, I thought to myself, "He is confusing me with Maurice like so many other people do." But as I began to speak to let him know who I was, I was interrupted, "You better not be talking back to us. We have a warrant out for your arrest!" shouted the officer, with an expression of certainty in his voice. "I am not Maurice," I responded defiantly. Holding a photo out beside my face, he insisted, "This is you! Stop lying." "That's my brother," I said, making sure that the intonation of my voice did not further increase the tension in the air. No matter what, I had to come out of this situation without getting jumped on or, worse, killed. I could not defend myself and was ganged up on by the officers. My mother intervened on my behalf. "Take the handcuffs off him," she demanded. "That is not Maurice! That's Jerome, my other son. Maurice doesn't live here." They ignored my mother's command.

Unconvinced, another police officer then demanded identification. I told him that my wallet was in my bedroom on the dresser. With my hands still cuffed behind my back, this particular officer and another one took me to the back room where I slept. My wallet sat on the dresser slightly opened with a dollar bill sticking out. They opened my wallet and quickly went through it, looking for any form of identification. Hastily searching, they seemed unable to locate my Alabama driver's license. Then one of them found something—my Alpha Phi Alpha fraternity membership card. One of the police officers, a Black male, looked at the membership card with a surprising facial expression. "You are an Alpha, and you went to college?" he asked with an intimation of surprise in his voice. "I am, and I graduated," I said. "My driver's license is right behind that piece of paper." But just before I made the statement, I could see that the Black police officer's demeanor had changed and that the tension in the room had begun to dissipate. "This is not Maurice," said the Black police officer to the white one.

The police officers nudged me forward, still ensuring I was in front of them, and led me out of the bedroom. They uncuffed my hands and returned my driver's license and fraternity card. They exited the front door as quickly and stealthily as they had come. I slumped into the couch. Disturbed by what had just happened, I vowed that I would contact the Birmingham police department's internal affairs office to report the incident. I took out my gray and bulky word processor that I had just bought to complete graduate school applications and began typing a letter to describe the police raid.

While writing the protest letter, I decided to delete the text because I had little confidence that anyone in the police department would even think I had a legitimate grievance. It was common knowledge that some officers had developed a reputation of forcing drug dealers to pay them not to get arrested. Why would they listen to me? Anyway, this was a so-called housing project, and nobody cared, even if there were Black faces in the mayor's office or on the city council. The police knew what was going on regarding the influx of drugs into Central City and other impoverished and predominantly Black communities in the United States. The economic conditions in Central City were dire, and selling drugs became a way that young people, particularly Black males, would attempt to combat poverty. Rather than get rid of poverty by providing job skills training and opportunities to young adults, the federal, state, and local governments waged the war on drugs, leading to the mass incarceration of multiple generations of Black people, particularly males.[1]

The selling of crack cocaine began in the Los Angeles area before spreading across the United States, damaging communities and families along its treacherous path.[2] There has been much debate about the extent to which the CIA supported drug traffickers and governments that then turned around and sold cocaine and crack in the United States to support anti-Sandinista rebels (the Contras) in Nicaragua. The U.S. government officially cut off the rebels' money, but U.S. president Ronald Reagan supported the Contras in their efforts to topple the Sandinista-led government. New Orleans and Atlanta—narcotics hot spots of the South—were where small-time Birmingham dealers could get their drugs. Some would drive down to these cities, whereas others waited for the drugs to arrive by the carload. The shameful part is that government officials knew about crack cocaine and marijuana shipments coming into these jobless communities and inner cities. And they knew that Black males, especially those who had been pushed out of school or were unemployed or underemployed, wanted some of the dope game's fast money.[3] Thus, the CIA and others turned their heads when these groups used cocaine to make money. Crack cocaine, produced more cheaply than pure cocaine, found a ripe market in U.S. urban areas where the people were seeking any relief from their blues.

I am not even sure that the small-time drug dealers in places like Central City knew the magnitude of U.S. governmental involvement in the drug enterprise, resulting in thousands of casualties in economically stressed communities. The young people caught up in this web mainly knew that they were getting paid and developing more street credibility than they had ever had. Many in Central City, some young and some old, found themselves jockeying for status and respect when these couldn't be found elsewhere, particularly in school or on the job.

I thought about how I had moved back to Central City after college to regroup. I was supposed to have been in Egypt for an entire year, but I stayed for only three months. Rather than learning about Arab politics and society and ancient African civilizations, I was sitting in my bedroom contemplating the problems of the ghetto and how law enforcers cared little about the rights and due process assurances of Black people in the United States. After the police raid, I went back into the bedroom, got into bed, covered my head, and attempted to fall back asleep, unsuccessfully.

I got out of bed again; this time it was around four o'clock in the morning. My mother and I called Maurice and told him to go downtown to turn himself in because the police were looking for him. Mau-

rice had been selling drugs—marijuana and crack cocaine in particular—and he had a lot of money compared to everyone else in our family.
He felt a semblance of economic freedom once he started getting paid
from "slanging." He had some money in his pocket, so he decided to
marry his girlfriend. He and his new wife were excited to be able to rent
an apartment and not live in the projects anymore. They bought a car,
purchased some goods for their new son, Junior, and gave both of their
mothers some money whenever they needed it. Still, I pleaded to Maurice to turn himself in. I let him know what had just happened. I loved
him and did not want anything to happen to him. Maurice decided to go
downtown to surrender.

Just as it had throughout the United States, crack cocaine tore
through housing projects such as Central City with a vengeance. It became the preferred escape for those experiencing abject poverty and
who wished to forget their daily problems. When those addicted to crack
cocaine did not have the money to support their habit, they resorted to
anything—even selling their bodies—to muster a few dollars to buy a
rock. Unlike U.S. governmental officials' recent response to opioid addiction, federal officials and state legislators showed little compassion
for Black people who had become addicted to crack cocaine. Today, federal, state, and local officials have decriminalized opioid abuse, made it
a medical and public health issue, and punished drug companies such
as Purdue Pharma that knew about and ignored opioids' consequences.
Opioid abuse overwhelmingly affects white people. In terms of crack cocaine, however, the U.S. government—as well as the U.S. public—waged
the war on drugs on disproportionately poor and Black and Brown communities. Black users and distributors were vilified, incarcerated for
long sentences, ostracized, and marginalized rather than rehabilitated.[4]

Illegal drugs were not something new that I had not seen or been
around. Growing up in Central City during the 1970s and early 1980s,
one might find oneself among friends who would suddenly pull out a
nickel (five dollars) or dime (ten dollars) bag of marijuana, place the
marijuana on a thin sheet of Top rolling paper, and roll a joint. They
would let you know they knew what they were doing by confidently running their tongue along the seam to seal the joint. But marijuana was
not like crack cocaine in the late 1980s and 1990s. Crack cocaine selling
and addiction would turn "good" people "bad," according to how it was
depicted as a drug of criminal-minded and morally neglect people. The
selling and usage of crack cocaine within a social structure that crimi-
nalized users and sellers led to a slew of deaths in Central City and other

impoverished communities of color. The drug turned Central City into sought-after turf. Crack cocaine made enemies of once close friends—as everyone vied for the opportunity to make some seemingly never-ending cash that flowed into and out of the city's various housing projects and other neighborhoods. Selling crack cocaine was a way for those who didn't have viable employment or sufficient schooling to earn money, impress their partners, buy something for their children, and help pay their mothers' bills. Crack cocaine had consequences, and it took an unimaginable toll on families, friends, and communities, even mine.

I spent the most time with Maurice of all my brothers while growing up. He was already well known throughout Central City because of his comedic nature and sociability. Maurice became more popular because many people, even family members, wanted some of that drug money he was making. On the other hand, I was making "chump change" in my job as a substitute teacher, and Maurice occasionally offered me some money. In our family, not unlike many in desperate need of cash and dealing with intergenerational poverty, giving money to a family member represented a strong display of love and loyalty. Although I needed more income after returning to Birmingham from college, I did not want Maurice's money. While he was hustling to make a living for himself, my mind would inevitably go back to when he made that fateful decision back in 1984.

That night Maurice and I sat on the bed that we shared—in the room we shared—in the dark, talking about his decision to stop attending high school. "Jerome, man, I ain't about to be no twenty-year-old graduating from high school. I can just get out and go to Job Corps or somewhere and learn a trade!" Maurice was behind a few classes in high school. He and I would now be graduating the same year. He didn't like that idea because everybody compared us to each other. We both enjoyed school—but in different ways. For him, school was a place to hang with friends and practice his carefully honed craft of cracking jokes on everyone, from students to teachers. But the fun he had in high school had taken an academic toll on him. He was now seventeen and still just a sophomore.

With the orange-tinted streetlights peeking through the bedroom window, I begged Maurice, "Man, if you don't finish up, then it will be hard to move on. You've got to hang in there and not worry about what everybody else's gonna say." At the time I didn't have a complete understanding to tell him how his future might unfold. I did not know that crack cocaine would be the culprit that would bring him down. All I knew was that leaving high school would not bode well for his future, but I was incapable at that time of fully describing how the entire scenario might play out for him.

Maurice stopped going to school at the end of the 1983–1984 academic year. He and one of our homeboys from Central City decided to join Job Corps, a vocational training program for young people between the ages of sixteen and twenty-four to go into industry-related jobs. Funded by the U.S. Congress, Job Corps advertised second chances for those who had not finished high school.[5] Maurice and our homeboy went to Jacksonville, Florida, for their second chance. As soon as they had arrived in Florida, Maurice and I would write letters to each other. He told me how beautiful and expansive Jacksonville was. I enjoyed receiving his letters, not just for the detailed content but also because of the care he took in writing them and the beautiful calligraphy-style penmanship he displayed. Maurice's letters were a work of art! He made sure to tell me that "Jacksonville has palm trees" and that it was "the nation's largest city based on landmass in the 48 states, not including Alaska."

Although Maurice and I grew up in the same household, did most things together when we were young, and had many of the same friends, our social and educational experiences diverged over time. I worried about the fate of my brother and other young Black males standing on Central City's street corners. A momentary slip in judgment could make one a victim of a system with no mercy for Black people. Instead of engaging in cultural and political development activities that helped them to see the forces that were creating their conditions, they remained in survival mode. I was learning how to see our experiences, like an outsider looking in, from reading books like Manning Marable's *How Capitalism Underdeveloped Black America*.[6] I was also reading Haki Madhubuti's *Black Men: Obsolete, Single, Dangerous?*[7] But books were not the only text that I studied. I also studied the lyrics written by hip-hop group Public Enemy. "Fight the Power" and "Brothers Gonna Work It Out" were my theme songs in college. I especially listened to what are now the old-school conscious rappers such as Queen Latifah, KRS-One, MC Lyte, and Kool Moe Dee. Moreover, I didn't have to go to college to find Black consciousness. I first discovered Black consciousness in Central City.

CHAPTER 16   BLACK CONSCIOUSNESS

Black consciousness, a sense of knowing who you are as a Black person and moving about in the world with this social and political awareness, has always existed among some Black people. In Central City, it was in the culture, the experiences, our souls, and our day-to-day stories of solidarity and surviving. Black consciousness was also learned by living, especially when we went beyond the boundaries of our neighborhood and interacted with white people.[1] Another kind of "consciousness," in terms of learning about the experiences of Black people, could be gained by reading books. Roderick, one of Richard Jr.'s close friends, personified this sense of consciousness. Richard Jr. and Roderick were the same age, and they immediately struck up a friendship when Roderick's mother moved into Central City in 1973. Roderick was eleven years old at the time and an only child. Like most children in Central City, Roderick attended Powell Elementary School; he would graduate from Phillips High School in 1980. Roderick took some college courses, first in 1982 at Livingston University in Livingston, Alabama, and then at the University of Alabama at Birmingham (UAB) in 1984.

Roderick's image personified that of a Black street intellectual. He wore dark shades and carried a backpack filled with conscious books. Joined by avid readers in the community such as Brother C.—a Black man who had served in Vietnam—Roderick occasionally invited me, though a teenager at the time, to participate in their book discussions. Our readings included Chinweizu's *The West and the Rest of Us* and Walter Rodney's *How Europe Underdeveloped Africa*. These books highlighted how enslavement and colonialism systemically extracted human and material resources for the benefit of European powers.[2] My five older brothers occasionally talked to me about life, mostly matters regarding girls and sports. Roderick spoke to me about issues in the world, especially the situation facing Black people. In the front room of his mother's apartment in Central City, we would sit for hours discussing ways to address issues in Black communities.

Interestingly, Roderick also combined a Black consciousness and intellectual curiosity with distinctive dress for a young Black male in the community at that particular time. His style included khaki or checkered pants, polo shirts, and penny loafers. About six feet tall but weighing only a hundred fifty pounds, Roderick knew that he had to hold his ground because of the reputation of some of his peers in Central City. He would not let anyone mistake his consciousness and style of dress as signs of weakness. In our community, we could gain a measure of respect by introducing a fashionable dressing style. Many of us copied Roderick's style and took it with us to Phillips High. There was an unofficial competition among Black students from the various communities served by Phillips, such as Southtown, Norwood, and Central City, for the "best dressed." We bought many of these clothes from Najjars, a discount clothing store located downtown.

After first getting rooted in Central City, my Black consciousness increased during my college years. My interactions with racially biased white professors and coaches introduced me to how racism looked in classrooms and on the playing field. I learned about Black politics from an intellectually gifted political science professor at Austin Peay named Dr. James Mock. I first read *The Autobiography of Malcolm X* during my second year in college and recited Malcolm's speeches verbatim during various campus events. Despite my growing Black consciousness in college, my family in Birmingham still lived in the projects. Their situation was always on my mind. I was increasingly aware of the conditions that influenced our predicament and impoverishment, and I wanted to know how I could help change these conditions.

By the time I went back to Central City in 1990 after college, I had begun to filter my analysis of the inequities facing communities like Central City through several personal and educational experiences. From my perspective, these inequities had caused many "good" people to do things they otherwise would not have done. One of those good people was a childhood friend whom I refer to as Fat Joe. He was about five feet seven inches tall, dark brown in complexion, and slightly chubby. Fat Joe was three years older than me, and I often hung out with him and his younger brother while growing up. Our families' lives and experiences paralleled each other in many ways. Like mine, his mother raised a lot of children alone. While our mother raised seven (six boys and one girl), Fat Joe's mother raised eight children: three boys and five girls. Like us, Fat Joe's family also came out of the Alley and the Court. Although our families struggled, it seemed as though Fat Joe and his siblings went through more than what my siblings and I had experienced. It wasn't as though we had a better life; it just looked like their clothes were a little more tattered and their struggle was a little more challenging. Most importantly, my siblings and I had grown up with our mother our entire childhoods; Fat Joe and his siblings had not.

Fat Joe and his siblings suffered a devastating loss when a man from the Alley murdered their mother. She was younger than forty at the time, Fat Joe just thirteen. Their mother's death left the eight children, especially the very young ones, orphaned. Consequently, Fat Joe and some of his siblings became wards of the state. State officials placed some of the children in foster care throughout Birmingham and Alabama. The older ones could care for themselves to a certain degree, but the younger ones had no choice but to accept placement in the foster care system. The siblings' separation seemed like a scene out of the 1977 television series *Roots* when white slave owners would snatch Black babies from their mothers and disperse the children throughout different plantations. In his autobiography, Malcolm X described a similar type of separation of his family.[3] For many of us who had formed close bonds with Fat Joe and his siblings, it was a sad sight to see an uncertain future on the children's faces. Fat Joe's younger brother and his sister—an outstanding student who resembled her mother—had to leave our school during the middle of the academic year.

Compared to his siblings, Fat Joe appeared to be the fortunate one. He was a close childhood friend of the Bast family, a Black family that owned a few houses near the Alley. They rented out houses to families and rooms to boarders, mostly men. The Bast family took Fat Joe in and raised him as their son and brother. The family's matriarch, Mrs. Bast, was a doting mother who would do just about anything to provide for her children and made them feel special. Mrs. Bast's youngest son was Fat Joe's best friend, and they even referred to each other as brothers. Mrs. Bast's husband, who lived with the family, seemed invisible compared to his wife's strong presence.

Mrs. Bast's food was legendary. A shrewd businesswoman who exchanged cash for food stamps at the rate of one cash dollar for two dollars' worth of food stamps, Mrs. Bast was well known for her pork chops, collard greens, and sweet potato pie. She made money selling home-cooked meals to employees at local organizations, including the Holsum Bakery across the street from her house, the Pollock Paper Company a block away, and UAB's hospital. Customers came from all over the city to get some of Mrs. Bast's food. She met a vital need for Black people in the community and the white and Black workers nearby. During the legal segregation era and afterward, Mrs. Bast and many other Black women would cook food that fed one's body and soul. As a Black woman, Mrs. Bast had seen and experienced how Black people were turned away or allowed only to purchase but not eat the meal in white-owned restaurants and establishments. Consequently, she started preparing and serving her signature dishes. Mrs. Bast's food was not only delicious but also affordable, and no one else, not even white restaurateurs, could boast of having the best food in town.

Mrs. Bast's entrepreneurial efforts allowed her to contribute to the family's finances and provide for her children. The family lived better than most Black families in the area. Whether cooking for their families, funerals, church fundraisers, or household income, Black women like Mrs. Bast have always used soul food to strengthen family ties, serve the community, and earn income.[4] And Mrs. Bast spent her money on her children, whether making sure that every child had a gold tooth in their mouth once they became teenagers or purchasing a used car for them to drive to high school. Also charitable, Mrs. Bast delighted when any children from the Alley and the Court graduated high school, always taking the time to send graduation cards with some money inside. I received cards from her when I graduated high school and college.

Like the rest of the Bast family members, Fat Joe received a gold tooth when he became a teenager. The family also purchased a used car for him that he drove just about everywhere, often through Central City. "Let me roll with you, man," I said to Fat Joe one day when he was passing through. As soon as I got inside of his car, Fat Joe asked me if I could drive. Determined to show him that I was not new at this, I replied foolishly, "Yeah, man, I can drive. Ain't nuthin to it." I was only fourteen at the time, and the only driving I had done was steering the joystick on the *Pac-Man* arcade games at the One Stop Convenience Store. I lied to Fat Joe, and I think he knew. But he didn't say anything or question me about it.

Fat Joe had learned how to drive through the "school of hard knocks." He just got inside the car and drove. He and my brother Michael, when they were much younger, would sneak into U-Haul trucks at the Exxon Service Station on Eighth Avenue and Twenty-Sixth Street and drive around town. "If they can drive at twelve and thirteen, I know that I can drive at fourteen," I thought to myself.

After riding around for some time, Fat Joe and I stopped at another service station, located near One Stop. "Jerome, look down there or somewhere between the seats to see if you can help me find any loose change on the floor," said Fat Joe. I looked and found a couple of quarters lodged between the seats. I handed them to Fat Joe. He passed the money to the attendant, a young white male rumored to like the young Black males in the area. After Fat Joe had finished pumping the gas, I asked if he would allow me to drive his car. "You know what you doing?" asked Fat Joe. "Yeah," I said. "Alright, jump in on my side," Fat Joe said encouragingly.

I walked around to the driver's side, hopped into the car, and turned the key. I then put the white Nova in reverse—thinking it was in drive—and then "Bang!" I hit a pole that protected the pump. I had accidentally scrubbed the driver's side door against the pole. "Stop, man; you gotta put it in drive!" shouted Fat Joe. Panicking, I quickly attempted to shift gears but further damaged the door by lodging it into the pole with a dull screeching sound. "Dang, man," I said. I had hit the pole once again. But this time was worse. Fat Joe looked at me, shook his head, and jumped out of the car to take over. "Mrs. Bast gonna be mad," sighed Fat Joe. He then paused and refused to disparage me. "Man, I'm sorry 'bout that. How much it's gonna cost to fix it?" I asked. Shocked at what had just happened to his car, Fat Joe knew there was little he could do to recoup his money. My mother was flat broke, and so was I. "Don't worry about it, Jerome," he said.

Throughout the whole ordeal, Fat Joe kept a slight smile on his face. Yet the smile that always showed the gleaming gold front tooth was now masking the hurt he felt. Fat Joe knew that he had to do some explaining to Mrs. Bast. And I felt terrible for what had happened and for the scolding he was going to receive. I had torn up this dude's car. But Fat Joe didn't even hate me for it; he forgave. However, this compassionate and understanding Fat Joe would be tested a few years later after I had gone off to college and then returned to Birmingham during some summer months.

◗

Word on the street was that Fat Joe had entered the lucrative crack co-caine game and that he, like many others, had set up base in Central City. He was making a lot of money in the area. However, another dealer in the area, nicknamed Hype, had vowed to take over the drug game in Central City after being released from prison. Hype had not grown up in the area but had a lot of street credibility from prison. Standing about six feet three inches tall with a slender build, Hype had not too long ago gotten out of prison. He was in his late twenties. Not long after being re-leased, Hype set up shop in Central City. By pulling guns on a couple of people, he instituted fear among those vying to sell in the area. We spoke when I saw him, but mostly about his younger brother, who had gone off to college. However, unlike his younger brother, Hype had become in-volved with criminal activity that landed him in prison. By the time he was freed, he was already determined to take over the Central City drug game. He wanted the area that Fat Joe worked, an area of Central City where he "made a killing" selling dope.

Hype kept a posse with him, and they all wanted to expand their daily cash flow. The money, women, clothes, and respect were too tempt-ing not to want it all. He decided to punk Fat Joe by letting him know that he had better get out of there or he was going to "get his fat ass whupped." At first the threats forced Fat Joe to stay cooped up in his old lady's apartment. But Fat Joe knew that he couldn't go on living like that for too long.

Fat Joe eventually had to face his fears. He walked down from the upstairs apartment where he lived. Seeing Fat Joe outside, Hype ap-proached him with a determination to let him know that Central City was now his territory: "I told you to take your fat ass back where you came from. I run this around here!" shouted Hype. Immediately, Hype pulled his right hand back and went forward with an open-faced palm slap across Fat Joe's face. As soon as Hype landed the blow, he shot Fat Joe once in the leg and then in the stomach. Determined to live, Fat Joe immediately reached for his pistol, tucked inside his pants, and pulled it out. Fat Joe unloaded a straight sniper bullet into Hype's forehead. Af-ter the first shot, which knocked Hype to the ground, Fat Joe stood over him and unloaded a barrage of bullets. Fat Joe was now inhabiting a darker world—a world tapping into an innate sense and desire to sur-vive, a world in which he had vowed not to die the way his mother had died. Fat Joe had entered a world whose laws included flight or fight. He was done fleeing because there was nowhere else to go. Central City, the Court, and the Alley were all that he had known. Fat Joe fought back.

The gunfire erupting from Hype's posse from across the street brought Fat Joe back into consciousness; then he felt pain in his stomach. He too had been struck by Hype's gun or by a bullet from Hype's boys. Another bullet struck a bystander, a young woman on the front porch with her children, in the head. Cars began screeching while bullets flew, and children and adults ran for cover, ducking everywhere. Fat Joe stumbled onto the stairs where his old lady lived and made his way back into the apartment, now bleeding profusely in the abdomen. He had conquered his fear and was still alive. But Fat Joe would be arrested and serve time in prison. He faced charges for killing Hype. But being challenged on the street would not be the last time for Fat Joe; prison was another world for him.

While incarcerated Fat Joe visited Donovan, his cousin who was serving time for murder. "Man, these dudes up here think they gonna turn me out," said Fat Joe. "I need you to get my back." In response, Donovan asked Fat Joe whether he was willing to protect his manhood and die for what he believed. Fat Joe reassured Donovan that he would fight. Fat Joe then told Donovan that he needed him to talk to the leader of the group and let them know what the deal is. "Okay, if you are down, then I am down. Give me a day or two; I'll go and talk to them," concluded Donovan.

The next day, Donovan met the group's leader to let him know that they "better not touch Fat Joe. First, he ain't no punk. Second, he is my cousin, so don't y'all fuck with him! If you do, you gonna have to see me. You think you got some big knives? I want you to know that I got knives bigger than any of y'all. So try me if you want to!" Donovan continued: "For that whole day, I sat in my cell waiting for one of them to come over and try me. I sat up with my two shanks and dared them. None of them dared me, and that's how it ended."

⬛

Fat Joe, Donovan, my brother Maurice, and many more Black men were doing time behind bars. But they were not the only ones incarcerated. Their mothers, wives, girlfriends, siblings, and children were also "doing time" with their absence.[5] Maurice's wife was now alone and raising their son on her own. And our mother, who had been raising Maurice's oldest son, would serve as the child's parent for the next seven years. To relieve our mother, who was raising him, I would bring Maurice's oldest son to Nashville during the summer months to live with Mary and me.

In addition to his father's incarceration, Maurice's oldest son's mother was battling a drug addiction. She would later make attempts to forge a relationship with her son when he became a teenager and young adult.

◗

I made the trip to Ventress Correctional Facility, near Alexander City, Alabama, about six months after Maurice's incarceration. My mother wrote and called me, asking me to take her to see Maurice the next time I came to Birmingham. As promised, I stopped in Birmingham to pick her up. She brought Maurice's oldest son along. Maurice's wife, and their son, also rode with me. Maurice would complain of how much he hated wearing the prison-issued flip-flop-style footwear, so I brought along a new pair of tennis shoes that I had purchased for him.

It seemed like a reunion of old friends and relatives at Ventress. A female cuz who once lived in Central City was visiting her husband at the prison. There were so many young men from Birmingham, young men who should have never been living their lives incarcerated. But they were there, many because of crack cocaine.[6] Birmingham Black, from the Norwood area of the city, was there. "Man, you still throwing that ball? I know you in law school and shit!" said Birmingham Black to me. "Nah man; I'm finna go to back to school to work on a degree in education policy. The law school thing didn't pan out the way I wanted. I'm focusing on the education of Black folks." "That's real; do your thing man," reassured Birmingham Black. He told me that he was in there for using drugs but was now doing his best to stay clean.

Before I left for the day, Maurice and I took a few minutes to reminisce about childhood, and we invariably brought up the teachers at Powell Elementary who were like "other mothers" to us.[7] These educators had grown up in Birmingham's Black communities, attended Black elementary and high schools, went to the historically Black colleges in Alabama, and understood the daily challenges facing our parents, especially our mothers.[8] They had done all they could to help our families to raise us. But something more potent than their teaching and love— something beyond what a school or educator could contend with—impacted our lives in very predictable and at times unfortunate ways. This something was inextricably a part of the American social fabric, and it had relegated many Black people to the economic dregs of U.S. society and attempted to steal our sense of identity and create a *social death* for us.[9] But we did not die. Just like Fat Joe, we survived and maintained our sense of humanity. Black consciousness, I would learn, was also about keeping your dignity and humanity while surviving in a hostile, anti-Black world and among, at times, dire social and economic conditions.

CHAPTER 17 CHOCOLATE OR WHITE MILK?

It was the 1991–1992 academic year. I was assigned to teach American history and government to eighth grade students at Treble Middle School (pseudonym)—a public school in Nashville serving seventh and eighth grades. At the time, Treble's student population numbered about five hundred, 60 percent Black and 40 percent white. Almost all of the students were from low-income backgrounds. On the other hand, the teacher composition was about 85 percent white and 15 percent Black. I was a member of the 8-White Team, which also consisted of three white female teachers in their early to mid-forties. The principal was John Thomas, a white male who was a strict disciplinarian. Newspaper articles on his office walls illustrated his previous successes at managing an "inner-city" school. Mrs. Sims, an African American woman and a veteran teacher of more than two decades, in her seventh year at Treble, served as assistant principal.

I was part of a unique teacher education program (organized by cohorts) at Peabody College of Vanderbilt University. This program allowed graduate students to earn a year's credit toward tenure as a teacher in Tennessee while attaining a master's degree. The program's motto was "Theory Meets Reality." The Peabody cohort consisted of seventeen students varying in age from twenty-two to forty-two. I was twenty-three at the time, the only nonwhite intern, and one of two males in the program. The other male was white and in his early forties. To ensure that we gradually eased into teaching since none of us had taught before, the program's coordinator placed each intern under the tutelage of a mentor teacher for an entire academic year. Additionally, the program included a supervisor who would visit the schools once a week to observe and evaluate the interns. My supervisor, a white male, was also the program's coordinator.

Throughout the first semester of the school year, I became more intentional in ensuring that my teaching could incorporate diverse cultural perspectives on various topics in American history. We used the books assigned to us, which provided a mainstream white view, with people of color such as Dr. Martin Luther King Jr. in the sidebars. I enjoyed teaching about Dr. King, but I also wanted the students to learn about more people and go beyond the often shallow depiction of Dr. King and the Civil Rights Movement.[1] My mentor teacher, a middle-aged white woman, expressed concerns when I presented her with my approach to teaching the American history unit that first semester. After reviewing my material, she asked, "Why did you only include additional information about African American people and not much about other groups?" I told her that I was making a conscious effort to include perspectives from diverse groups. Given my increasing knowledge of African American history, I wanted to incorporate that perspective since it was absent from the textbooks we were using. I especially wanted the Black children to have more than a sidebar of their history.

Tensions intensified when some Black teachers and I invited a student group from a nearby high school to present during our Black History Month celebration. The high school students, primarily African American, performed skits, recited poems, and sang African American spirituals. Immediately following the program, Mr. Thomas stopped me in the teachers' lounge and asked, "Mr. Morris, didn't you think that program was very offensive to the white teachers and students in the audience?" He had caught me somewhat off guard, but I was not surprised by the question. "No, I did not witness anything that they said that I thought was offensive to white people." He was visibly upset based on the way his face had turned red. He continued, "You can't tell me that when Black students get up on stage and talk about how their ancestors had been stolen from Africa and how white men raped the women, that it is not offensive. What if white people would have gotten up there on stage and then said the same things about Black people? How would you have felt?" I then answered his question: "That couldn't have occurred because the emotional reaction from Black people as a result of slavery would have been different. Africans were enslaved by white people and not vice versa. Basically, you are asking me to create a hypothetical that didn't exist. Therefore, I can't tell you how African Americans would have felt because Africans never enslaved white people systematically in the United States." Mr. Thomas shouted in return: "I was about to stop the program right in the middle of the performances! There will never be a program like that again at the school, and if any teachers proposed such programs, I would have to look it over thoroughly before approving it!"

The following day, Mr. Thomas called a meeting with the various teaching teams to discuss the program. During the meeting with our team, he emphasized how displeased he was with the program and said he believed it could incite friction between Black and white students because "the Black children live in the projects, and the poor white students live in trailer homes." He felt that the program would enflame what he described as hidden frustrations. I asked him whether he believed we could teach children in a vacuum. For me, schools are the place where young people should be learning about different groups' histories. Mr. Thomas, on the other hand, believed that race and racial matters should not be taught in schools: "Yes, I believe that we can teach them in a vacuum by ignoring race!" After Mr. Thomas's statement, a team member of mine (a white woman) said she had already noticed the tension in the school. "I overheard one Black student tell another Black student to get chocolate milk instead of white milk because chocolate milk was better." I found this teacher's association of a Black student's statement about preferring chocolate milk over white milk with the school assembly far-fetched. But this was her thinking.

I informed Mr. Thomas that it appeared that the only people who expressed disappointment with the Black History Month program were some of the adults in the school, specifically the white teachers. I talked about how shortly after the program I had discussed the assembly with my students, who had enjoyed the program. "We need these kinds of programs to teach about important topics in the Black experience that are rarely in textbooks." I looked around and got tacit agreement from one Black teacher. The meeting ended with everyone just walking out.

About a week later I met with my mentor teacher and my supervisor, a white male who had been a middle school social studies teacher and coach. This meeting overwhelmingly focused on what the coordinator and mentor teacher considered my "emphasis on the Black perspective." "Jerome, you are way too far to the side of being only interested in Black people's concerns. You should try to move a little more toward the middle," he cautioned me. I remembered how Mr. Thomas and my team members seemingly expressed joy at my presence on the team when I had first arrived. They said the African American males needed a positive role model like me. Additionally, they asked me to coordinate some of the Black History Month activities, which I did. However, I now felt castigated for fulfilling my role as a teacher and role model for Black children.

My supervisor continued to question my focus and motives with a statement that seemed to come from nowhere. "Jerome, one of the teachers on your team said that you agreed with Sister Souljah's statement that Black people can't be racist and that they can only show prejudice." "What did this question have to do with the issue at the school?" I thought to myself. They were attempting to gauge my politics and where I stood on Black issues by bringing up a comment I had said a while back. During the 1990s, Sister Souljah, a hip-hop pioneer, scholar, published author, and speaker, made statements about racism having a power dimension. She received pushback in the media when she said Black people could not be racist because they, collectively, do not wield power over white people. She also became well known because of her statements about the U.S. government's unwillingness to stop the killing within Black communities related to drugs and gangs. She mentioned that if Black people began killing white people, the U.S. government would do something about it. Bill Clinton, presidential candidate at the time, weighed in on the situation and criticized her comments. Sister Souljah countered Clinton, calling him a "hypocrite."[2]

I informed my supervisor that I agreed with Sister Souljah's comments about Black people not being racists. Still, he was emphatic that Black people and white people can both be racists. I then went into political science mode. I pulled from readings in the Black politics courses during my undergraduate years at Austin Peay. I began describing how one of the tenets of racism implies that one has a base to control others. Historically, Black people have not been in control over white people in the United States. Later, this statement, and the conversation between my supervisor and me, would resurface.

Shortly afterward, an array of issues emerged that seemed to have resulted from the Black History Month program and my approach to teaching. Some Black teachers said that Mr. Thomas approached them individually and asked them whether they thought the Black History Month program should have been allowed. He was especially disturbed when he found that none of the Black teachers felt offended by the program. Mr. Thomas's questioning of my Black colleagues about my approach to teaching, I felt, represented a way to control Black people. One day in the hall, Mrs. Sims, the assistant principal, approached me. She told me that she wanted to see how "you integrate the curriculum. I want to make sure you teach according to the state curriculum guidelines."

As a new teacher, I felt under surveillance for affirming Black history and culture. My style of teaching was ostracizing for some of the white adults. I had entered the school under the assumption that Treble's administrators wanted quality teaching and a positive role model for the Black children. Did they want this, or was it a facade? Was it worth it to be involved in that kind of confrontation with colleagues for the Black students to get some semblance of their history? The answer for me was an emphatic yes! Was there another way in which we could have all reached a mutual understanding about the matter? Possibly.

I had made my decision about whether to teach the following school year. I was not interested in working where the administration wanted no teaching concerning Black people. I was beginning to read about the shortage of Black teachers in schools, and I felt some degree of responsibility to help minimize this disparity. My idea of the sacredness of teaching had been shaped by Black educators in Birmingham who taught me at Powell Elementary and Phillips High. Like Black educators throughout history, the educators at those schools in Birmingham had demonstrated a deep and abiding commitment to us, our families, and our communities.[3] After the experience at Treble, I developed greater clarity about the practice of teaching, Black children's education, and U.S. schools. When white school administrators and teachers, for the most part, made statements about wanting more Black teachers, they were really saying they wanted teachers who were Black only in physical appearance. There was little desire for Black teachers who centered the experiences of Black people when teaching Black children. They did not welcome Black teachers who affirmed Black identity and culture.

Once the school year ended, I informed my middle school team members that I would not accept the district's job offer to teach. Instead, I enrolled in the doctorate program in educational policy at Peabody College of Vanderbilt University. My studies and research focus would examine how larger forces such as race, racism, politics, and economics impact education. I wanted to learn more about how educational policies and reforms influenced African American children's schooling experiences and outcomes.

At Vanderbilt University, I received scholarly guidance about education's social and political contexts from excellent faculty members. However, there were few Black faculty members, so I sought insights related to Black education from faculty members at other universities throughout the United States. My sense of community in graduate school became enhanced through Vanderbilt's Organization of Black Graduate and Professional Scholars (OBGAPS), for which I served as president.

But Vanderbilt was not my only world during the early to mid-1990s. Mary and I lived in a predominantly Black South Nashville community—a community that is now majority white. During that period, we became members of several Black- and African-centered groups in the city. Collectively, we sought ways to strengthen our communities and positively impact the lives of young people. One such effort involved my cofounding with a group of other Black males the PEAKS program. PEAKS used concepts from an Afrocentric perspective to guide middle school Black males in their development. The work we were doing with PEAKS became affirmed in 1995 when minister Louis Farrakhan galvanized a new generation of Black people with the Million Man March. As founders of PEAKS, some of us traveled to join other Black men—and some women—at that historic gathering in Washington, D.C.

In reflecting on that year teaching at Treble Middle School in 1991–1992, I see that the opposition I experienced from some of the white administrators and teachers still exists but in a different form today. Today's opposition comes from those who rail against critical race theory (CRT) in U.S. public schools. However, CRT is a legal theory primarily taught in graduate and law schools, not K–12 schools. Those against the teaching of Black people's experiences are merely using CRT to camouflage their efforts to hold onto white racial mythology about U.S. history. Resistance to teaching about "race" has become codified through bills and enacted through dozens of statutes, including in Alabama, Tennessee, Missouri, Michigan, and New York.[4] Some are even suggesting that teaching about Black people and enslavement would make white children feel bad about themselves and their history. The teaching of Black people's history, however, must not be predicated on making its presentation acceptable to white people. Furthermore, it is important to note that CRT should not be conflated with African American history and the 1619 Project, which centers enslavement and Black people's contributions in the larger story of the United States.

White families and educators who say they are committed to racial justice should also be outraged at the miseducation that is taking place related to U.S. history. They should not attempt to shield white school children from a factual account of a history that includes genocide against Indigenous people and the enslavement of African people.

Moreover, those pushing the agenda to exclude teaching related to race and racism reinforce misunderstandings about Black people's role in U.S. and world history and ignore the importance of Black children seeing themselves within that history. As historian Dr. John Henrik Clarke notes, "History is a clock the people use to tell their political and cultural time of day. . . . It tells them where they are, but more importantly, what they must be."[5] My white colleague at Treble Middle in Nashville, Tennessee, should not have misinterpreted the Black student's remark that "chocolate milk is better than white milk" as a statement about race. Teachers must not be color-blind, particularly when it comes to preparing Black children educationally, culturally, and societally. An essential goal for any teacher in charge of the education of Black children must include connecting these children to their historical and cultural lineages and inspiring them to make their communities better.

CHAPTER 18 BIG MEATY

Boone, a former neighbor in Central City and one of my brother Ronnie's close friends, stopped by his old neighborhood to say hello to us. It was the summer of 1995, and I was in Birmingham to pick up my niece and nephew to take them to Nashville to spend the summer with Mary and me. "What's up, Big Meaty?" Boone asked while looking up to our second-floor apartment. Big Meaty was my brother Michael's nickname. Almost five years older than me, Michael was the middle child of the seven of us. Just about every day as an adult, Michael would sit on the front porch, smoke cigarettes, drink alcohol, play his music, and eat. Michael turned down the volume on his boom box just enough to respond to Boone: "What's happening, Boone? You still shooting lights out?" referring to Boone's deadly basketball jump shot.

"What did Big Meaty eat for lunch?" Boone asked rhetorically—a joking question he had asked ever since our childhood. While laughing and in one breath with rapid fire, Boone responded to his own question: "Big Meaty ate two Big Macs, three Whoppers, one Orange Ade, two cupcakes, three scoops of ice cream, five chicken wings, and washed it down with a gallon of purple Kool-Aid!"

Laughter erupted. Michael then grinned from ear to ear, accepting Boone's joking as a gesture of warmth. After everyone left, and dusk began to set in, Michael rewound the cassette tape on his boom box and continued where he had left off from Harold Melvin and the Blue Notes' song "Miss You." Later that night, Michael entered the front room to the apartment in Central City and fell asleep on the floor. Michael was thirty-one years old but looked to be about fifty. Every day he drank almost a bottle of Thunderbird or Wild Irish Rose wine and smoked a pack of Benson & Hedges cigarettes. When he got hold of a good amount of money or wanted to celebrate, he bought and drank Jack Daniel's Tennessee Whiskey. However, the liquor, smoking, and a rough life had taken a toll on him in such a short period. To support his drinking and smoking habits, Michael had learned how to fix almost anything mechanical to earn money; he was our family's and the neighborhood's handyman. Lil Maurice, our nephew, fetched anything that Michael needed—his cigarettes, his cup with liquor in it, and his food.

⌐

The year, 1975. We rode in a car to get to the Juvenile Detention Center where Michael had been sent for stealing. We referred to the facility using one word: "juvenile." Juvenile was only a few miles away from Central City, although the ride seemed much longer to me as a child. Our mother had brought Maurice, Shelda, and me with her to visit Michael. We rode up to the place in a car, passed through a gate, got out of the car, and then walked into a brick building. We waited a few minutes. Then Michael came out. He was chubby—always had been—and tall. Michael gave each of us a nudge, glad that we were there. He and our mother talked some before we left. Our mother handed one of the employees an envelope with Michael's name on it. As we began to depart, her eyes glistened. We got back into the car with the driver and drove away.

Michael had been sent away to juvenile for some months. The police caught him and some of the boys he would hang out with stealing from department stores. This time in juvenile was not Michael's first; he had already been there multiple times, even at only twelve. A couple of years before, Aunt Maxine and Uncle Monroe had allowed Michael to live with them to help out our mother. Our mother never wanted to be considered an "unfit mother" because of the challenges she experienced raising Michael and the rest of us. But she had no choice but to allow Aunt Maxine and Uncle Monroe to take a chance with raising Michael. They lived in an apartment in the Fountain Heights / Druid Hills area about a couple of miles from Central City.

Aunt Maxine and Uncle Monroe, who had no children, had steady employment. Aunt Maxine worked in janitorial services at a nearby hospital and later became a licensed practical nurse. Uncle Monroe got a job at the downtown post office in late 1968. They had a car, had an apartment, and were doing well compared to the rest of our family members. They stepped in to relieve our mother of the pressure of raising seven children alone. To me, it seemed as though Michael perceived the move as more of a punishment and not as an opportunity to leave the abject poverty we were experiencing in the housing projects. Occasionally, Michael would ride his yellow ten-speed bicycle from Aunt Maxine and Uncle Monroe's apartment to be with us in Central City. In the Fountain Heights / Druid Hills area, Michael had also found camaraderie among a group of friends that he said were members of his gang. Still, Michael continued to get into trouble. After a few months, he was arrested, along with his friends, and sent to juvenile. Aunt Maxine and Uncle Monroe eventually sent Michael back to Central City to live with us. A judge warned Michael that, after numerous stints in juvenile, he would go to prison the next time he got into trouble. That was all that our mother needed to hear for the next few years.

Rather than risk Michael going to prison, our mother had another plan, a plan that would be difficult for the rest of us—Michael's six siblings—to fully comprehend. Our mother was determined to save Michael for as long as she could. She would go through almost any measure to give him money, even if it was her last dime. As siblings at the time, we could not fully understand why. "Michael, take these five dollars. Now don't ask me for a goddamned thing again!" said our mother angrily. While displeased, she still gave Michael money, even if he used it to buy cigarettes and liquor. Ronnie often fussed at our mother for the way she reacted to Michael: "I give you money, and you give it to Michael; I can't understand that," he would say. Michael was only sixteen, and as long as he was not in the streets or getting into any trouble, that seemed sufficient for our mother.

Years later, I began interpreting our mother's doting on Michael as her way of dealing with regrets and as one way to discourage Michael from engaging in activities that could put him in danger of returning to juvenile, going to prison, or being killed. Her fear was not unlike the fear that many Black mothers have for their sons. She seemed to view Michael as that one lost sheep whom she was determined not to let stray again. Like the good shepherd from the Parable of the Lost Sheep, our mother would risk life and limb to bring Michael back into the fold.[1]

"Jerome: You have a telephone call." Someone had tacked the note on my mailbox in the Fusz Hall dormitory on Saint Louis University's campus. The date was June 4, 1996. I resided in the campus dorm while collecting research data for my dissertation. I had gone to St. Louis to finalize the data collection for my study of the city's desegregation plan's impact on Black families' connections with schools.

A knot began forming in my stomach after honing in on the 205 area code, seeing the number, and recognizing that the call was from Aunt Maxine. I prayed that nothing was wrong. "Maybe it's a surprise birthday party for Ronnie since his birthday is June 6—two days from now," I had hoped. But out-of-the-blue calls of joy were rare, and for Aunt Maxine to call me in St. Louis was unusual. I had come to view telephone calls from Birmingham as ominous or financial, such as when a family member called me from the auto dealer to borrow a down payment for a new car. I retrieved my calling card and began dialing Aunt Maxine's telephone number. "Hello?" answered the calming voice. "Hey Aunt Sandra, this is Jerome. Y'all called me today?" "Hey, baby! Maxine 'nem called you because Michael is real sick and all. Let me go and get Maxine, and she can explain everything to you. You take care now, okay?" "I will," I said while anxiously waiting for Aunt Maxine to get to the telephone. "Jerome, Michael needs a kidney. I know you out of town, but do you think you can get down here to see if y'all got a matching kidney?" Pause. "A kidney from me? Did anyone else have a match? Drinking is the cause for the kidney failure, isn't that right?" I asked. "Yeah, you know Michael. But we just need to know if you can see if you've got a match or not," said Aunt Maxine. "I'll get down there within a few days." "Okay then; we'll be waiting for you."

The very next day, a new note had been placed in my dormitory's mailbox: "Jerome: Call Aunt Maxine." I retrieved the message, then dialed the number, listened for the dial tone, and punched in my calling card number. "Ring. Ring. Ring." "Hello?" "Hey, Aunt Maxine, how is Michael doing now?" "Come on down now, Jerome! The doctors are only giving him a few days to live." "Are you for real? Why did no one tell me how urgent it was? I thought he was in the hospital and had a little while." They had downplayed the seriousness of Michael's illness. Was it because none of us could have imagined Michael being so sick? Though only thirty-two years of age, Michael had been a heavy drinker and smoker for more than half of his life, and I was not surprised that it had come to this. Although Aunt Maxine's morbid tone conveyed that she too was hoping that Michael would recover from this episode, she seemed to have accepted the inevitable. Michael drank like it was nobody's business, and although I dared not voice it in front of anyone, I felt that Michael would drink away another kidney if someone donated it to him.

I packed my bags, placed them in the rental car, and left St. Louis, eventually driving nonstop to Nashville to pick up Mary. With a kiss and a hug, my wife greeted me at the entrance to the home that we rented with the news that I did not want to hear. "Jerome, they called to tell me that Michael died." My brother had passed away before I had the chance to say goodbye. As Mary and I got into the car and began heading down I-65 to Birmingham, Stevie Wonder's song "Love's in Need of Love Today" came over the radio, and I began to cry.

During the drive to Birmingham, I thought about how Michael's premature death was not just from the alcohol but also from poverty, a racist structure, a longing to belong, and the way society often treated young Black boys as though they were adults.[2] Michael stood about six feet two inches and weighed about three hundred pounds by the age of fourteen. Family and friends gave Michael nicknames such as Meaty Brain and Big Meaty because of his size. In the seventh grade, he was suspended from school for using profanity toward the principal, a white male. After this suspension from school, Michael would never return. He just found jobs working with mechanics, and they employed him without taking issue with the fact that he was still an adolescent. Throughout the remainder of his short life, Michael performed sporadic mechanical jobs.

As I listened to Stevie Wonder's beautiful song, I replayed through my mind my mother's sorrow after losing two sons, first Steve Morris, who was stillborn, and now Michael. I replayed Michael's life through my mind. After arriving in Central City from Nashville, I walked up the steps to the apartment's second-story floor and onto the front porch. My brother Kenneth, who had moved back in with our mother a few months earlier, greeted and comforted me with a hug. Such a hug was a rare expression of brotherly love. My sister's three-year-old son was there beside his uncle Kenneth.

Uncle Monroe had brought some of his clothes over to Central City so that the mortician could dress Michael up. Both Uncle Monroe and Michael were big men. Along with donations from extended family members and neighbors, my brothers and I pooled our money to pay for Michael's funeral. While viewing Michael's body at the funeral home, I overheard some people talking about how the mortician had "done a good job with Big Meaty!" We all seemed to conclude that if Michael could not have the nice things in life, then at least he could have them in death. But this still did not take away the sense of loss we all felt about our brother's premature death. No one could find Richard Morris Sr. to tell him about his son's passing and the funeral.

Michael Morris (aka Big Meaty) standing with Aunt Sandra. (Source: Author's collection.)

Jerome, Maurice, Shelda, Richard Jr., Ronnie, and Kenneth standing in the Central City community (Metropolitan Gardens) after Michael's funeral. (Source: Author's collection.)

After the service, we gathered at Central City's Community Center and ate the repast meal that our Central City neighbors and family members had prepared for everyone. We ate, took pictures, and became reacquainted with each other. Michael had some of his old friends in attendance from throughout Birmingham, including his former girlfriend and former members of his gang—a once loosely organized group of teenagers that Michael had been a member of and whom he also considered his brothers.

CHAPTER 19   BUILDING SOME NEW APARTMENTS FOR Y'ALL

> From Africa, to America, new name?
> Section 8, Hope VI, then Katrina came
> Moved in, moved out, and moved away
> Now back to the city and here to stay.
>
> Re-gentrify, redevelop, and renewal
> Of bad hoods, bad people, and bad schools?
> Once minority, now urban, no real change
> It's all the same, but a different name
>
> New Orleans, Nashville, or New York
> Different city, same state, that's how it worked
> Whether policy, promises, or a shovel
> As James Baldwin said, it is still Negro Removal
> —JEROME E. MORRIS, "All the Same" (©2009)

I wrote this poem while collecting data for the Central City Research Project and after the world witnessed the horrific treatment and scattering of Black people from New Orleans in 2005. Hurricane Katrina represented a continuation of events, policies, and practices that inevitably dispersed Black people, going back to the African slave trade. Years before the storm touched land, however, New Orleans's public housing officials had already displaced residents to other areas of the city for years.[1] Katrina served as the so-called natural disaster that city officials used as rationale for grabbing coveted urban spaces.[2] Using as official policy HOPE VI—a housing program developed during the Clinton administration that favored mixed-income development—the city had already moved almost seven thousand residents out of New Orleans's public housing units between 1996 and 2005.[3] The fate of the Black poor in other cities' public housing projects such as Techwood Homes in Atlanta and Metropolitan Gardens (formerly Central City and later renamed Park Place) paralleled the displacement of Black people from New Orleans's communities such as the St. Bernard Housing Projects.[4]

During the mid-1990s, just like in New Orleans, Birmingham Housing Authority officials applied for and received federal Housing Opportunities for People Everywhere (HOPE VI) funds to revitalize its public housing communities. Officially known as the Urban Revitalization Demonstration Project, HOPE VI began in 1993 and was a product of the U.S. Congress and the U.S. Department of Housing and Urban Development (HUD).[5] The program emerged from federal efforts to reform social services for the American poor. During the 1980s and 1990s, Democrats and Republicans supported housing policies like HOPE VI that would eventually undermine President Franklin Delano Roosevelt's New Deal and leave poor residents at the mercy of private enterprise. By 2005, HOPE VI's administrators had distributed to cities 446 federal block grants totaling $5.8 billion. An argument made by those supporting HOPE VI was that concentrated areas of poverty bred hopelessness, helplessness, and crime. HOPE VI proponents aimed to transform so-called distressed public housing by reducing concentrated poverty in an area.[6] The program involved removing inner-city residents from public housing into so-called better neighborhoods. The problem with such a nice-sounding effort was that an entire community would be demolished and never replaced to accommodate populations needing affordable housing. For example, one of the earliest studies of HOPE VI, produced by the Urban Institute in 2004, revealed that of the 49,828 demolished units, only 21,000 were replaced.[7]

Housing reformers had their eyes on places like Central City because it was located in an up-and-coming real estate area. After receiving HOPE VI funds, Birmingham Housing Authority (BHA) officials began informing Central City's residents during a series of community meetings in the late 1990s that the area would be revitalized. They told residents that they could return to a much better Central City—if they so desired. Slowly, the overwhelmingly Black residents trickled out of Central City, some with Section 8 vouchers, some willingly and hoping for a new start on life, others with great reluctance. Section 8 is a federal government program that provides a housing voucher to residents based on income to subsidize their rent.

Like many predominantly Black communities located in now coveted urban centers, Central City would become vilified leading up to the announcement of the HOPE VI grants. For example, in the effort to host the 1996 Olympics, civic and business officials in Atlanta painted pejorative portrayals of public housing residents who lived in what would become Olympic spaces.[8] Similarly, Birmingham's news programs highlighted crimes in Central City, mainly focusing on young adult males' arrests for marijuana and crack cocaine. The push for HOPE VI and the support for the so-called war on drugs ultimately created a situation that would have dire consequences for families, communities, and even schools. For example, nearby Powell Elementary and Phillips High were shuttered due to residents' displacement and the subsequent declining student population. The HOPE VI housing program would take a personal toll on families from Central City, including mine.

◻

I was completing my dissertation and making plans to graduate the following year, 1997. "Ring. . . . Ring." I reluctantly rose from my fixation on the computer screen to answer the telephone. My mother was on the other line. When we began talking, she said she had called to see whether I was still coming home to Birmingham for the Thanksgiving holiday break. I told her that I would be there. After I asked about my sister and her three children, my mother then told me her real reason for calling: "Jerome, I need a favor from you. When you come down, I need you to go over to the rent office to pay for a cheap ass door that was broken here at the apartment!" My mother had called to tell me that the Birmingham Housing Authority, specifically the people at the Central City rent office, had said that she had to pay for a damaged door to move into the planned new apartments. The rent office staff had billed my mother a hundred dollars for the door and informed her that she had to pay it no later than the day after Thanksgiving.

I asked my mother for the name of the person she had spoken with at the rent office regarding the door. In a calm tone so that I wouldn't just raise hell, she said, "Jerome, I don't need you to do any overanalyzing, just go on over there and pay them because I don't want them trying to hold something over my head." "Okay. I'll be down there the day before and talk to the people in the rent office," I reassured her. "Thanks. I love you, son." "I love you too." We both hung up.

I awakened early and left Nashville Wednesday morning, the day before Thanksgiving. I drove on Interstate 65 for approximately two hours and forty-five minutes to Birmingham. I went directly to Central City's rent office—located across the street from the front entrance to Phillips High School—to inquire about my mother's door bill. There was tension between my mother and the rent office personnel this time. Her relationship with the rent office staff in the 1990s differed from what she experienced in the late 1960s, throughout the 1970s, and into the early 1980s. During those times, my mother would sometimes go into the rent office and speak to the managers, first a white male and then a Black male. They seemed to understand when she had an apartment issue or was a little behind on her rent.

But things had changed by the mid-1990s. Central City's new manager, a white male, did not care to know the residents as well. After entering the rent office, I mentioned to the manager that my mother did not have the money to pay for the door, and I asked why they were asking residents to pay such bills knowing they were going to demolish the place. He went into the personal responsibility mode: "Well, that is what family members are supposed to do. They need to help take care of these kinds of responsibilities. They need to step up!" all the while raising his voice. "But you never answered my question," I countered. It was clear he did not want to answer. I then told him that the housing authority needed to "step up" and stop lying to people and telling them they would be able to move back there once the area was renovated. He and I both knew the real deal. I placed five $20 bills on the table, demanded a receipt, and walked out the door.

Keenly aware of how Birmingham officials (Black and white ones) had deceptively presented the information to residents about the promise of returning, I still made the payment for the damaged door on my mother's behalf. I wanted to ease her fears about not being able to move back into Central City. I was a full-time graduate student and had no other means of paying for the door other than my monthly $900 stipend and a student loan. As a doctorate student, I had some promises of a decent salary in the future, but it was still a challenge to come up with that $100. My mother expected one of her children to pay for the door. Proud that I was away working on my doctorate, she viewed my stipend as decent money.

After arriving in Birmingham earlier that day, I spent the night on the couch in the front room of my mother's three-bedroom apartment, located on the second floor. Eight of us were in there: my mother, my sister and her three children, a nephew, and my brother Kenneth. Upon waking the following day, I opened the metal front door and stepped onto the front porch. The November morning sun was just enough to knock off the chills. After eating a light breakfast, I walked across the street to get ready for the game.

Everyone was ready to get their fun in, soon to prepare for their family members coming over later in the day to eat turkey, ham, cornbread, sage dressing, macaroni and cheese, collard greens, cranberry sauce, and sweet potato pie. Our mother had cooked a small meal. Later on, I would get a bite at my Aunt Maxine and Uncle Monroe's house, a common gathering place for many of our family members during the holidays. But first we had to play in what we referred to as Central City's annual Turkey Bowl.

I played my usual position, quarterback. One of the players on my team stood in the backfield, and the other was spread out wide—both of them good friends since childhood. We were at it again, albeit ten years since last playing together in high school. The "new-school" ballers—just two or three years out of high school—were on the opposing team and wanted revenge for last year's loss. A crowd formed on both sides of the park, separated by age and the Central City section they represented: east side versus west. I was the east side quarterback and began to bark: "Blue eighty-four, blue eighty-four. Hut, hut."

While sprinting backward—just a millisecond slower than when I was in high school and college—I dodged to the left, to the right, pivoted, pumped, and scrambled. Sneaky reached and Lil Chub reached. "I still got it!" I thought to myself. Ten yards, then 20 yards later, I twisted and turned. Then all of a sudden, a breeze had come across my back and front sides. I began to spin, and threads began to unravel with each turn. In Sneaky's palm was a lump of black-and-white cloth from the shorts and underwear I had been wearing. Before I crossed the goal line, I stopped and stood naked in Central City! Everybody looked at me as I looked down.

"Ah man, take my pants!" exclaimed Sneaky. All the while, everybody was running around laughing hysterically at me. I laughed with them because it was the only thing I could do. To get another laugh due to this very embarrassing moment, Richard Jr. telephoned Mary and two of my sisters-in-law using the colossal cell phone that he carried with him.

After the game and a day of laughter, I said goodbye to everyone and promised to return the following year. "Jerome, man, you can keep those sweatpants," said Sneaky jokingly. I got a bite to eat at my mother's place and then visited my aunt and uncle's house. After seeing family that day, I headed north on Interstate 65, back to Nashville.

Fall 1998. I had graduated with my doctorate the year before and was in my second year as an assistant professor in the College of Education at the University of Georgia. My sister, Shelda, and her three children had come to live with Mary and me in our Atlanta-area two-bedroom apartment. After witnessing the struggles that my sister experienced while raising three children alone, we decided to assist her as much as we could. Shelda's children at the time were three, five, and twelve. Mary and I knew that helping my sister would also benefit the children—our two nieces and nephew. None of the children's fathers were in their lives or had contributed anything financially to them. One of them, an older man who my sister said worked for the city of Birmingham, denied he was the youngest child's father.

Nevertheless, many of our family members in Birmingham seemed to experience a sense of relief after Shelda and her children had moved in with Mary and me. She was having a tough time being a single parent in Birmingham, even though she received some support from our mother. Shelda was four years younger than me, and we were very close siblings. I felt obligated to help my sister. I convinced my wife to help me to support Shelda. Mary agreed, even though she was enrolled in graduate school at Emory University's School of Public Health. I also had to commute an hour and fifteen minutes—each way—to my job in Athens, Georgia.

Still, Mary and I took the time to help my sister make the transition from Birmingham. We assisted her in getting a job at a Dollar General store and enrolled her in a GED program. We then enrolled my sister's children in schools up the street from our apartment complex. I also assisted Shelda in setting up a bank account to deposit her entire biweekly salary. Mary and I slept in one of the bedrooms in the apartment, and my sister and her children took the other bedroom.

After about the first month of living with us, Shelda repeatedly called our mother to tell her how I was "too strict" with her. Our mother listened to Shelda's perspective. Shelda interpreted my demands as strictness. On the other hand, I viewed what I was doing as a way for her to become more focused in life. Our mother and Shelda were missing each other, and Shelda was also not used to being away from our mother. Although my sister was technically grown and had three children, our mother had served as a coparent to the children, which was not unusual from what she had seen other grandmothers in Central City, the Alley, and the Court do. I tried reassuring my sister that Mary and I were there for her.

Shelda was supposed to be living with us for good in Atlanta. That was the plan until she refused to come back with us after visiting Birmingham over the 1998 Thanksgiving holiday. Before having left for Birmingham, Shelda and I developed a plan, which entailed driving her and the children to Birmingham for Thanksgiving. We would visit family. Then on Thanksgiving Day I would leave Birmingham to return to Atlanta. Shelda and the children would ride the Greyhound bus back to Atlanta a few days later. On the Wednesday before Thanksgiving, Shelda and the children piled into the 1979 Toyota Corolla that Mary and I owned. We headed west on I-20 to Birmingham to ease my sister's homesickness and visit family for Thanksgiving. I would be there for only one day because I would drive back to Atlanta to spend time with Mary, who had stayed behind to complete assignments for graduate school.

Friday passed, and Shelda had not called. Saturday afternoon passed, still without word. Then on Saturday night, I called. "I ain't going back, Jerome. I miss my folks; I miss my Momma!" said Shelda emphatically. "Let me speak to our mother," I pleaded to my sister. I began to fuss at my mother: "You gotta tell Shelda that she's going to have to come on back on the bus!" "Jerome, Shelda wants to be here with me and take care of me." "Are you for real?" I asked our mother. "How is she going to take care of you? You have been taking care of her all of her life!" I shouted. Our mother was determined to come up with any justification for why Shelda should remain in Birmingham. There was little hope in changing her mind. As Shelda's brother, I felt that I was doing all I could to help her. I was trying to support my sister in parenting her children and transitioning from under our mother's care. Although several of our family members in Birmingham were eager for Shelda to move in with me and Mary because of our prior experiences of bringing nieces and nephews to live with us during the summertime in Nashville, I would find out that our mother still wanted Shelda and the children by her side. As the grandmother to Shelda's children, she still wanted to play an active role in raising them.[9]

The door among the debris. The demolition of Metropolitan Gardens.
(Courtesy, Richard Lee Morris Jr.)

Although Shelda had saved almost a thousand dollars in about three months, she never bought those bus tickets to come back to Atlanta. The Monday morning after Thanksgiving, I drove back to Birmingham to pick up Santana, Shelda's oldest child, who was in seventh grade. Santana was still enrolled in a middle school in an Atlanta suburb and needed to finish out the semester. Once the Christmas holiday came, I withdrew Santana from the middle school and drove her back to Birmingham to be with her mother, sister, brother, and grandmother.

⬛

The Birmingham Housing Authority moved my mother, sister Shelda, and Shelda's three children into the Tuxedo Court public housing community—infamously nicknamed the Brickyard. Tuxedo Court had cinderblock construction and a reputation as one of Birmingham's most dangerous housing projects. In the fall of 1999, demolition crews began tearing down 2510 Apartment C, 6th Court North in Central City—the community we had called home for more than three decades. Richard Jr. captured the demolition of Central City. He even took photos of the sink, the bathtub, and even the hundred-dollar door scattered among the debris.

⬛

The BHA displaced the mostly Black and low-income residents of Central City, even those who had called Central City home for three decades, in an effort to turn the property, and eventually Tuxedo Court, into mixed-income developments. Most of the residents never returned home. Our mother had hoped to come back after being moved temporarily into the Brickyard. This uprooting from a place where they had lived for three decades and displacement into another housing project that they were unfamiliar with took a devastating toll on our mother's health and on Shelda's and her children's overall circumstances.[10] In February 2000, our mother eventually moved in with Ronnie—the oldest of us—after becoming ill with congestive heart failure. My brothers and I made arrangements to make our mother as comfortable as possible while her health declined. Maurice and Richard Jr. visited her weekly, ensuring she had food and other necessities. Since I lived out of town, I would provide Ronnie with a monthly allowance to offset his expenses, but I still went to Birmingham to see my mother just about every weekend. When our mother moved in with Ronnie, she had to leave Shelda and her three children behind in the Brickyard. Leaving Shelda and the children was excruciating for our mother because she always worried about what would become of them if she were no longer around.

Ronnie eased our mother's transition from the Brickyard into his apartment, despite our mother fussing with him about any and everything. As the oldest son, Ronnie understood and fulfilled his duty. Mary, my spouse who was expecting our first child, had to go on bed rest due to complications with the pregnancy. I would travel weekly to Birmingham to see my mother while ensuring that Mary did not need anything. I continued this routine for about three months. Everyone was stressed. Once our first child, our daughter Amadi, was born, our mother willed herself to be able to travel to Atlanta to attend Amadi's African naming ceremony.

Our mother, Joann Steele Morris, passed away on March 30, 2001, at the age of fifty-eight from congestive heart failure and what we suspected was a broken heart, partly from Michael's untimely death at the age of thirty-two and partly from the psychological toll of displacement from Central City. Our mother's passing was even more devastating for Shelda in comparison to the rest of us. Without our mother's constant presence and support, Shelda attempted to raise children in a neighborhood where she had no roots or connections. Everyone in Central City had known and would look out for Shelda and her children—even Powell's educators and staff. But the Brickyard and the schools in that area were new places, where Shelda was anonymous. She felt isolated and

Park Place, at the site where Central City and Metropolitan Gardens once stood. (Courtesy, Derrick Collins.)

vulnerable in the Brickyard and had to fend for herself. Ronnie later assumed custody of the three children for a few years.

◖

In the former Central City housing project now stands the newly named mixed-income development known as Park Place, whose total number of units is less than Central City had. There was never a one-to-one replacement of housing units because Congress had repealed this provision of the law.[11] Of the newly created seven hundred housing units in Park Place, BHA reserved only forty-seven for low-income families, and the vast majority were offered for "market rate." Critics of the Park Place plan, particularly from the Greater Birmingham Ministry (GBM), felt that the tenant council's leader, a longtime resident, did not fully represent the residents' aims. According to one GBM representative, "The president of Central City's tenant association during the 1990s could have told the people there that they could have stayed in their apartments and fought against what was happening. But they were dealing with so many personal things in terms of their own family and was just trying to make sure they made out okay with everything."

CHAPTER 20 THAT'S HOME

"I don't like staying here [in this new residence]. I miss Central City. I miss home. I want to go back. But then I don't want to go back." Those words from Tabatha, a childhood friend from Central City, captured the ambivalence that Black women often experience about living in and then moving out of public housing. They struggle to reconcile the sense of community with the negative perceptions of public housing communities. Unfortunately, these perceptions often portray Black women and mothers in stereotypical ways, ignoring that they are mothers, daughters, wives, and sisters.[1] Moreover, Black women in public housing have to fight against images that depict them as lazy welfare queens and as promiscuous. Tabatha did not want to go back to the projects (Central City), not because it was a place she despised but because Black women in public housing always have to fight for their dignity and respect. It mattered not if they supported their families by working or staying at home to raise their children.[2]

My interviews with Tabatha and another childhood friend, Charlene, further illustrate Black women's resistance to stereotypical images and reaffirm the home that Central City had become for generations of Black people. By 2005, a few years after the Birmingham Housing Authority had converted Central City into Park Place, most of the people I had known while growing up no longer lived there. As part of the research study that I was leading on the displacement of Black families from Central City, I stopped by the Birmingham Housing Authority's offices to inquire about where the former residents from Central City had moved. I exchanged messages with the staff, but no one provided any information that I found helpful. I contacted the office of the mayor and spoke to a

Black woman in the economic development office, who said, "Honestly, I don't know if people really wanted to know where those people from Central City went." After speaking with this employee, I realized that one of the strategies of displacing people is to not keep any records of their new places of residence or their housing situation. I then reached out to the HOPE VI program's project manager, a Black male I had met. I tried interviewing him, but he too refused to provide any information or agree to an interview with me.

Numerous researchers attempting to investigate and evaluate HOPE VI have noted the challenges related to accountability due to the lack of adequate records and record keeping.[3] After the difficulty of gathering accurate information from the mayor's offices, Birmingham Housing Authority staff, and the HOPE VI's program manager, I resorted to using what is called a snowball approach to securing interviews with former residents. I contacted one person who knew the whereabouts of other people, and then that person would lead me to yet others. Fortunately, a Central City neighbor and school classmate had the telephone numbers of many of the people in the area. I talked to and interviewed several former residents. I especially highlight my interviews with Tabatha and Charlene, two women whose lives, though similar in many ways, became impacted in different ways. Both women were second-generation Central City public housing residents. Their mothers had moved into the community during the early 1970s.

Summer of 2006. I exited my 1999 green Honda Accord, parked in the gravel driveway. Immediately, I waved to Tabatha and her boyfriend to let them know I had made it. "Y'all way out here?!" I exclaimed. "What's up, Tabatha?" I asked. "I'm good, Jerome. It's good to see you!" I stepped onto the front porch of a small white wooden house in a section of West Birmingham where Tabatha lived. Out from the front door came Tabatha's boyfriend and the father of her youngest son. "Man, it's good to see you," I said. He reciprocated, "Good to see you too, man." Tabatha and her boyfriend would get married a few years later.

Now thirty-eight years old, one year older than I was, Tabatha was still her old self. Her dark-brown skin possessed the same youthful glow from childhood. A gold encasing (the crown type) on one of her center teeth gleamed through her still-white smile. Tabatha's hair had a slick black sheen to it. Her family had first moved into Central City in 1973.

She, her mother, her sister, and two brothers first lived there. During the late 1970s, her stepfather—the neighborhood football and softball coach known as Sugar Man—moved in when he got out of prison. Tabatha's grandparents lived in another apartment in Central City. We both attended Powell Elementary and graduated from Phillips High School together. Tabatha was the mother of three children. Her oldest child, a daughter, was twenty years old and had a child herself. Tabatha's middle child, a tall and lean young male, resembled Tabatha a lot. Tabatha and her boyfriend had one child together, a son who was the youngest of the three children.

"I sho' miss Mrs. Joann, Jerome." "Thank you, Tabatha. Every time I think about my momma, I smile. She was something else!" "Yeah, I can see Mrs. Joann right now," said Tabatha. "Your mother would say, 'Shelda, get your ass back in this house!'" Tabatha and I both laughed hysterically.

I asked Tabatha about all she knew related to people leaving Central City. She recalled conversations with housing officials about tearing the projects down around 1999. They asked her if she wanted to live in another housing project, and she said, "No! I want to have Section 8; I did not want to live in some other projects. We just went to the rent office to fill out the application, and they automatically gave it to us. I first went to live in Section 8 in West End and then over here to the Ensley area where I live [now]." Tabatha told me that she had moved into that part of the city four years after getting a Section 8 voucher and described how flyers had been posted in Central City to inform people that they could move into other housing projects such as Collegeville and High Chaparral. Tabatha rejected the offer and stated that she "did not want to move out of one project and into another project. I wanted to put my children into a house."

I understood how Tabatha felt because I also aspired to place my family in a house. During our conversation, Tabatha asked me about living in Atlanta, and I let her know that it was fine living there, just congested with a lot of traffic. I told her that Mary and I bought a house in the Atlanta area a month before our daughter was born in 2000. Tabatha later described how housing authority officials misled Central City's residents into believing they could move back into Central City. "They knew those folks couldn't move back. They were checking records and everything to try to see if they had a bad record, you know like warrants or whether they got busted for drugs or something," said Tabatha. While a few people moved back, many went to other housing projects throughout the city. Housing authority officials moved many older adults into the Smithfield housing project. Whereas the housing authority maintained vague records on who went where, some of the families ended up living in Southtown Court, located on the city's South Side near the University of Alabama at Birmingham and St. Vincent Hospital. Those families would be moved again when developers in December 2021 began demolishing the twenty-six-acre, 445-unit Southtown Court to create hotel and office space, residential units, a hotel, and retail stores and restaurants.[4]

Toward the end of our almost two-hour interview, I asked Tabatha to describe living in her new place compared to living in Central City. In a solemn and reflective tone, she responded, "I don't like it, Jerome." "You don't like what?" I further asked. "I don't like staying here. I miss Central City. I miss home. I want to go back. But then I want to go back, but I don't want to go back. Do you see what I am saying, Jerome?" I immediately told Tabatha, "I understand *exactly* what you mean."

Like so many Black residents of public housing throughout the United States, Tabatha contended with the stigma associated with living in the housing "projects," which played a significant role in her not wanting to move into any other public housing complex throughout the city.[5] Tabatha resisted dominant narratives about her experiences and what she wanted in life. As a Black woman and mother, she had been stigmatized her entire life and was tired of bearing this burden. She too wanted to provide a house for her children. She tried to accomplish this while maintaining her dignity. Moving out of the projects and into a house was almost everyone's desire, even mine. Although she was now living in Section 8 subsidized housing, Tabatha experienced a void in her life. She missed the sense of community that Central City provided.

Charlene, another longtime resident whose family had lived in Central City for twenty-five years, echoed Tabatha's sentiments. I met with Charlene also during the summer of 2006. She rented a small wooden house near an airplane museum on the eastern side of town. She and her three children, two sons and a daughter, lived there. While greeting each other again, Charlene and I hugged after not seeing each other for a few years. She invited me into the front room, illuminated by a lamp that gave off a yellowish hue. Her daughter sat in a chair while we shared a couch for the interview.

Charlene is the mother of three children. In 1997, she and her three children moved out of her mother's Central City apartment before the families had to leave. Using her resources, Charlene moved into an apartment on another side of town, hoping to provide a more respectable and safer environment to raise her two teenage sons and her daughter. However, she found the transition into the new apartment too much of a social and economic stressor for her. Although she worked, Charlene did not earn sufficient income to afford a rental place other than public housing. Besides, she did not know any of her neighbors in the new location and felt isolated. Eventually, Charlene would have to move back into Central City to assist her ailing mother, ease the financial stress that she was experiencing, and be among people she knew and who knew her.[6] When reflecting on living in Central City, Charlene talked more about it as a "good and bad experience." It was "bad" for her because she lived in what she called a "low-income situation." The lack of economic resources was real. The "good" part about living in Central City was that it pushed her to expand her outlook on life: "Some people do not want to expand their lives to a higher level. It taught me better so that when I expanded out again, I will be better prepared." For Charlene, living in Central City served as a motivating force for improving her life circumstances. An example of this motivation is Charlene's decision, approximately fifteen years after my interview with her, to go back to school. She finished high school and subsequently enrolled in a junior college.

Like Tabatha, Charlene was very familiar with the numerous conversations about revitalizing Central City so that the former residents would have a better place to stay. She linked the redevelopment of the housing project with efforts to revive downtown Birmingham: "They [developers] were going to make it into like mini condominiums to upgrade downtown." After moving back in with her mother, Charlene became engaged in the issues regarding the moving of people out of Central City. She and her mother attended the meetings together. I asked Charlene about the messages residents received from housing officials during the various community meetings. She responded, "They said that folks who lived there will be the first ones with the option to move back in. I was taking my mother back and forth to the meeting. The residents were fed a situation on how this could be a better neighborhood. I don't know if they got the full thing on what was going to happen." Charlene especially did not like the income stipulation with the new mixed-income development and felt that none of the new apartments should have been rented at market rate. She rhetorically raised the question about new residents affording the rent: "They have one-bedroom apartments for five hundred dollars. How are they going to afford that?"

After living back with her mother, Charlene and her children would eventually move out of Central City. She and her two sons helped her mother with the move. She never received reimbursement for the move, which the housing authority had promised. However, Charlene's mother chose not to move into the new Park Place Apartments because of all the rules regarding relatives living there. Her mother had a lot of siblings who sometimes visited.

Moreover, Charlene did not want to "risk being put out" if someone living there had a criminal record or bad credit or if she made too many requests for maintenance. Rather than deal with the inconvenience, her mother moved into another public housing complex. Charlene and her three children would also leave and move into a rental house on the city's eastern side.

CONCLUSION

The U.S. federal government has abandoned its public housing model that has been prevalent for the past sixty years. "By 2012, close to 260,000 units of public housing have been demolished or sold."[1] The failure to ensure one-to-one public housing replacement in places like Central City sends a clear message that the U.S. government has abandoned public housing for its low-income citizens. Policies that move people to so-called opportunities do not end poverty. People are still poor and often become disconnected from their neighbors. Moreover, by withholding resources and information and tearing down public housing, housing authority personnel further place vulnerable groups at risk.

Birmingham's civic and business leaders have begun marketing their downtown, including the new "Central City," as an up-and-coming commercial and business district. This new Central City district is increasingly becoming a white and gentrified place. These changes have resulted in the closing of schools, the creation of urban community gardens, and the transformation of an urban landscape that is pushing the Black poor away from the area.[2]

For example, the Birmingham public school system closed Powell Elementary in 2001, supposedly due to a declining student population and low academic achievement. After sitting idle for a decade, the building suffered a devastating fire in 2011. Developers purchased the building with the intention of converting it into lofts. In 2021, Powell was still sitting in the middle of the city, rotting away, two decades since being closed. Like community members in other cities that have experienced the closing of their neighborhood schools due to gentrification and the presence of charter schools, we mourned the closing of Powell.

First Central City was torn down; then Powell was closed.[3] When policy makers remove a school from vulnerable people and communities, they remove one of the few stable institutions within these spaces. A call for Black Lives Matter means that Black people in some of the most neglected schools and neighborhoods should also matter.[4]

The school system converted Phillips High School into Phillips Academy—an academically enriched prekindergarten to eighth grade school that selectively admits students from across the city. The city refurbished Marconi Park, converted Phillips's gym into a YMCA Family Center, and supported the development of an urban community garden. The garden, founded by a group of white people affiliated with a nonprofit organization, occupies an entire city block. Strategically placed barrels catch rainwater used to irrigate crops. The gardeners use several machines and tools to till and amend the soil. Abundant vegetables, plants, and foliage spring from the ground. During the early 2000s, reformers throughout the United States began to transform blighted urban areas into mixed-income "oases" where residents were to have access to quality homes, shopping centers, schools, and community gardens. These reformers presented community gardens as a way to supposedly reengage urban residents in their communities and promote healthier lifestyles. Some of these gardens have emerged organically from the residents' desires to combat the numerous so-called food deserts in these communities. Others sprang from efforts driven by people who lived outside the communities.

Jones Valley Urban Gardens emerged from people outside the Central City community. This garden sits in Birmingham along Seventh Avenue and Twenty-Fifth Street North with well-outfitted equipment, beautiful plots, corporate sponsorship, and well-spoken and credentialed founders. Jones Valley Urban Gardens attracts grants from federal agencies and foundations; students from schools near and far volunteer, and visitors stop by to witness the flowering of the foliage and the yielding of the fruits and vegetables. On the garden's website, which has since been modified, the founders initially stated how in 2007 they "transformed three and a half acres of vacant downtown property into a budding urban oasis, driven by the singular vision of making our community a healthier place. In no time, the Farm was teeming with organic produce and flowers, to the delight of local restaurants and citizens alike."[5]

Well, part of the above passage is a bit of an exaggeration. Contrary to the history depicted on the Jones Valley Urban Gardens' website, the land was not vacant or unused before the present garden. As early as the mid-1990s, the same plot of land once served as a community garden that was spearheaded by and for Central City's Black residents. Residents tilled the land and grew fruits and vegetables. They could walk across the street to pick their homegrown tomatoes, collard greens, and okra. Unfortunately, the garden started by the Black and mostly low-income residents of Central City never received the corporate, governmental, philanthropic, and public support that the white-led Jones Valley Urban Gardens in Park Place is receiving today. These white-led community gardens, initially presented under the guise of social justice for the Black, Brown, and low-income residents, too often lead to "unintended" outcomes such as gentrification. Higher income potential residents find community gardens an attractive aspect of a neighborhood.[6] Given that the garden was led by people from outside the community, I knew years ago that its presence would foreshadow the gentrification that the downtown area of Birmingham is now undergoing.

Charitable organizations like the Greater Birmingham Ministry (GBM) that Mrs. Sarah Price, mentioned earlier, worked for find it challenging to counter these larger changes that are taking place in downtown Birmingham and the adverse effects on the poor and the homeless. Though vital to deal with the immediate needs and provide short-term support to families affected by disruptions, GBM and similar organizations temporarily soothe the pain caused by unfair housing, schooling, and economic policies and practices. To begin bringing about change, we must address systemic and intergenerational racism and poverty and create structural and institutional supports that help counter large-scale processes such as housing displacement and gentrification.

Efforts at change must include place-based interventions that further provide economic and housing support for low-income Black families and communities. We have already seen such financial assistance through the multiple stimulus packages passed in 2020 and 2021 to support families and businesses adversely affected by the COVID-19 pandemic. These stimulus packages came about with the clear recognition that some groups suffered more than others due to the pandemic. We must apply this same thinking and commitment to systematically excluded groups in U.S. society. Some groups, positioned differently due to their race and social class, need more assistance than others at a particular time. Professor john a. powell, a legal scholar who focuses on policy issues related to race and equity, refers to this approach of assisting vulnerable groups as "targeted universalism." As further noted by powell and his colleagues, Black people have historically been positioned in marginalized ways within U.S. society. A targeted universalism approach means investing in the entire ecosystem of Black community life, which includes families, schools, young people, employment, economics, and health.[7] Moreover, the United States has entered a moment of racial reckoning over the past few years due to the highly publicized killings of Black people, including Breonna Taylor, Ahmaud Arbery, and George Floyd. We must have substantial efforts to strengthen Black community life as an affirmation and concrete statement that Black lives matter. Public statements about supporting Black institutions and communities ring hollow when scores of Black families face gentrification, housing displacement, school closings, and economic neglect.

Today, the Central City housing project in Birmingham no longer exists. Park Place, a different set of buildings occupied by residents who have little intergenerational memory of the former community, now stands in its place. No physical marker or monument chronicles our more than three decades there. To remember our past, present, and purpose, we drive to the area from another side of town, another city, or another state. This pilgrimage back to our roots places us, once again, with family and friends. Annually, we symbolize our bonds by attending Central City reunions. We have immortalized our relationships by having children together, attending weddings and birthdays, posting on Facebook, and paying our respects at funerals. In Central City we felt the pain. But that pain was softened by the joy coming from the people, who remind us that we remain a community and that nothing will change that.

THE END

EPILOGUE

A lot has happened since I first began writing this book in 2013. The area in Birmingham that was once known as Central City and Metropolitan Gardens has now become Park Place. Yet remnants of Central City's identity remain in the people and their memories. People who once lived in Central City are slowly passing away. However, to remember their community and roots, those who once lived there sometimes ensure funeral processions for the departed pass through Central City. People park their cars and get out to say a prayer or release balloons to the heavens. They always acknowledge "home" before heading to the funeral services and then to the cemetery to bury their loved ones. My family members and I stopped there in April 2001 before burying our mother, who died on March 30, 2001. We stopped there in February 2020 on the way to bury my brother, Richard Jr., who passed at the age of fifty-eight. Richard Jr., a brother I looked up to when I was a little boy, remained closely connected to many people from the old Central City community. He was instrumental in providing crucial parts of the history for this book and helping me secure some of the photos. Richard documented the demolition of Central City with his camera. I feel the effects of Richard's passing daily. Supremely talented and intelligent, he could have written a book like this one. I miss him.

While completing the book before sending it to the publisher, several other notable deaths occurred in my family and among people mentioned in this book. Mrs. Sarah Price, who positively affected the lives of so many through her guidance and advocacy for vulnerable families while working with Greater Birmingham Ministries, passed away in September 2021 at eighty-three.[1] James and Leola, the owners of One

Stop Convenience Store, both have passed. The many children who hung out at their store will never forget them. A very close cousin of mine and former high school football teammate, Devon Collins, passed away in December 2019 at age fifty. One of my brothers on the Clency side of my family, Bobby "Bebop" Clency, passed away in March 2020. He was fifty-nine. Several of the amazing teachers who taught us at Powell Elementary School and Phillips High School are no longer here.

In October 2021, another elder and pillar in our family, Aunt Maxine, passed. Whereas my Aunt Maxine, who lived to seventy-six, had lived longer than any recent family members, her passing left a sense of emptiness. She kept the family together through thick and thin. Her home served as the gathering place for family for more than forty years. Although she and her husband Monroe had had no children, Aunt Maxine had taken over as the matriarch of the family after our grandmother, Oceola Collins, passed away in 1982. Over the years, Maxine and her husband Monroe would take in family members who were down on their luck. They supported Aunt Maxine's younger sister (Aunt Sandra) and Sandra's two sons. It seemed like just about every family member in Birmingham who had gone through challenging times found refuge by living with Aunt Maxine and Uncle Monroe for a few weeks or even a few months. The passing of these family members and friends left voids in our families and our communities. But through social media, we continue to celebrate the lives of family members and former residents from Central City, the Alley, and the Court. We keep them alive by continuing to say their names.

My sister, Shelda, was a pivotal person in this book. As noted earlier, the "Brickyard" housing projects where she had to live became a challenging place for Shelda and her three children. The Birmingham Housing Authority evicted her due to drug-related and other issues. Shelda would go in and out of drug rehabilitation. Still in recovery, Shelda has her good days and her bad days. But just as the gospel song "I Won't Complain" says, many of Shelda's good days are now outweighing her bad days. At the beginning of Shelda's struggles in the early 2000s, Ronnie, our oldest brother, would take temporary custody of our sister's three children—two daughters and a son. The children lived with Ronnie in a family-based foster care arrangement for a few years. Shelda's oldest child and daughter eventually moved out from Ronnie and got herself an apartment. She would graduate Carver High School with honors, attend college for a few years, and now has two teenage daughters. She has worked several jobs, such as in retail and apartment management, and is doing very well as an entrepreneur, including owning a hair-braiding business.

Shelda's two younger children, a boy and a girl, continued living in foster care arrangements, eventually moving in with Ronnie's girlfriend's family, who assumed foster care custodianship of Shelda's two younger children. The son experienced several challenges at home and in school and spent time incarcerated. He is a bright young man, and we still pray for and support his eventual release.

Shelda's youngest child, a daughter, completed high school and eventually graduated from the University of Alabama in 2021. Through prayers and support, she persisted through her college education. She received guidance and support from a woman whom I call Ms. J. While our extended family in Birmingham and my immediate family have maintained close connections with Shelda and her three children, a family does not always consist of one's blood relatives. When we say "family," we mean kinfolks by blood-related and non-blood-related family. Ms. J. and her children were another family to Shelda's youngest daughter.

Two of the women whose excerpted interviews are included in this book, Tabatha and Charlene (pseudonyms), continue to live their lives. It is especially important to note that Charlene not only has finished high school but is presently enrolled in junior college. She accomplished these milestones after the passing of her mother. Charlene views her educational persistence as a way to model to herself and her children the importance of taking advantage of opportunities. Unfortunately, Tabatha's husband died in 2021.

A lot has changed in my immediate family and professional life since I began writing this book. In 2015, after eighteen years at the University of Georgia, I moved into an endowed professorship at the University of Missouri–St. Louis, a position that allowed me to work directly with Black communities and schools in urban areas. I moved to St. Louis out of deep concern about Black people's issues and the need to be near those places where my skills and talents were most needed and wanted. St. Louis, located only ten miles from Ferguson, Missouri, where a police officer killed unarmed Michael Brown, was placed in the national spotlight due to the killing. I was excited about moving back to a city where I had begun my earlier research on Black families, schools, and communities. My family was excited about the move to St. Louis. Amadi, my daughter, was fifteen, and Kamau, my son, was about to turn thirteen. They have since finished high school, and Amadi attended and graduated from Washington University in St. Louis, and Kamau is a student at Stanford University in California. My wife, Mary, has found St. Louis to be a welcoming place where she can pursue her research interests on Black women's and children's health.

In the end, I hope this book serves as one record of our stories and lives in Central City. I thank everyone mentioned and some not mentioned in this book for their guidance and for taking the time to listen to or read parts of the book. I aimed to capture people's lives in ways that demonstrated how we were once, and continue to be, a powerful community of Black people from an area in downtown Birmingham known as Central City.

ACKNOWLEDGMENTS

My wife, Mary Muse, and our children, Amadi MuseMorris and Kamau MuseMorris, believed in this project from the very start. Researchers and scholars in your respective areas, you all provided immediate, and critical, feedback whenever I was stumped by a particular section of the book. I am deeply grateful to the generous people from Central City, the Alley, and the Court that made this book possible. Many of you helped to see this book to fruition, provided important facts and interviews, filled in gaps, and always told me how much you could not wait to read that "book about Central City." Please understand that I could not mention all of your names and had to change many of them because the stories and research involved actual people from Central City and Birmingham. As a researcher, I must protect people's privacy and identities. But do know that I thank you for your willingness to share your lives, thoughts, and experiences. The stories presented captured our collective experiences. Several of you connected me with participants, corrected errors, and provided invaluable feedback and analysis. I appreciate your scholarly and practical wisdom!

Several scholars, inside and outside the academy, listened, provided research guidance and support, advised me on the book's structure, and read sections. They include the anonymous reviewers whose scholarly insight and wisdom pushed me beyond the planned destination, as well as Derrick Alridge, Robert L. Crowson, Na'ilah Nasir, Ayanna F. Brown, Samuel Brown, Dave Bloome, Elaine Brown, and Rebecca Rogers.

I thank members of my research teams (whether at the University of Georgia or the University of Missouri–St. Louis) who were there during the formative years of writing this book (including Wanda McGowan,

Melissa Garcia, and jeff carr). You listened to earlier parts, and some of you, particularly jeff, have been with me through the finish line. Thanks, jeff, for listening to the spur-of-the-moment ideas about the book's structure, scope, and content. Your assistance has been immeasurable! Moreover, thanks to members of my research team affiliated with the Communally Bonded Research Project and Center who read chapters and offered feedback, specifically Zori Paul, Tiffany Simon, Jacquelyn Lewis-Harris, Tenille-Rose Martin, Nicole Misra, Luimil Negrón, Joan Dodgson, and Claire Martin. Directly and indirectly, a group of former graduate students (now faculty members and researchers) offered insightful comments and suggestions, including Adeoye Adeyemo, Benjamin Parker, and Sara Woodruff.

As researchers, we inevitably rely on the wisdom, resourcefulness, intelligence, and patience of librarians and archivists. This book benefited from the insights and information provided by Jim Baggett and his team in the Department of Archives and Manuscripts at Birmingham's Linn-Henley Research Library.

The Editor at the University of Georgia Press, Mick Gusindy, and the team there, including Jon Davies, Joseph Dahm, and Kaelin Broaddus, collectively shepherded this project to the finish line. Thank you for believing in this book and welcoming the creative lens I aimed to offer.

Finally, I owe an immense debt of gratitude to Dan Zettwoch for reading an unsolicited email from me about the creation of maps for this book. You listened to and read excerpts from the book, as well as met with me on several occasions to get the feel for what I wanted in this book. What you produced was beyond what I could have imagined. Thank you for creating the amazing maps to help the reader to visualize the changes within Central City, and a section of the Birmingham landscape, over time!

Joann Steele Morris (participant, resident, interviewee; interviewed on
    April 3, 1998—before the study began and before she passed in 2001)
Ronald Steele, also referred to as Ronnie (participant, resident,
    interviewee)
Richard Lee Morris Jr. (participant, resident, interviewee)
Kenneth Morris (participant, resident, interviewee)
Maurice Morris (participant, resident, interviewee)
Shelda Morris (participant, resident, interviewee)
Santana Morris (participant, resident, interviewee)
Maxine Steele Wright (interviewee)
Sandra Collins (interviewee)
Clara Clency (resident, interviewee)
Cleo Clency (interviewee)
Charles Clency, also known as Panky (interviewee)
Joe Harris, also known as Sugar Man (participant, neighborhood
    association president, resident, interviewee)
Elizabeth Leonard Harris (participant, neighborhood association
    leader, resident, interviewee)
Mary Muse (interviewee)
Laura Smith (participant, resident)*
Scott Douglas (participant, community organization leader and
    advocate, interviewee)
Sarah Price (participant, community organization leader and advocate,
    interviewee)
Charles Foster Jr. (interviewee)
James Goldthwaite (business owner, interviewee)

Dionne Goldthwaite (business owner, interviewee)
Derrick Collins (interviewee)
Fat Joe (resident, interviewee)*
Donovan (resident, interviewee)*
Vanessa Parker (resident, community liaison)
Tabatha (participant, resident, interviewee)*
Charlene (participant, resident, interviewee)*
Eugene Sanders (resident, interviewee)
Rosie Lee Jackson (participant, resident, interviewee)
Roderick Jackson (participant, resident, interviewee)
Ms. Shay (teacher, interviewee)*
Mrs. Gede (teacher, interviewee)*
Government and economics teacher (teacher, interviewee)*
Lucille H. Turrentine (teacher, interviewee)
Ruth LaMonte (professor, civic leader)
Preston Lawley (business owner, interviewee)
Johnnie Lockett (resident, interviewee)
Greg Hamlet (resident, interviewee)
Keith Denson (resident, interviewee)
Nate Kelly Jr. (interviewee)

*Indicates pseudonym

NOTES

Preface

1. For excellent discussions related to reflexivity, positionality, and researching one's own community, see the following: L. N. Chaudhry, 1997, "Researching 'My People,' Researching Myself: Fragments of a Reflexive Tale," *International Journal of Qualitative Studies in Education*, *10*(4): 441–453; D. P. Alridge, 2003, "The Dilemmas, Challenges, and Duality of an African-American Educational Historian," *Educational Researcher*, *32*(9): 25–34; J. E. Dodgson, 2019, "Reflexivity in Qualitative Research," *Journal of Human Lactation*, *35*(2): 220–222.

2. Black residents who lived in Central City between the late 1960s and early 1980s almost always referred to the renovated and newly named Metropolitan Gardens, which occurred in the early to mid-1980s, as Central City. Many of the Central City residents remained in Metropolitan Gardens throughout the renovation, and a great deal of the renovation focused on modernizing the complex. The original Central City building structure was kept. To us, only the name had changed; the people and buildings remained.

Chapter 1. The Poorest Zip Code in America

1. Charles Connerly, 2005, *The Most Segregated City in America: City Planning and Civil Rights in Birmingham, 1920–1980* (Charlottesville: University of Virginia Press).

2. One of the four girls killed was decapitated, and a fifth girl who survived the bombing, Sarah Collins, was partially blinded. For more on Collins, see Sarah Collins Rudolph, 2017, "In New Book, 'Fifth Little Girl' Describes First Hand Account of Horrific Church Bombing," *Birmingham Times*, September 14, https://www.birminghamtimes.com/2017/09/fifth-little-girl-gives-first-hand-account-of-horrific-church-bombing/. State-sanctioned violence in Birmingham a few hours after the church bombing continued when a Black boy, Johnny Robinson, was shot by a white policeman and another Black boy, Virgil Ware, was

shot by a group of white males while riding his bicycle. For more on the murder of these two Black boys, please see William O. Bryant, 1963, "Six Negro Children Killed in Alabama," *Time-News*, September 16.

3. D. S. Massey and N. A. Denton, 1989, "Hypersegregation in United States Metropolitan Areas—Black and Hispanic Segregation along 5 Dimensions," *Demography, 26*(2): 373–391.

4. One might argue that the movement, as demonstrated by the Poor People's Campaign, had included a more critical analysis of the intersection of racial and economic inequality.

5. Howell Raines, 1977, *My Soul Is Rested: Movement Days in the Deep South Remembered* (New York: Penguin).

6. For a discussion of these dilemmas facing many young Black people growing up in poverty and playing sports, please see the following: H. Edwards, 1980, *The Struggle That Must Be* (New York: Macmillan); R. G. Kelley, 1997, *Yo Mama's Disfunktional! Fighting the Culture Wars in Urban America* (Boston: Beacon); C. K. Harrison, 2000, "Black Athletes at the Millennium," *Society, 37*(3): 35–39.

7. Dr. Adeoye Adeyemo and I have led research on Black male students who participate in sports. See J. E. Morris and A. Adeyemo, 2012, "Touchdowns and Honor Societies: Expanding the Focus of Black Male Excellence," *Phi Delta Kappan, 93*(5): 28–32; A. Adeyemo and J. E. Morris, 2020, "Researching the Neighborhood and Schooling Experiences of Black Male High-School Students Who Play Sports in Atlanta and Chicago," *Teachers College Record, 122*(8): 1–52.

8. Still in existence, the Ain Shams Community Centre provides social services such as English classes, job preparation training, and medical support for families, mothers, and children.

9. Alex de Waal (ed.), 2007, *War in Darfur and the Search for Peace* (Cambridge, Mass.: Harvard University Press); Gerard Prunier, 2005, *Darfur: The Ambiguous Genocide* (Ithaca, N.Y.: Cornell University Press).

10. While the focus on inner-city communities besides the South is often the direction of much of the research on Black people in urban areas, many researchers have led incredible work in these northern and midwestern areas. Some of these scholars include E. Anderson, 2000, *Code of the Street: Decency, Violence, and the Moral Life of the Inner City* (New York: Norton); A. Kotlowitz, 1992, *There Are No Children Here: The Story of Two Boys Growing Up in the Other America* (New York: Anchor); W. J. Wilson, 1987, *The Truly Disadvantaged: The Inner City, the Underclass, and Public Policy* (Chicago: University of Chicago Press); Valerie Kinloch, 2009, *Harlem on Our Minds: Place, Race, and the Literacies of Urban Youth* (New York: Teachers College Press).

11. For an insightful discussion and analysis of the Blues and its ability to capture Black people's lived experience, see B. Brian Foster's 2020 book *I Don't Like the Blues: Race, Place and the Backbeat of Black Life* (Chapel Hill: University of North Carolina Press).

12. Also see Glenn Askew, 1997, *But for Birmingham: The Local and National Movement in the Civil Rights Struggle* (Chapel Hill: University of North Carolina Press); and Connerly, 2005.

13. Derrick A. Bell, 1992, *Faces at the Bottom of the Well: The Permanence of Racism* (New York: Basic Books).

14. Patrick Sharkey, 2013, *Stuck in Place: Urban Neighborhoods and the End of Progress toward Racial Equality* (Chicago: University of Chicago Press).

15. The methodology allowed 35203 to be designated as the poorest zip code in the United States. With a poverty rate greater than 72 percent in the 1990s, Metropolitan Gardens (aka Central City) was the only residential area included in zip code 35203. Mostly commercial buildings populated the area.

16. For additional analyses and readings on poverty and the inner city, see Wilson, 1987. Also see William Julius Wilson, 1996, *When Work Disappears: The World of the New Urban Poor* (New York: Knopf).

17. Numerous researchers have described the intergenerational effects of parental exposure to severe environmental and psychophysiological trauma. See Joy DeGruy, 2005, *Post Traumatic Slave Syndrome: America's Legacy of Enduring Injury and Healing* (n.p.: Joy DeGruy Publications). Also, researchers studying Jewish Holocaust survivors have noted how the consequences of such trauma are not just physical but may also manifest at the genetic level. For additional reading on the lingering effects of trauma and oppression, please see Rachel Yehuda, Nikolaos P. Daskalakis, Linda M. Bierer, Heather N. Bader, Torsten Klengel, Florian Holsboer, and Elisabeth B. Binder, 2016, "Holocaust Exposure Induced Intergeneration Effects on FKBP5 Methylation," *Biological Psychiatry, 80*(5): 372–380.

18. Charles Murray, 1984, *Losing Ground: American Social Policy, 1950–1980* (New York: Basic Books).

19. W. A. Darity and Melba J. Nicholson, 2005, "Racial Wealth Inequality and the Black Family," in Vonnie C. McLoyd, Nancy E. Hill, and Kenneth A. Dodge (eds.), *African American Family Life: Ecological and Cultural Diversity,* 78–85 (New York: Guilford); Melvin L. Oliver and Thomas M. Shapiro, 2006, *Black Wealth, White Wealth: A New Perspective* (New York: Routledge).

20. W. E. B. Du Bois, 1933, "The Field and Function of the Negro College," in Herbert Aptheker (ed.), *The Education of Black People: Ten Critiques, 1906–1960,* 111–133 (New York: Monthly Review).

21. R. Rothstein, 2017, *The Color of Law: A Forgotten History of How Our Government Segregated America* (New York: Norton). Also see the following authors: Wilson, 1987; Wilson, 1996; Kotlowitz, 1992; R. Y. Williams, 2004, *The Politics of Public Housing: Black Women's Struggles Against Urban Inequality* (New York: Oxford University Press).

22. Words by Frankie Beverly, recorded 1980.

23. I. Wilkerson, 2020, *Caste: The Origins of Our Discontents* (New York: Random House).

24. W. E. B. Du Bois, 1903/1994, *The Souls of Black Folk* (New York: Dover).

25. W. A. Darity (ed.), 2008, "Ghetto," *International Encyclopedia of the Social Sciences 3*(2): 311–314; D. S. Massey, 2004, "Segregation and Stratification: A Biosocial Perspective," *Du Bois Review, 1*(1): 7–25.

26. S. D. Kassow, 2007, *Who Will Write Our History? A Hidden Archive from the Warsaw Ghetto* (Bloomington: University of Indiana Press).

27. M. Karenga, 1982, *Introduction to Black Studies* (Los Angeles: Kawaida Publications).

Chapter 2. Before the Projects

1. G. Wright, 1983, *Building the Dream: A Social History of Housing in America* (Cambridge, Mass.: MIT Press).

2. A paper by Elliott Anne Rigsby at the Century Foundation describes the consequences of exclusionary zoning in creating discriminatory housing. Rigsby, 2016, "Understanding Exclusionary Zoning and Its Impact on Concentrated Poverty," June 23, https://tcf.org/content/facts/understanding-exclusionary-zoning-impact-concentrated-poverty/?agreed=1&agreed=1. For additional discussion, see Richard Rothstein's 2017 book, *The Color of Law: A Forgotten History of How Our Government Segregated America* (New York: Norton).

3. Some U.S. cities provided publicly funded housing before 1937. One of the earliest public housing complexes in the United States was Techwood Homes, located in Atlanta, Georgia, and completed in 1936. Other U.S. cities that provided some of the earliest publicly funded housing include New York and Philadelphia. The federal government modeled the national housing program after some of these earlier developments. The funds used to support public housing construction came from the U.S. Public Works Administration (PWA), which provided approximately $4 billion for the construction of hospitals, courthouses, and educational buildings. For additional historical information on public housing, see J. A. Stoloff, 2004, "A Brief History of Public Housing" (paper, American Sociological Association, San Francisco, August).

4. A. Bickford and D. S. Massey, 1991, "Segregation in the Second Ghetto: Racial and Ethnic Segregation in American Public Housing, 1977," *Social Forces*, 69(4): 1011–1036.

5. Charles Connerly, 2005, *The Most Segregated City in America: City Planning and Civil Rights in Birmingham, 1920–1980* (Charlottesville: University of Virginia Press).

6. W. Johnson, 2020, *The Broken Heart of America: St. Louis and the Violent History of the United States* (London: Hachette).

7. Connerly, 2005.

8. Marco Williams, 2006, *Banished: How Whites Drove Blacks out of Town in America* (California Newsreel).

9. Jennifer E. Brooks, 2022, *Resident Strangers: Immigrant Laborers in New South Alabama* (Baton Rouge: Louisiana University Press).

10. C. Fox and Thomas A. Guglielmo, 2012, "Defining America's Racial Boundaries: Blacks, Mexicans, and European Immigrants, 1890–1945," *American Journal of Sociology*, 118(2): 327–379.

11. Lynne B. Feldman, 1999, *A Sense of Place: Birmingham's Black Middle-Class Community, 1890–1930* (Tuscaloosa: University of Alabama Press).

12. For a detailed discussion on Black family structure in the United States, see A. Billingsley, 1992, *Climbing Jacob's Ladder* (New York: Simon & Schuster).

13. Architecturally, the kinds of shotgun-style houses in the United States that

we lived in first appeared in the early 1800s in New Orleans, Louisiana. One commonly held belief is that shotgun-style housing refers to the idea that one could open the front door of the house and fire a shotgun, and the bullet would pass through each room and out the back. Another view is that the word "shotgun" originates from a word in the Dahomey area of West Africa, "do gun," or "to gun," which means "to assemble." Enslaved Black people from Haiti then brought this style of dwelling with them to New Orleans after the Haitian Revolution, around 1803. By 1810, Black residents of New Orleans outnumbered their white counterparts more than two to one and commonly used this "do gun" construction style. Eventually, builders adopted the shotgun style throughout the South because such houses were cheaper to build and less expensive in terms of property taxes, which were based on a building's width. Birmingham's industrialists used shotgun dwellings to house their workers throughout the city. For more of this history, please see John Michael Vlach, 1976, "The Shotgun House: An African American Architectural Legacy," *Pioneer America*, 8(1): 47–56.

14. Parker High School has had various names, including Negro High School and Industrial High School. For additional information on education in Birmingham, see T. Loder-Jackson, 2015, *Schoolhouse Activists: African American Educators and the Long Birmingham Civil Rights Movement* (Albany: State University of New York Press).

15. H. Huntley and D. Montgomery (eds.), 2004, *Black Workers' Struggle for Equality in Birmingham* (Urbana: University of Illinois Press).

16. H. M. McKiven Jr., 2011, *Iron and Steel: Class, Race and Community in Birmingham, Alabama, 1875–1920* (Chapel Hill: University of North Carolina Press).

17. W. E. B. Du Bois, 1899, "The Negro in the Black Belt," *Bulletin of the Department of Labor*, May 22, 405–415.

18. The A. G. Gaston Motel, owned by the state's first Black millionaire and a meeting place for leading civil rights figures during the 1960s, would not be built until 1955.

19. The school system was founded in 1905 by the Josephites, formally St. Joseph's Society of the Sacred Heart, the Roman Catholic clerical society of priests that was founded in 1871 to "minister to newly freed slaves" after the Civil War. See S. J. Ochs, 1993, *Desegregating the Altar: The Josephites and the Struggle for Black Priests, 1871–1960* (Baton Rouge: Louisiana State University Press).

20. Jacqueline Jones, 2010, *Labor of Love, Labor of Sorrow: Black Women, Work and the Family from Slavery to the Present* (New York: Basic Books). Also see Patricia Hill Collins, 1990, *Black Feminist Thought: Knowledge, Consciousness, and the Politics of Empowerment* (New York: Routledge).

21. L. Harris, 2016, *Sex Workers, Psychics, and Numbers Runners: Black Women in New York City's Underground Economy* (Urbana: University of Illinois Press).

22. Harris, 2016.

23. Anthropologist and playwright Zora Neale Hurston even wrote about the prevalence of this way of thinking among Black people. Please see her book

Color Struck, republished in 2008 in Jean Lee Cole and Charles Mitchell (eds.), *Zora Neale Hurston: Collected Plays* (New Brunswick, N.J.: Rutgers University Press).

24. Colorism has been explored by a number of scholars, and as early as the 1950s by sociologist E. Franklin Frazier in *The Black Bourgeoisie* (New York: Free Press). For an insightful discussion of colorism as social capital, see Margaret Hunter, 2002, "'If You're Light You're Alright': Light Skin Color as Social Capital for Women of Color," *Gender and Society*, 16(2): 175–193. In general, colorism is a function of a society that values whiteness. On the plantations, white slave owners divided Black people into distinct groups, based on the tasks they performed, their willingness to comply with the brutal slave system, and their skin color. The darker the enslaved African, the greater the chances he or she worked in the fields. Closer in complexion to white people, and often related to them in familial ways as a result of the wanton and routine raping of young Black females by white slave masters, fairer complexioned Black people sometimes received reprieve from the grueling work that accompanied field work. They cooked white people's food, nursed their babies, and tended to their elderly. These class cleavages based on the plantation system set the foundation for the "colorism" that has endured for hundreds of years.

25. E. F. Frazier, 1968, *The Negro Family in the United States*, rev. and abridged ed. (Chicago: University of Chicago Press).

Chapter 3. Convergence

1. T. Branch, 2007, *At Canaan's Edge: America in the King Years, 1965–68* (New York: Simon & Schuster).

2. C. Anderson, 2016, *White Rage: The Unspoken Truth of Our Racial Divide* (New York: Bloomsbury).

3. For the most part, white people—barring the few who cannot afford to move and the elderly—flee an area as soon as a critical mass of Black people desires to live there. Social scientists call this a "tipping point," and it slightly varies by metropolitan area. For more on the tipping point in housing segregation, see Thomas C. Schelling, 1971, "Dynamic Models of Segregation," *Journal of Mathematical Sociology*, 1: 143–186; David Card, Alexandre Mas, and Jesse Rothstein, 2008, "Tipping and the Dynamics of Segregation," *Quarterly Journal of Economics*, 123(1): 177–218; and Gary S. Becker and Kevin M. Murphy, 2000, *Social Economics: Market Behavior in a Social Environment* (Cambridge, Mass.: Harvard University Press). This tipping point holds even if the Black people come from a higher social class than the whites and no matter if the school quality, housing stock, and perceived safety of the neighborhood all remain the same. For middle- and upper-class Black people, their social class status can temporarily minimize the effects of this caste-like status, but only if they remain a tiny number in the community—usually one or two Black families in a mostly white neighborhood. See John Eligon and Robert Gebeloff, 2016, "Affluent and Black and Still Trapped by Segregation," *New York Times*, August 20, p. 20.

4. W. E. B. Du Bois, 1920, *Darkwater*, republished in David R. Roediger, 1998, *Black on White: Black Writers on What It Means to Be White* (New York: Penguin).

5. In addition to W. E. B. Du Bois's analysis regarding whiteness, see the following works by scholars who have researched whiteness: C. I. Harris, 1993, "Whiteness as Property," *Harvard Law Review*, June 10, 1707–1791; Z. Leonardo, 2002, "The Souls of White Folk: Critical Pedagogy, Whiteness Studies, and Globalization Discourse," *Race Ethnicity and Education*, 5(1): 29–50.

6. N. Hannah-Jones, 2012, "How the Government Betrayed a Landmark Civil Rights Law," *ProPublica*, October 28. For a history of the Fair Housing Act, see U.S. Department of Housing and Urban Development, "History of Fair Housing," https://portal.hud.gov/hudportal/HUD?src=/program_offices/fair_housing _equal_opp/aboutfheo/history. The act was expanded in 1974 to include gender and in 1988 to include families with children and people with disabilities.

7. See M. Krysan, 2015, "Racial Residential Segregation and the Housing Search Process" (Institute of Government and Public Affairs, University of Illinois, December 3), https://igpa.uillinois.edu/wp-content/uploads/2022/03 /Research-Spotlight-Krysan_Housing-Search.pdf. Also see Alvin Chang, 2017, "White America Is Quietly Self-Segregating: Everyone Wants Diversity, but Not Everyone Wants It on Their Street," *Vox*, January 18, http://www.vox.com/2017 /1/18/14296126/white-segregated-suburb-neighborhood-cartoon.

8. Maulana Karenga describes this ability by Black people to adjust to structural and ideological racism and yet still hold on to aspects of their culture and beliefs as "adaptive vitality." See his 1982 book *Introduction to Black Studies* (Los Angeles: Kawaida Publications).

Chapter 4. A Link in the Chain

1. M. J. Friedman, P. P. Schnurr, and Coyle A. McDonagh, 1994, "Post-traumatic Stress Disorder in the Military Veteran," *Psychiatric Clinics of North America*, 17(2): 265–277.

2. D. D. Blake, T. M. Keane, P. R. Wine, C. Mora, K. L. Taylor, and J. A. Lyons, 1994, "Prevalence of PTSD Symptoms in Combat Veterans Seeking Medical Treatment," *Journal of Traumatic Stress*, 3(15): 15–27.

3. Friedman, Schnurr, and McDonagh, 1994.

4. John Morrow, 2003, *The Great War: An Imperial History* (New York: Routledge).

Chapter 5. Blue Black

1. Laurie B. Green, 2007, *Battling the Plantation Mentality: Memphis and the Black Freedom Struggle* (Chapel Hill: University of North Carolina Press); S. J. Little, 1993, "The Freedom Train: Citizenship and Postwar Political Culture, 1946–1949," *American Studies*, 34(1): 35–67; J. White, 1999, "Civil Rights in Conflict: The 'Birmingham Plan' and the Freedom Train, 1947," *Alabama Review*, 52(2): 121–141.

Chapter 6. Sankofa

1. Before slavery's legal ending, many enslaved Black people did not have official last names. White slave owners divided Black families frequently as people were bought and sold. It was common for Black people to have different last names, and these names would change due to them being sold from plantation to plantation. In *Help Me to Find My People: The African American Search for Family Lost in Slavery*, historian Heather Andrea Williams described how the newly freed Black people would travel throughout the South searching for family and at times placing costly advertisements in newspapers in the hope of reconnecting with their loved ones who had been sold or stolen. Knowing the names of family members, the plantations' locations, and slave owners' names would be crucial to reconnecting. See H. A. Williams, 2012, *Help Me to Find My People: The African American Search for Family Lost in Slavery*.

2. 1860 U.S. Slave Census.

3. U.S. Department of the Interior, Bureau of the Census, 1900, Twelfth Census of the United States, p. 529. Also see H. M. McKiven Jr., 2011, *Iron and Steel: Class, Race and Community in Birmingham, Alabama, 1875–1920* (Chapel Hill: University of North Carolina Press).

4. D. A. Blackmon, 2009, *Slavery by Another Name: The Re-enslavement of Black Americans from the Civil War to World War II* (New York: Anchor).

5. Jacqueline Jones, 2010, *Labor of Love, Labor of Sorrow: Black Women, Work and the Family from Slavery to the Present* (New York: Basic Books). Also see Patricia Hill Collins, 1990, *Black Feminist Thought: Knowledge, Consciousness, and the Politics of Empowerment* (New York: Routledge).

6. Hayes High School was named after Carol W. Hayes, Birmingham's former "Director of Negro Schools." See Tondra Loder-Jackson, 2015, *Schoolhouse Activists: African American Educators and the Long Birmingham Civil Rights Movement* (Albany: State University of New York Press).

7. See William Julius Wilson, 1996, *When Work Disappears: The World of the New Urban Poor* (New York: Knopf).

8. R. Fry and D. Cohn, 2010, "Women, Men and the New Economics of Marriage" (Pew Research Center, January 19); Michael Greenstone and Adam Looney, 2012, "The Marriage Gap: Impact of Economic and Technological Change on Marriage Rates" (Hamilton Project, February).

9. Isabell Wilkerson, 2011, *The Warmth of Other Suns* (New York: Vintage).

10. The following sources provide additional information about the Gullah Geechee people and how their traditions survived the Middle Passage and enslavement: M. A. Gomez, 1998, *Exchanging Our Country Marks: The Transformation of African Identities in the Colonial and Antebellum South* (Chapel Hill: University of North Carolina Press); Philip Morgan (ed.), 2010, *African American Life in the Georgia Lowcountry: The Atlantic World and the Gullah Geechee* (Athens: University of Georgia Press); R. Crook, C. Bailey, N. Harris, and K. Smith, 2003, *Sapelo Voices: Historical Anthropology and the Oral Traditions of Gullah-Geechee Communities on Sapelo Island, Georgia* (Carrollton: State University of West Georgia).

11. Katherine Scott Sturdevant, 2020, "Walls Tumbling Down: Teaching Black Family History and Genealogy in Social History Context," *Black History Bulletin*, 83(2): 30–47.

12. Spirituals Project at the University of Denver, "African Tradition, Proverbs, and Sankofa" (archived from the original on April 20, 2011).

13. Spirituals Project at the University of Denver, "African Tradition, Proverbs, and Sankofa."

Chapter 7. Black and Proud

1. Greater Birmingham Ministries, "Greater Birmingham Ministries Story" (2022), http://gbm.org/about/history/.

2. Howell Raines, 1977, *My Soul Is Rested: Movement Days in the Deep South Remembered* (New York: Penguin).

3. M. A. Manis, 1999, *A Fire You Can't Put Out: The Civil Rights Life of Reverend Fred Shuttlesworth* (Tuscaloosa: University of Alabama Press).

4. T. Loder-Jackson, 2015, *Schoolhouse Activists: African American Educators and the Long Birmingham Civil Rights Movement* (Albany: State University of New York Press).

5. J. E. Morris, 2008, "Research, Ideology, and the Brown Decision: Counternarratives to the Historical and Contemporary Representation of Black Schooling," *Teachers College Record*, 110(4): 713–732.

6. Oral history interview with Rev. Fred L. Shuttlesworth at the Birmingham Civil Rights Institute, date unknown, YouTube, uploaded July 21, 2020, https://www.youtube.com/watch?v=HM7FvZ1ISZw.

7. W. H. Frey, 1979, "Central City White Flight: Racial and Nonracial Causes," *American Sociological Review*, 44(3): 425–448; J. E. Morris, 2010, "White Flight," in K. Lomotey (ed.), *The Encyclopedia of African American Education*, 2:667–669 (Newbury Park, Calif.: Sage).

8. J. E. Morris, 2009, *Troubling the Waters: Fulfilling the Promise of Quality Public Schooling for Black Children* (New York: Teachers College Press).

9. Bruce Drake, 2013, "Incarceration Gap Widens between Whites and Blacks" (Pew Research Center, September 6), http://www.pewresearch.org/fact-tank/2013/09/06/incarceration-gap-between-whites-and-blacks-widens/.

10. Michelle Alexander, 2010, *The New Jim Crow: Mass Incarceration in the Age of Colorblindness* (New York: New Press).

11. Donald Braman, 2007, *Doing Time on the Outside: Incarceration and Family Life in Urban America* (Ann Arbor: University of Michigan Press).

12. Charles Connerly, 2005, *The Most Segregated City in America: City Planning and Civil Rights in Birmingham, 1920–1980* (Charlottesville: University of Virginia Press).

13. Connerly, 2005.

14. J. L. Franklin, 1989, *Back to Birmingham: Richard Arrington, Jr., and His Times* (Tuscaloosa: University of Alabama Press); Connerly, 2005.

15. H. Huntley and D. Montgomery (eds.), 2004, *Black Workers' Struggle for Equality in Birmingham* (Urbana: University of Illinois Press).

16. P. Hoose, 2009, *Claudette Colvin: Twice Toward Justice* (New York: Square Fish).

17. J. A. G. Robinson, 1989, *The Montgomery Bus Boycott and the Women Who Started It: The Memoir of Jo Ann Gibson Robinson* (Knoxville: University of Tennessee Press).

18. V. L. Crawford, J. A. Rouse, B. Woods, and B. Butler (eds.), 1993, *Women in the Civil Rights Movement: Trailblazers and Torchbearers, 1941–1965* (Bloomington: Indiana University Press).

19. The Impressions, "We're a Winner" (1967), from the album *We're a Winner* (1968).

Chapter 8. Fists, Knives, Neck Bones, and Collard Greens

1. E. Wald, 2012, *The Dozens: A History of Rap's Mama* (New York: Oxford University Press); Geneva Smitherman, 1977, *Talkin and Testifyin: The Language of Black America* (Boston: Houghton Mifflin).

2. R. Majors, 2017, "Cool Pose: Black Masculinity and Sports," in Gary A. Sales (ed.), *Contemporary Themes: African Americans in Sport*, 15–22 (New York: Routledge).

3. Richard Majors and Janet Mancini Billson, 1992, *Cool Pose: The Dilemmas of Black Manhood in America* (New York: Lexington Books).

4. R. Wright, 1992, *Stolen Continents: The "New World" through Indian Eyes since 1492* (New York: Houghton Mifflin); Russell Thornton, 1987, *American Indian Holocaust and Survival: A Population History since 1492* (Norman: University of Oklahoma Press).

5. R. Horsman, 1981, *Race and Manifest Destiny: Origins of American Racial Anglo-Saxon* (Cambridge, Mass.: Harvard University Press).

6. H. Rap Brown later converted to Islam and changed his name to Jamil Al-Amin. For the exact quote, please see "Violence Is as American as Cherry Pie: The Words of Imam Jamil Al-Amin (H. Rap Brown)," YouTube, https://www.youtube.com/watch?v=4jNfaSeZwlk.

7. D. Carnegie, 1937, *How to Win Friends and Influence People* (New York: Simon & Schuster).

8. Carter G. Woodson, 1990, *The Mis-education of the Negro* (Trenton, N.J.: Africa World Press).

9. For an excellent discussion of this word and its usage, see Randall Kennedy, 2003, *Nigger: The Strange Career of a Troubled Word* (New York: Vintage); also see Jabari Asim, 2008, *The N-Word: Who Can Say It, Who Shouldn't, and Why* (New York: Houghton Mifflin).

10. Bob Marley and the Wailers, "Them Belly Full (But We Hungry)," on *Natty Dread* (1974).

11. Based in Oakland, California, the Black Panther Party not only provided a free breakfast program but also offered health clinics to people living in poverty. For more on the Black Panther Party and its work for Black liberation, please see the following book by Elaine Brown, the first and only female head of the Black

Panther Party: Elaine A. Brown, 1992, *A Taste of Power: A Black Woman's Story* (New York: Anchor).

12. Grandmaster Flash and the Furious Five, "The Message," on *The Message* (1982).

Chapter 9. Going to School

1. M. Shujaa (ed.), 1994, *Too Much Schooling, Too Little Education: A Paradox of Black Life in White Societies* (Trenton, N.J.: Africa World Press). Also, in one of her most quoted statements, late poet Maya Angelou remembered what her mother said about intelligence and schooling: "My mother said I must always be intolerant of ignorance but understanding of illiteracy. That some people, unable to go to school, were more educated and more intelligent than college professors."

2. Developed by the Italian physician and educator Maria Montessori (1870–1952), the Montessori Method emphasizes using a child's initiative and natural abilities for learning through practical play. See Maria Montessori, 2008, *The Montessori Method* (Radford, Va.: Wilder).

3. C. Tilley, 2005, "For Improving Early Literacy, Reading Comics Is No Child's Play," *University of Illinois News*; also available at *ScienceDaily*, www.science daily.com/releases/2009/11/091105121220.htm.

4. B. Cider, 2013, *Lost Birmingham* (Charleston, S.C.: History Press).

5. For an in-depth discussion of African American Vernacular English (AAVE), please see the following: J. Baugh, 2000, *Beyond Ebonics: Linguistic Pride and Racial Prejudice* (New York: Oxford University Press); Sonja Lanehart, 2001, "State of the Art in African American English Research: Multi-disciplinary Perspectives and Directions," in Sonja Lanehart (ed.), *Sociocultural and Historical Contexts of African American English, Varieties of English Around the World*, 1–20 (Amsterdam: John Benjamins); John Rickford and Russell Rickford, 2000, *Spoken Soul: The Story of Black English* (New York: John Wiley); Geneva Smitherman, 1977, *Talkin and Testifyin: The Language of Black America* (Boston: Houghton Mifflin).

6. M. Foster, 1997, "Ebonics and All That Jazz: Cutting through the Politics of Linguistics, Education, and Race," *The Quarterly*, 19(1): 7–12.

7. "Martin Luther King Junior Elementary School Children v. Michigan Board of Education: Extension of EEOA Protection to Black-English-Speaking Students" (1980), *William and Mary Law Review*, 22(3): 161–175, https://scholarship.law.wm.edu/wmlr/vol22/iss1/6.

8. W. G. Cowan and J. B. McGuire, 2008, *Louisiana Governors: Rulers, Rascals, and Reformers* (Jackson: University Press of Mississippi).

9. Sung by greats such as activist and singer Paul Robeson and opera singer Jessye Norman, "The Gospel Train" is a traditional African American spiritual first published in 1872 as a song by the world-famous Fisk Jubilee Singers.

10. James Weldon Johnson, 1959, *God's Trombones* (New York: Viking).

11. P. L. Dunbar, 1913, *The Complete Poems of Paul Laurence Dunbar* (New York: Dodd, Mead).

12. For additional insights on Dr. Carter G. Woodson, please see Pero Gaglo Dagbovie's 2007 book *The Early Black History Movement, Carter G. Woodson, and Lorenzo Johnston Greene* (Urbana: University of Illinois Press) and LaGarret J. King, Ryan M. Crowley, and Anthony L. Brown's 2010 article "The Forgotten Legacy of Carter G. Woodson: Contributions to Multicultural Social Studies and African American History," *Social Studies, 101*(5): 211–215. Also see Jarvis R. Givens's 2021 book *Fugitive Pedagogy: Carter G. Woodson and the Art of Black Teaching* (Cambridge, Mass.: Harvard University Press).

13. See E. B. Goldring and C. Smrekar, 1995, "Parental Choice: Consequences for Families, Schools, and Communities" (Technical Summary Report to the Spence Foundation). Moreover, incentives to encourage the voluntary transfer of Black and white students were approved by two federal courts in *Arthur v. Nyquist* (1976) in Buffalo, New York, and by *Amos v. Board of Directors of the City of Milwaukee* (1976). Also see J. E. Morris and E. B. Goldring, 1999, "Are Magnet Schools More Equitable? An Analysis of the Disciplinary Rates of African-American and White Students in Cincinnati Magnet and Nonmagnet Schools," *Equity & Excellence in Education, 32*(3): 59–65.

14. For a discussion of Black teachers' roles in the sociopolitical development of Black children, please see the following: T. Beauboeuf-Lafontant, 1999, "A Movement Against and Beyond Boundaries," *Teachers College Record, 100*(4): 702–723; M. Foster, 1997, *Black Teachers on Teaching* (New York: New Press); J. J. Irvine, 1989, "Beyond Role Models: An Examination of Cultural Influences on the Pedagogical Perspectives of Black Teachers," *Peabody Journal of Education, 66*(4): 51–63; M. McKinney de Royston, T. C. Madkins, J. R. Givens, and N. I. S. Nasir, 2020, "'I'm a Teacher, I'm Gonna Always Protect You': Understanding Black Educators' Protection of Black Children," *American Educational Research Journal, 58*(1), https://doi.org/10.3102/0002831220921119.

15. G. Ladson-Billings and W. Tate, 1995, "Toward a Critical Race Theory of Education," *Teachers College Record, 97*(1): 47–68; Jessica T. Decuir-Gunby, Thandeka K. Chapman, and Paul A. Schutz (eds.), 1992, *Understanding Critical Race Research Methods and Methodologies: Lessons from the Field* (New York: Routledge); Derrick A. Bell, 1992, *Faces at the Bottom of the Well: The Permanence of Racism* (New York: Basic Books).

16. See the following for a discussion on Black educators and researchers' counternarratives related to public school desegregation: J. E. Morris, 2001, "Forgotten Voices of Black Educators: Critical Race Perspectives on the Implementation of a Desegregation Plan," *Educational Policy, 15*(4): 575–600; J. E. Morris, 2008, "Research, Ideology, and the Brown Decision: Counter-narratives to the Historical and Contemporary Representation of Black Schooling," *Teachers College Record, 110*(4): 713–732.

17. For a similar observation, see interviews in T. Loder-Jackson, 2015, *Schoolhouse Activists: African American Educators and the Long Birmingham Civil Rights Movement* (Albany: State University of New York Press).

18. Ann A. Ferguson, 2000, *Bad Boys: Public Schools in the Making of Black*

Masculinity (Ann Arbor: University of Michigan Press); also see C. R. Monroe, 2006, "African American Boys and the Discipline Gap: Balancing Educators' Uneven Hand," *Educational Horizons, 84*(2): 102–111; and Monique Morris, 2016, *Pushout: The Criminalization of Black Girls in Schools* (New York: New Press).

19. Paulo Freire, 2005, *Teachers as Cultural Workers: Letters to Those Who Dare to Teach* (New York: Routledge).

20. G. S. Boutte, 2015, *Educating African American Students: And How Are the Children?* (New York: Routledge).

21. See my research on other Black schools that served as pillars in Black communities: J. E. Morris, 1999, "A Pillar of Strength: An African American School's Communal Bonds with Families and Community since Brown," *Urban Education, 33*(5): 584–605.

22. V. S. Walker, 1996, *Their Highest Potential: An African American School Community in the Segregated South* (Chapel Hill: University of North Carolina Press); K. Lomotey, 1987, "Black Principals for Black Students: Some Preliminary Observations," *Urban Education, 22*(2): 173–181.

23. Mary Scott Hodgin, 2016, "Eva Hardy Jones: Powell School's Legendary Principle," WBHM, May 13, https://wbhm.org/feature/2016/eva-hardy-jones -powell-schools-legendary-principal/.

24. J. E. Morris, 2004, "Can Anything Good Come from Nazareth? Race, Class, and African American Schooling and Community in the Urban South and Midwest," *American Educational Research Journal, 41*(1): 69–112.

25. Morris, 2004; J. E. Morris, 2009, *Troubling the Waters: Fulfilling the Promise of Quality Public Schooling for Black Children* (New York: Teachers College Press). Also see J. E. Morris, 2021, "Reclaim, Recenter, and Restore: An Imperative for Affirmation, Equity and Excellence in the New Fight for Urban Education," in H. R. Milner and K. Lomotey (eds.), *The Handbook of Urban Education* (New York: Routledge).

26. Bell, 1992.

27. J. Anyon, 2014, *Radical Possibilities: Public Policy, Urban Education, and New Social Movement*, 3rd ed. (New York: Routledge).

Chapter 10. The Sugar Jets

1. *Roots* was a 1977 miniseries that aired on ABC and was based on the 1976 novel *Roots: The Saga of an American Family* by Alex Haley.

2. D. P. Alridge and J. B. Stewart, 2005, "Introduction: Hip Hop in History: Past, Present, and Future," *Journal of African American History, 90*(3): 190–195; J. Chang, 2007, *Can't Stop Won't Stop: A History of the Hip-Hop Generation* (New York: St. Martin's).

3. Regina Bradley, 2021, *Chronicling Stankonia: The Rise of the Hip-Hop South* (Chapel Hill: University of North Carolina Press); B. L. Love, 2012, *Hip Hop's Li'l Sistas Speak: Negotiating Hip Hop Identities and Politics in the New South* (New York: Peter Lang); R. Sarig, 2007, *Third Coast: Outkast, Timbaland, and How Hip-Hop Became a Southern Thing* (Cambridge, Mass.: Da Capo Press).

4. The Carver Theatre opened in 1935 to provide opportunities for African Americans, who were excluded from the city's whites-only theaters, to watch motion pictures. All of these theaters, the Carver, Melba, and Empire, would close in the early 1980s due to the overall economic decline of downtown Birmingham.

5. For us, ideas of a family often went beyond blood-related individuals to include fictive kinfolks. Black people still use endearing terms such as "brother," "sister," "aunt," "uncle," and "cousin" when referring to non-blood-related individuals. For readings on and examples of these familial and fictive kinships among Black people, see the following: Linda M. Chatters, Robert Joseph Taylor, and Rukmalie Jayakody, 1994, "Fictive Kinship Relations in Black Extended Families," *Journal of Comparative Family Studies*, 25(3): 297–312; E. Anderson, 1978, *A Place on the Corner* (Chicago: University of Chicago Press); J. Aschenbrenner, 1975, *Lifelines: Black Families in Chicago* (New York: Holt, Rinehart & Winston); Carol B. Stack, 1974, *All Our Kin: Strategies for Survival in a Black Community* (New York: Harper & Row); B. D. Tatum, 1987, *Assimilation Blues: Black Families in a White Community* (Westport, Conn.: Greenwood).

6. A. Caliver, 1931, "Largest Negro High School," *School Life*, 17(4): 73–74, retrieved from Birmingham Public Library Digital Collections, Newspaper Vertical File Collection.

7. W. K. McNeil, 2005, *Encyclopedia of American Gospel Music* (New York: Routledge).

8. For a list of the all-state football players from Phillips High School, please see the website for the Alabama High School Football Historical Society: http://www.ahsfhs.org/teams2/allstate.asp?Team=Phillips%20Birmingham.

9. "New Life," copyright by Olivia Walker and Shirley Walker (1985).

Chapter 11. First Impressions

1. J. Hayman, 1998, *Doing unto the Least of These: The Story of Birmingham's Jimmie Hale Mission* (Montgomery, Ala.: Black Belt Press); Thomas Spencer, 2007, "Address Changes, Mission Doesn't," *Birmingham News*, January 14.

Chapter 12. Inner-City Church Joys and Pains

1. The term "sanctified" often implies members of the Church of God in Christ.

2. "Jesus Met the Woman at the Well," traditional African American gospel song.

3. J. H. Cone, 1991, *The Spirituals and the Blues: An Interdisciplinary* (Maryknoll, N.Y.: Orbis Books).

4. Luke Flood, "A Brief History of the Church Bus Ministry in America," *Help4Today*, https://help4today.org/a-brief-history-of-the-church-bus-ministry-in-america/.

5. From the hymn "Jesus Loves the Little Children."

6. See J. H. Cone, 1970, *A Black Theology of Liberation*, 20th anniversary ed. (repr., Maryknoll, N.Y.: Orbis Books, 1990).

7. A. B. Pollard, 2011, "The Negro Church: An Introduction," in W. E. B. Du Bois (ed.), *The Negro Church*, ix–xxxii (Eugene, Oreg.: Cascade Books).

8. M. W. D. Shomanah and M. Dube, 2012, *Postcolonial Feminist Interpretation of the Bible* (n.p.: Chalice Press).

9. J. E. Morris, 2004, "Can Anything Good Come from Nazareth? Race, Class, and African American Schooling and Community in the Urban South and Midwest," *American Educational Research Journal*, *41*(1): 69–112.

10. From numerous conversations with Dr. Alton B. Pollard III.

Chapter 13. April Fools' Day

1. Job Corps was established by the Economic Opportunity Act of 1964, as part of Lyndon B. Johnson's War on Poverty.

2. L. M. Burton, 1990, "Teenage Childbearing as an Alternative Life-Course Strategy in Multigeneration Black Families," *Human Nature*, *1*(2): 123–143.

Chapter 14. Player No More

1. For more on Black students' racial identity development, see the following: W. E. Cross Jr., 1995, "The Psychology of Nigrescence: Revising the Cross Model," in J. G. Ponterotto, J. M. Casas, L. A. Suzuki, and C. M. Alexander (eds.), *Handbook of Multicultural Counseling*, 93–122 (Thousand Oaks, Calif.: Sage); S. L. Mitchell and D. M. Dell, 1992, "The Relationship between Black Students' Racial Identity Attitude and Participation in Campus Organizations," *Journal of College Student Development*, *33*(1): 39–43; T. A. Parham and J. E. Helms, 1985, "Relation of Racial Identity Attitudes to Self-Actualization and Affective States of Black Students," *Journal of Counseling Psychology*, *32*(3): 431–440, http://dx.doi .org/10.1037/0022-0167.32.3.431; T. A. Parham and J. E. Helms, 1981, "The Influence of Black Students' Racial Identity Attitudes on Preferences for Counselor's Race," *Journal of Counseling Psychology*, *28*(3): 250–257, http://dx.doi.org /10.1037/0022-0167.28.3.250.

2. R. W. Irvine and J. J. Irvine, 1983, "The Impact of the Desegregation Process on the Education of Black Students: Key Variables," *Journal of Negro Education*, *52*(4): 410–422.

3. S. R. Harper, 2015, "Black Male College Achievers and Resistant Responses to Racist Stereotypes at Predominantly White Colleges and Universities," *Harvard Educational Review*, *85*(4): 646–674.

4. Some of these players would go on to become professors, lawyers, engineers, and military leaders.

5. This experience with the English professor, and others that would take place, represented what William Cross and other scholars refer to as a phase of Black racial identity development. For more on this, see W. E. Cross Jr. and B. J. Vandiver, 2001, "Nigrescence Theory and Measurement: Introducing the Cross Racial Identity Scale (CRIS)," in J. G. Ponterotto, J. M. Casas, L. A. Suzuki, and C. M. Alexander (eds.), *Handbook of Multicultural Counseling*, 371–393 (Thousand Oaks, Calif.: Sage).

6. Vincent High School was closed in 1969 with the enforcement of *Brown v. Board of Education*. Black students then had to attend the all-white Chester County High School. Most of the Black educators and staff who had previously

worked in the county's Black schools would not be hired to work in the white schools. They lost their jobs like Black educators and school staff across the country after school desegregation became enforced. See J. E. Haney, 1978, "The Effects of the Brown Decision on Black Educators," *Journal of Negro Education*, 47(1): 88–95.

7. M. J. Dumas, 2014, "'Losing an Arm': Schooling as a Site of Black Suffering," *Race Ethnicity and Education*, 17(1): 1–29.

8. For more discussions of teachers' expectations of students by race, see the following studies: H. R. Tenenbaum and M. D. Ruck, 2007, "Are Teachers' Expectations Different for Racial Minorities Than for European American Students? A Meta-Analysis," *Journal of Educational Psychology*, 99(2): 253; S. Gershenson, S. B. Holt, and N. W. Papageorge, 2016, "Who Believes in Me? The Effect of Student–Teacher Demographic Match on Teacher Expectations," *Economics of Education Review*, 52: 209–224; J. J. Irvine, 1990, *Black Students and School Failure: Policies, Practices, and Prescriptions* (Westport, Conn.: Greenwood).

9. See J. E. Morris, 2001, "African American Students and Gifted Education: The Politics of Race and Culture," *Roeper Review*, 24(2): 59–62; D. Y. Ford, T. C. Grantham, and G. W. Whiting, 2008, "Culturally and Linguistically Diverse Students in Gifted Education: Recruitment and Retention Issues," *Exceptional Children*, 74(3): 289–306.

10. A. Lewis and J. Diamond, 2015, *Despite the Best Intentions: How Racial Inequality Thrives in Good Schools* (New York: Oxford University Press).

11. L. C. Ross, 2001, *The Divine Nine: The History of African American Fraternities and Sororities* (New York: Kensington Books).

12. C. H. Wesley, 1929, *The History of Alpha Phi Alpha: A Development in College Life, 1906–1979* (Baltimore: Foundation Publishers).

13. U.S. Department of Education, "Federal Pell Grant Program" (2022), https://www2.ed.gov/programs/fpg/index.html.

14. Although he had an outstanding college career playing for the University of Washington, Warren Moon was not drafted by any National Football League teams. He would go on to play in the Canadian Football League, where he would lead his team to five championships. Moon would later be provided the opportunity to play quarterback with the U.S.-based National Football League.

15. E. Mercurio and V. F. Filak, 2010, "Roughing the Passer: The Framing of Black and White Quarterbacks Prior to the NFL Draft," *Howard Journal of Communications*, 21(1): 56–71.

16. A. Adeyemo and J. E. Morris, 2020, "Researching the Neighborhood and Schooling Experiences of Black Male High-School Students Who Play Sports in Atlanta and Chicago," *Teachers College Record*, 122(8): 1–52. In our article, Dr. Adeoye Adeyemo, a former graduate student who worked with me and is now leading cutting-edge research in the sociology of sports, and I coined the phrase "students who play sports" when referring to Black male students playing school sports. We argue that such a shift humanizes young Black people rather than treating them as commodities.

17. For additional insightful studies and critiques of this topic, see the following: B. Hawkins, 2010, *The New Plantation: Black Athletes, College Sports, and Predominantly White NCAA Institutions* (New York: Palgrave Macmillan); T. C. Howard, 2014, *Black Male(d): Peril and Promise in the Education of African American Males* (New York: Teachers College Press); H. Edwards, 2000, "Crisis of Black Athletes on the Eve of the 21st Century," *Society, 37*(3): 9–14; L. Harrison, C. K. Harrison, and L. N. Moore, 2002, "African American Identity and Sport," *Sports, Education and Society, 7*(2): 121–133; T. S. Johnson and T. A. Migliaccio, 2009, "The Social Construction of an Athlete: African American Boy's Experience in Sport," *Western Journal of Black Studies, 33*(2): 98–109.

18. Staff Reports, 2020, "30 Years Today, TSU Students Took over Campus to Demand Change," *Tennessean*, February 21, https://www.tennessean.com/story/news/education/2020/02/21/tsu-nashville-protests-1990-students-took-over-campus-change/4830466002/; Brad Schmitt, 2017, "Activist Jeff Obafemi Carr's First Protest: Shutting Down TSU," *Tennessean*, March 30, https://www.tennessean.com/story/news/local/davidson%20/2017/03/30/activist-jeff-obafemi-carrs-first-protest-shutting-down-tsu/99257492/.

19. Jimmie Settle, 1990, "APSU Students March to Back TSU Strikers," *Leaf-Chronicle*, March 1.

Chapter 15. The Joys and Pains of Central City

1. Michelle Alexander, 2010, *The New Jim Crow: Mass Incarceration in the Age of Colorblindness* (New York: New Press).

2. Gary Webb, 1996, "Cocaine Pipeline Finance Rebels: Evidence Points to CIA Knowing of High-Volume Drug Network," *San Jose Mercury News*, August 22.

3. Webb, 1996.

4. Donna Murch, 2019, "How Race Made the Opioid Crisis," *Boston Review*, August 27.

5. According to its website, www.jobcorps.gov, Job Corps is funded by Congress and administered by the Department of Labor. It is a no-cost educational and vocational training program that trains young people between the ages of sixteen and twenty-four for industry-related jobs. Job Corps' mission also includes providing young people who have not finished high school with a second opportunity to develop job-related skills.

6. Manning Marable, 1983, *How Capitalism Underdeveloped Black America* (Boston: South End Press).

7. Haki R. Madhubuti, 1990, *Black Men: Obsolete, Single, Dangerous? Afrikan American Families in Transition: Essays in Discovery, Solution, and Hope* (Chicago: Third World Press).

Chapter 16. Black Consciousness

1. In *The Souls of Black Folk*, Du Bois writes about Black people's awareness of racist structures as a sort of double consciousness. Antiapartheid activist Steve Biko espoused Black consciousness as a galvanizing force for Black people and

form of resistance to white supremacy in South Africa. Steve Biko, 2015, *I Write What I Like: Selected Writings* (Chicago: University of Chicago Press). Several scholars, including Lewis Gordon, write about this awareness by Black people of the embedded nature of racist structures. See L. R. Gordon, 2022, *Fear of Black Consciousness* (London: Penguin).

2. Chinweizu Ibekwe, 1975, *The West and the Rest of Us: White Predators, Black Slavers and the African Elite* (New York: Vintage); Walter Rodney, 1972, *How Europe Underdeveloped Africa* (London: Bogle-L'Ouverture).

3. In the book, Malcolm X attributes his mother's mental issues partly to the stress of raising him and his siblings after the murder of their father by a group of white men. See Malcolm X and Alex Haley, 1966, *The Autobiography of Malcolm X* (New York: Grove Press).

4. Psyche A. Williams-Forson, 2006, *Building Houses out of Chicken Legs: Black Women, Food, and Power* (Chapel Hill: University of North Carolina Press).

5. Donald Braman, 2007, *Doing Time on the Outside: Incarceration and Family Life in Urban America* (Ann Arbor: University of Michigan Press).

6. See the following for more discussion: Lawrence Bobo and Victor Thomas, 2006, "Unfair by Design: The War on Drugs, Race, and the Legitimacy of the Criminal Justice System," *Social Research*, 73(2): 445–472; Kenneth B. Nunn, 2002, "Race, Crime and the Pool of Surplus Criminality: Or Why the War on Drugs Was a War on Blacks," *Gender, Race & Justice*, 6: 381–446; Jonathan Rothwell, 2014, "How the War on Drugs Damages Black Social Mobility," *Social Mobility Memos*, September 30, https://www.brookings.edu/blog/social-mobility-memos/2014/09/30/how-the-war-on-drugs-damages-black-social-mobility/.

7. For more on the concept of "other mothers," see Jacqueline Jordan Irvine's 1999 work "The Education of Children Whose Nightmares Come Both Day and Night," *Journal of Negro Education*, 68(3): 244–253; Patricia Hill Collins, 2000, *Black Feminist Thought: Knowledge, Consciousness, and the Politics of Empowerment*, 2nd ed. (New York: Routledge); C. G. Stanford, 1997, "Successful Pedagogy in Urban Schools: Perspectives of Four African American Teachers," *Journal of Education for Students Placed at Risk*, 2(2): 107–119.

8. G. Ladson-Billings, 1994, *The Dreamkeepers: Successful Teachers of African American Children* (San Francisco: Jossey-Bass).

9. In his book, sociologist Orlando Patterson describes enslavement as an extreme form of social death because it includes domination and has the ability to change people's views of themselves over time. For more discussion, see O. Patterson, 1982, *Slavery and Social Death: A Comparative Study* (Cambridge, Mass.: Harvard University Press).

Chapter 17. Chocolate or White Milk?

1. See the work by the following scholars regarding the one-dimensional representation of civil rights leaders such as Dr. King: D. P. Alridge, 2006, "The Limits of Master Narratives in History Textbooks: An Analysis of Representations of Martin Luther King, Jr.," *Teachers College Record*, 108(4): 662. Also see K. D. Brown and A. L. Brown, 2010, "Silenced Memories: An Examination of the So-

ciocultural Knowledge on Race and Racial Violence in Official School Curriculum," *Equity & Excellence in Education*, 43(2): 139–154.

2. Sheila Rule, 1992, "The 1992 Campaign: Racial Issues; Rapper, Chided by Clinton, Calls Him a Hypocrite," *New York Times*, June 17, A22.

3. M. Foster, 1997, *Black Teachers on Teaching* (New York: New Press); J. J. Irvine, 1989, "Beyond Role Models: An Examination of Cultural Influences on the Pedagogical Perspectives of Black Teachers," *Peabody Journal of Education*, 66(4): 51–63.

4. Sarah Schwartz, 2021, "Map: Where Critical Race Theory Is Under Attack," *Education Week*, June 11, https://www.edweek.org/policy-politics/map-where -critical-race-theory-is-under-attack/2021/06.

5. Cornell University Library, "John Henrik Clarke Bibliography," last updated September 14, 2022, https://guides.library.cornell.edu/clarke.

Chapter 18. Big Meaty

1. Cain Hope Felder (ed.), 2007, *The Original African Heritage Study Bible* (Valley Forge, Pa.: Judson Press). In this parable, Jesus describes how the shepherd leaves behind the ninety-nine sheep in order to find the one that is lost. The shepherd delights in finding the one lost sheep and shares the good news with neighbors, family, and friends.

2. Ann A. Ferguson, 2000, *Bad Boys: Public Schools in the Making of Black Masculinity* (Ann Arbor: University of Michigan Press).

Chapter 19. Building Some New Apartments for Y'all

1. J. E. Morris, 2012, "God's Will or Government Policy?," in William F. Tate IV (ed.), *Research on Schools, Neighborhoods, and Communities: Toward Civic Responsibility*, 455–477 (Lanham, Md.: Rowman & Littlefield).

2. J. E. Morris, 2008, "Out of New Orleans: Race, Class, and Researching the Katrina Diaspora," *Urban Education*, 43(4): 463–487.

3. A. Goodman, D. Smith, J. Gonzalez, and B. Wright, 2005, "Race in New Orleans: Shaping the Response to Katrina," *Democracy Now!*, September, http://www.democracynow.org/2005/9/2.

4. Charles Connerly, 2005, *The Most Segregated City in America: City Planning and Civil Rights in Birmingham, 1920–1980* (Charlottesville: University of Virginia Press).

5. Sheila Crowley, 2003, "The Affordable Housing Crisis: Residential Mobility of Poor Families and School Mobility of Poor Children," *Student Mobility: How Some Children Get Left Behind*, special issue of *Journal of Negro Education*, 72(1): 22–38.

6. National Commission on Severely Distressed Public Housing, 1992, "The Final Report of the National Commission on Severely Distressed Public Housing: A Report to the Congress and Secretary of Housing and Urban Development" (Washington, D.C.: National Commission on Severely Distressed Public Housing, August).

7. Susan J. Popkin, Bruce Katz, Mary K. Cunningham, Karen D. Brown, Jer-

emy Gustafson, and Margery Augstin Turner, 2004, "A Decade of HOPE VI: Research Findings and Policy Challenges" (Washington, D.C.: Urban Institute and Brookings Institution, May). Also see James Tracy's 2008 paper "Hope VI Mixed-Income Housing Projects Displace Poor People," *Who Owns Our Cities?*, 15(1), https://www.reimaginerpe.org/node/1811.

8. S. Gustafson, 2013, "Displacement and the Racial State in Olympic Atlanta: 1990–1996," *Southeastern Geographer*, 53(2): 198–213, https://www.jstor.org /stable/10.2307/26229061.

9. L. M. Burton, 1990, "Teenage Childbearing as an Alternative Life-Course Strategy in Multigeneration Black Families," *Human Nature*, 1(2): 123–143.

10. A number of researchers studying public housing demolition have captured the social isolation that results from being uprooted from places in which multiple generations of families would live. For more on this work as it relates to the HOPE VI program, see the following: S. Greenbaum, W. Hathaway, C. Rodriguez, A. Spalding, and B. Ward, 2008, "Deconcentration and Social Capital: Contradictions of a Poverty Alleviation Policy," *Journal of Poverty*, 12(2): 201–228, doi:10.1080/10875540801973609; S. Clampet-Lundquist, 2004, "Moving Over or Moving Up? Short-Term Gains and Losses for Relocated HOPE VI Families," *Cityscape*, 7(1): 57–80, www.scopus.com.

11. National Housing Law Project, Poverty & Race Research Action Council, Sherwood Research Associates & Everywhere and Now Public Housing Residents Organizing Together, 2002, *False HOPE: A Critical Assessment of the HOPE VI Public Housing Redevelopment Program* (Oakland, Calif.: National Housing Law Project).

Chapter 20. That's Home

1. For a discussion of the roots and pervasiveness of these controlling images and Black women, please see the following: P. H. Collins, 2004, *Black Sexual Politics* (New York: Routledge); Adia H. Wingfield, 2007, "The Modern Mammy and the Angry Black Man: African American Professionals' Experiences with Gendered Racism in the Workplace," *Race, Gender & Class*, 14(1/2): 196–212.

2. Black women across all socioeconomic classes fight against controlling images. Black professional women contend with images of the modern mammy, expected to sacrifice their personal life in professional settings for the sake of the institution or of their white boss. And Black women who stay at home to care for their children and receive federal or state assistance have been called welfare queens and viewed as bad mothers. Black women are more complex than these narrow depictions. They have resisted such narratives while supporting their families and communities. For a discussion on these roles and images, please see A. Cammett, 2016, "Welfare Queens Redux: Criminalizing Black Mothers in the Age of Neoliberalism," *Southern California Interdisciplinary Law Journal*, 25(2): 363–393, as well as R. Y. Williams, 2004, *The Politics of Public Housing: Black Women's Struggles Against Urban Inequality* (New York: Oxford University Press).

3. Lawrence J. Vale, Shomon Shamsuddin, and Nicholas Kelly, 2018, "Broken Promises or Selective Memory Planning? A National Picture of HOPE VI Plans and Realities," *Housing Policy Debate*, 28(5): 746–769, https://doi.org/10.1080/10511482.2018.1458245; U.S. Government Accountability Office (GAO), 2003a, "Public Housing: HOPE VI Resident Issues and Changes in Neighborhoods Surrounding Grant Sites" (GAO-04-109, November); GAO, 2003b, "Public Housing: HUD's Oversight of HOPE VI Sites Needs to Be More Consistent," https://www.gao.gov/products/GAO-03-555; "When Hope Falls Short: HOPE VI, Accountability, and the Privatization of Public Housing," 2003, *Harvard Law Review*, 116(5): 1477–1498, https://doi.org/10.2307/1342733.

4. In December 2021, developers began demolishing the twenty-six-acre, 445-unit public housing community known as Southtown Court, which was located on the city's south side near the University of Alabama at Birmingham and St. Vincent's Hospital. Developers plan to construct office space, residential units, a hotel, and retail space and restaurants. See the following news story: Greg Garrison, 2021, "Demolition Begins on Southtown Public Housing," *Birmingham Real-Time News*, December 17, https://www.al.com/news/birmingham/2021/12/demolition-begins-on-southtown-public-housing.html.

5. Williams, 2004.

6. D. E. Keene and A. T. Geronimus, 2011, "Community-Based Support among African American Public Housing Residents," *Journal of Urban Health*, 88(1): 41–53, https://doi.org/10.1007/s11524-010-9511-z.

Conclusion

1. Edward G. Goetz, 2012, "The Transformation of Public Housing Policy, 1985–2011," *Journal of the American Planning Association*, 78(4): 452–463, https://doi.org/10.1080/01944363.2012.737983.

2. Please see the following regarding the ways that policies and practices are working against vulnerable families and communities: C. Gordon, 2009, *Mapping Decline: St. Louis and the Fate of the American City* (Philadelphia: University of Pennsylvania Press); J. R. Henig, R. C. Hula, M. Orr, and D. S. Pedescleaux, 1999, *The Color of School Reform: Race, Politics, and the Challenge of Urban Education* (Princeton, N.J.: Princeton University Press); W. F. Tate, 2008, "'Geography of Opportunity': Poverty, Place, and Educational Outcomes," *Educational Researcher*, 37(7): 397–411; R. Rothstein, 2017, *The Color or Law: A Forgotten History of How Our Government Segregated America* (New York: Norton).

3. E. Ewing, 2018, *Ghosts in the Schoolyard: Racism and School Closings on Chicago's Southside* (Chicago: University of Chicago Press). For other readings on Black school closings, please see E. M. Duncan-Shippy (ed.), 2019, *Shuttered Schools: Race, Community, and School Closures in American Cities* (Charlotte, N.C.: Information Age).

4. J. E. Morris, 2021, "Closures of Black K–12 Schools across the Nation Threaten Neighborhood Stability," *The Conversation*, June 25 , https://the conversation.com/closures-of-black-k-12-schools-across-the-nation-threaten

-neighborhood-stability-162072. For an in-depth scholarly analysis of the historical pattern of Black school closures, please see J. E. Morris, B. D. Parker, and L. M. Negrón, 2022, "Black School Closings Aren't New: Historically Contextualizing Contemporary School Closings and Black Community Resistance," *Educational Researcher*, *51*(9): 575–583.

5. The original Jones Valley Teaching Farm's website that provided this quote has since been modified. However, I was able to retrieve this information from a 2013 job advertisement that was placed on AmeriCorps' website. Please see the first two sentences at the following website: https://my.americorps.gov/mp /listing/viewListing.do?id=48420.

6. T. H. Braswell, 2018, "Fresh Food, New Faces: Community Gardening as Ecological Gentrification in St. Louis, Missouri," *Agriculture and Human Values*, *35*(4): 809–822.

7. According to john powell and colleagues, "Within a targeted universalism framework, universal goals are established for all groups concerned. The strategies developed to achieve those goals are targeted, based upon how different groups are situated within structures, culture, and across geographies to obtain the universal goal." See j. a. powell, S. Menedian, and W. Ake, 2019, *Targeted Universalism: Policy and Practice* (Berkeley: Haas Institute for a Fair & Inclusive Society, University of California, Berkeley).

Epilogue

1. "Community Activist Sarah Price Remembered for Work with Greater Birmingham Ministries," 2012, CBS 42, September 16, https://www.cbs42.com/news /local/community-activist-sarah-price-remembered-for-work-with-greater -birmingham-ministries/.

INDEX

Notes: Page numbers in italics refer to photographs and illustrations. The term "schools" refers to elementary schools and high schools, while postsecondary institutions are referred to as "colleges and universities."

Adair, Uretta, 64
Adeyemo, Adeoye, 208, 226n16
African American spirituals, xi, 86–87, 105, 122, 124. *See also* church(es); soul(s)
A. H. Parker High School. *See* Parker High School
Alley, the (neighborhood), xiii, *xviii*; author's family history in, 17, 19–26, 48, 70; overview, 15–17; relationships formed in, 28, 38, 53, 76, 99, 161–162. *See also* Twenty-Ninth Court
"All the Same" (J. E. Morris), 182
Alpha Phi Alpha fraternity, 137–141, 152
American Freedom Train, 41
Angelou, Maya, 79, 221n1
APSU. *See* Austin Peay State University
Arbery, Ahmaud, 202
Arrington, Richard, 62, 117
athletic scholarships, 129, 132, 133, 138, 144–145. *See also* coaches; football
Atlanta, Ga., 154, 182, 184, 187–189, 195, 214n3
Austin Peay State University (APSU): author's Black consciousness and, 160, 171; author's experiences at, 4–5, 131–134, 136,

141–146; Black student organizations at, 138, 146–148
Autobiography of Malcolm X, The (with Haley), 160, 161, 228n3

Barbara (classmate), 88–89
Bast, Mrs. (neighbor), 161–162, 163
Bell, Derrick, 7
Beulah Missionary Baptist Church, xiv, 118–120
Bevel, James, 148
BHA. *See* Birmingham Housing Authority
Big Brother Steve (fraternity member), 139, 140
Big Meaty (brother). *See* Morris, Michael
Big Willie (neighbor), 75
Biko, Steve, 227n1 (chap. 16)
Billson, Janet Mancini, 67
Birmingham, Ala., xvi; America's poorest zip code in, 8, 213n15; as Civil Rights Movement epicenter, 1–2; downtown, xiii–xiv, *xvii*, *xviii*, 98, 199–201, 224n4 (chap. 10); industries of, 17, 20, 47; public bus system in, 63; represented by author in Japan, 3, 115, 116–117; shotgun houses of, 14, 17, *18*, 19, 214n13; siblings' departures from, 48–50, 85, 187–189. *See also specific neighborhoods*
—city government: first Black mayor of, 62; Red Mountain Expressway and, 58–60; study abroad program and, 3, 113, 114. *See also* Birmingham Housing Authority

Birmingham, Ala. (*continued*)
—police: author's family's interactions with, 29, 34, 48, 151–153, 154–155, 176; Black men as viewed by, 114–115; Black prison labor and, 47; Carter's murder and, 61–62; payments to, 15, 26, 153; violence and, 1, 55, 56, 211n2 (chap. 1). *See also* incarceration
—public housing communities: as Black communities, 11; Central City residents displaced to other, 189–190, 195–196, 198; Civil Rights Movement's neglect of, 2; crack-cocaine epidemic in, 155–156; culture of, 98, 99, 120–121; history of, 12–13, 15; police abuses in, official indifference to, 153; poverty in, 6, 8, 9–10, 71; racist managers of, 60. *See also specific public housing communities*
—public school system: Black students neglected by, 78; HOPE VI and school closures, 199–200; magnet schools embraced by, 91–92; segregation/desegregation and, 55–57, 82–83, 89; study abroad program supported by, 3, 114; Woodson's books adopted by, 90. *See also* Black students: school; schools; *and specific schools*
—residents, Black: as activists, 1–2, 53–54, 56, 59–60, 61–62; civil organizations of, 115, 129; crack-cocaine epidemic and, 154, 166; culture of, 83–84, 98, 121–122, 162; as domestic workers, 21, 23, 31, 62–63, 78, 110; education and schools for, 89–90, 91–92, 102; history of, 13, 15–17, 47–48; housing of, 17, 19, 27–28, 30, 41, 199–202, 214n13; as industrial workers, 20, 22, 25, 47; middle-class, 17, 90, 115; poverty among, 1–2, 6–7, 8–9, 71, 153, 155, 156, 160, 199, 213n15; racism encountered by, 54–55, 62–64; represented by author in Japan, 115. *See also* Central City residents; *and specific individuals*
—residents, white: at American Freedom Train, 41; anti-Black violence of, 54–55, 211n2 (chap. 1); Black domestic workers and, 31, 62–63, 78, 110; Carter's murder and, 61–62; flight from Black residents, 30, 31, 33, 57, 82–83, 92, 216n3; gentrification and, 199–201; in Greater Birmingham Ministry, 59; housing of, 13, 28–29, 59; as police officers, 26, 34, 55, 61–62;

racism of, 61–64; Red Mountain Expressway and, 58, 59; schools and, 55–56, 82–83, 89, 91, 103. *See also specific individuals*
Birmingham Black (friend), 166
Birmingham Housing Authority (BHA): author's family's experiences with, 184–185, 204; Central City football team and, 99; Central City's demolition and, ix, 183–184, 189, 191, 193–194, 195, 197–198; history of, 12, 13, 15; Red Mountain Expressway and, 58–60. *See also* Birmingham, Ala.: public housing communities
Black children, 2, 20, 23–24, 161. *See also* Black families; Black females; Black males; Black students: school
Black colleges and universities. *See* colleges and universities: historically Black
Black communities, low-income: in the Alley and the Court, 16–17; Central City as example of, x–xii, 10, 11, 206; children in, 2, 20, 23–24, 161; drugs and, 6, 153, 154–156, 171; government food programs in, 71; HOPE VI policy and, 182–184, 193–194, 199–202; relationships as wealth in, 16; resilience and vitality of, 10–11, 33, 166–167; schools as pillar of strength for, 94–96; targeted universalism to assist, 201–202; violence in, context of, 67–68. *See also* Birmingham, Ala.: public housing communities; Black families; Black poverty; downtown neighborhoods; public housing; *and specific communities*
Black consciousness, 134, 157–158, 159–160, 166–167, 225n5
Black culture: adaptive vitality of, 217n8; in Birmingham, 83–84, 98, 121–122, 162; Black consciousness and, 134, 157–158, 159–160, 166–167; church in, 17, 118–124; colorism in, 23–24; "nigger," use of term, and, 69; spirituals in, xi, 86–87, 105, 122, 124; teaching of, 86–90, 169–172, 173–174. *See also* Black history
Black educators. *See* educators: Black
Black families: crack-cocaine epidemic and, 6; displacement of, 13, 15, 184; familial and fictive kinships among, 205, 224n5 (chap. 10); genealogy of, 51–52; households of, 20, 128, 156; incarceration and, 165–166, 177; intergenerational trauma and, 8–10, 213n17; schools as support for,

94–96; targeted universalism to assist, 201–202. *See also* Black children; Black communities, low-income; Black females; Black males

Black females: as activists, 59–60, 63–64; as competitors for scarce males, 38; as domestic workers, 21, 23, 31, 62–63, 78, 110; as entrepreneurs, 21, 162; ideas about / images of, 21, 23–24, 230n2; mistreatment of, 47–48; as mothers and grandmothers, 20, 45, 53–54, 126, 128, 176–177, 188; in public housing, stigmatization of, 193, 195, 196; sexual exploitation of, 23–24, 169, 216n24; as teachers, 83, 95, 166. *See also* Black children; Black families; Black males

Black history, 13, 15–17, 47–48, 86–90, 169–172, 173–174. *See also* Black culture; enslavement

Black Lives Matter, urban landscape and, 200, 202

Black males: Alpha Phi Alpha as organization of, 137–138; as athletes, 4, 133–135, 137, 141–145, 226n16; Black teachers and, 170–171, 172; drugs and, 6, 153, 154–155; employment of, 20, 47, 49–50; as fathers, 45; incarceration of, 3, 47, 48, 58, 153; masculinity and, 66–67, 82, 139–140; PEAKS program for young, 173; police brutality toward, 152; scarcity of, reasons for, 38; sexual exploitation by, 23–24; vilification of, in HOPE VI program, 184; violence between, 99; young, 98–99, 112, 126, 157, 160, 179. *See also* Black children; Black families; Black females

Black Men (Madhubuti), 157

Black Panther Party, 71, 220n11

Black people. *See* Birmingham, Ala.: residents, Black; Black children; Black communities, low-income; Black culture; Black families; Black females; Black history; Black males; Black students; educators: Black; *and specific individuals*

Black poverty: athletics as way out of, 4, 133; in author's family, 2, 71–72, 93, 156, 176; in Birmingham, 1–2, 8; drugs and, 6–7, 153, 154, 155, 156; global parallels to, 3, 5–6, 11; HOPE VI and, 182–184, 199–202; incarceration and, 58; intergenerational, 8–10, 201–202, 213n17; premature deaths and, 179; public awareness of,

27–28. *See also* Black communities, low-income; middle-class Black people; opportunities; public housing; survival

Black schools. *See* schools

Black spirituals, xi, 86–87, 105, 122, 124. *See also* church(es); soul(s)

Black students:
—college and university: abilities of, perceived, 133–134, 136–137; as activists, 141, 146–148; Alpha Phi Alpha and, 137–138; identities of, 133; sports and, 133, 134–135, 137, 141–145, 226n16. *See also* colleges and universities; educators: Black
—school: abilities of, perceived, 90, 92, 136–137; African American Vernacular English (AAVE) in teaching of, 83–84; Black history in education of, 86–89, 169–172, 173–174; Black teachers as support for, 94–96, 170–171, 172; desegregation and, 56–57, 82–83, 225n6; disciplining of, 93; female, teenage pregnancy and, 126; with learning challenges, 78–79, 84–85; in predominantly white schools, 91–92, 136–137, 225n6; psychological violence inflicted on, 68–69; textbooks inadequate for, 169, 170. *See also* Black children; educators: Black; schools

Blue (football player), 108

Boone (friend), 175

Brickyard, the (Tuxedo Court housing project), 189, 190–191, 204

Brown, Charles, 34

Brown, H. Rap (Jamil Al-Amin), 68

Brown, Michael, 205

Brown v. Board of Education (1954), 56, 57, 92, 225n6

Burks, Mary Fair, 64

Cairo, Egypt, 5–6

carr, jeff, 124, 147, 207–208

Carruba, Paul, 59

Carruba Grocery, xiv, 15, *16*

Carter, Bonita, 61–62

Carver Theatre, 224n4 (chap. 10)

CBSM (Communally-Bonded Schooling Model), 96

Central City Poppers (CCP), 98

Central City public housing community (later Metropolitan Gardens), xiii, *xvii*, *xviii*, *14*, *32*, *180*; construction of, 13; as home to Black community, 11, 193–194;

Central City public housing community
(*continued*)
    HOPE VI project and, 183–184, 189;
    as microcosm, 10; name change, xi, 38,
    221n2 (preface); Red Mountain Express-
    way and, 58–60; renovation of, 60–61
Central City Research Project, ix–xii, 193–
    194
Central City residents: Black community
    of, ix–xii, 28–31, 58, 159–160, 196, 206;
    block parties held by, 97–99; church and,
    118, 120–121, 123; community garden run
    by, 201; daycare and schools serving, xiii,
    80–81, 91–92, 94–95; displacement of,
    183–185, 189–190, 191–192, 193–194, 197–
    198; drugs and, 6–7, 153, 154–156, 164–
    165; fights between, 36–37, 65–67, 68–71,
    72–73, 75–76, 99; football and, 99–100,
    104, 107, 186–187; government food pro-
    grams used by, 71–72; post-displacement,
    194–198, 199–200, 201–202; poverty of,
    2, 6, 8, 10, 11, 71–72, 213n15; racist vio-
    lence toward, 54–55; Red Mountain Ex-
    pressway and, 58–60; as supportive, 114,
    133, 181, 207; white, 28–30, 31, 33, 55;
    young, 23, 66, 74–75, 98–99, 109, 128. *See
    also specific individuals*
Charlene (friend), 196–198, 205, 210
Chicken George (neighbor), 97, 98
children, Black. *See* Black children
Chinweizu, 159
chocolate milk, versus white milk, 170
Chubby, Ms. (neighbor), 35–37
church(es), 17, 118–122, 123–124. *See also*
    African American spirituals; soul(s)
cities, U.S., 30, 57; Black rebellion in, fol-
    lowing MLK's assassination, 27; Black
    versus white housing/neighborhoods in,
    12–13, 15–17, 57; crack-cocaine epidemic
    in, 154; gentrification of, 199–202; HOPE
    VI policy and, 182–184, 193–194, 199–
    202; magnet schools developed by, 91–
    92; neglected areas of (inner cities), 10–
    11, 13; public housing in, 15, 214n3; white
    flight from, 31, 33, 57. *See also* downtown
    neighborhoods; public housing; schools;
    and specific cities
Clancy, Annie (great-grandmother), 47
Clancy, Charlie Ray, Sr. (grandfather), xv
Clancy, Lillian (grandmother), 47
Clancy, Nathan (great-grandfather), 46–47

Clancy, Thomas G. (slave owner), 46
Clarke, John Henrik, 174
Clency, Bobby "Bebop" (brother), 204
Clency, Charles (Panky; brother), xv, 48–
    50, 209
Clency, Charlie Ray, Jr. (father), xv, 25–26,
    40–45, 47–48
Clency, Clara (sister), 209
Clency, Cleo (nephew), 209
Clinton, Bill, 171, 183
Coach C. (football coach), 131, 132
coaches, 99, 100, 134, 141–145. *See also* ath-
    letic scholarships; educators; *and specific
    individuals*
Cole, Echol, 27
colleges and universities (*see also specific
    universities*):
—historically Black: Black teachers edu-
    cated at, 80, 89, 91, 95, 166; student pro-
    tests at, 147–148. *See also* Black students:
    college and university; educators: Black;
    schools
—predominantly white: Alpha Phi Alpha
    at, 137–138; Black males as sports players
    at, 133–135, 137, 141–145, 226n16. *See also*
    Black students: college and university;
    educators: white
Collins, Addie Mae, 1
Collins, Alonzo (uncle), xv, 17, 25
Collins, Derrick (DC), 103, 104–107, 210
Collins, Devon (cousin), 104, 204
Collins, Eddie Steele (uncle), xv, 17
Collins, Oceola Steele (Mama, Ms. OC,
    Alice Mae Hendrix; grandmother), xv;
    adulthood, 19, 20–21, 23, 25, 78, 83, 128;
    death and funeral, 121; early life and edu-
    cation, 19–20, 51
Collins, Sandra (aunt), xv, *180*, 209; life
    events, 78–79, 136, 178, 204; quoted,
    28
Collins, Sarah, 221n2 (chap. 1)
Collins, William (grandmother's spouse),
    19–20, 23, 78
Collins Hotel, xiv, *xviii*, 20–21, 70
Colvin, Claudette, 2, 64
Communally-Bonded Schooling Model
    (CBSM), 96
communities. *See* Black communities, low-
    income; downtown neighborhoods; *and
    specific communities*
Connerly, Charles, 60

consciousness, Black. *See* Black consciousness

Cool Pose (Majors and Billson), 67

Court, the (neighborhood). *See* Twenty-Ninth Court

crack cocaine. *See* drugs

"Creation, The" (Johnson), 87, 88

crime. *See* Birmingham, Ala.: police; drugs; incarceration

Crouch, Treddia Clency (niece), 50

culture, Black. *See* Black culture

CW (nephew/playmate), 41, 42–43, 44

Damien (neighbor), 66

DC (Derrick Collins), 103, 104–107, 210

Denson, Keith, 210

desegregation: of housing, 27–30, 31, 33; of schools, 54, 55–57, 82–83, 91, 92, 136, 225n6. *See also* segregation

DeYampert, Moses, 19

discrimination. *See* racism; segregation

Donald (neighbor), 66

Donovan (neighbor), 54–56, 57–58, 165, 210

Douglas, Scott, 209

Downtown Farmers Market, xiv, 109–110, 111

downtown neighborhoods: Black masculinity in, 67; crack-cocaine epidemic in, 6, 154; fights in, 65–66; in global context, 10–11; government food programs and, 71; HOPE VI policy and, 182–184, 193–194, 199–202; magnet schools in, 91–92; urban renewal efforts in, 13; white flight from, 57. *See also* Black communities, low-income; public housing

DP (neighbor), 74–76

drugs: crack-cocaine epidemic, 6, 164–165, 166; war on, 58, 153, 154–156, 184. *See also* incarceration

Dube, Musa W., 123

Du Bois, W. E. B., 10, 227n1 (chap. 16)

Dunbar, Paul Laurence, 88–89

education. *See* Black students; educators; schools

educators:

—Black: Black communities supported by, 94–96; Black history taught by, 169–172; Black students supported by, 92, 137, 166, 170–171, 172; desegregation and, 136, 225n6; at Phillips High School, 92–93; at Powell Elementary School, 82–83, 85–90, 91–92; race not considered in academic evaluations by, 134; sacredness of teaching and, 94, 172; social class and, 90. *See also* Black students; coaches; schools; *and specific individuals*

—white: low expectations of Black students, 92, 133–135, 136–137; teaching Black history and culture, 169–172. *See also* coaches; colleges and universities: predominantly white; *and specific individuals*

elementary schools. *See* schools

Elyton Village, 13

enslavement: in author's family history, 46–47, 51; Black consciousness and, 159–160; Black people dispersed by, 182; colorism and, 216n24; intergenerational effects of, 9–10, 213n17; last names and, 218n1; modern comparisons with, 58, 161; as social death, 228n9; spirituals about, 122; teaching about, 169–170, 173–174; violence of, 67. *See also* Black history; racism

families, Black. *See* Black families

Fat Joe (neighbor), 161–163, 164–165, 210

federal government. *See* United States government

females, Black. *See* Black females

First Afrikan Presbyterian Church, 123–124

Fisk Jubilee Singers, 86–87

Fleming, Vinton, 146

Floyd, George, 202

food scarcity, 71–74, 76–77

football: APSU, 4–5, 141, 144–146; Central City, 75, 97–98, 99, 100; Phillips High School, 100–107, 108; Turkey Bowl, 186. *See also* athletic scholarships; coaches

football scholarships. *See* athletic scholarships

Foster, Charles, Jr., 209

Freire, Paulo, 94

GBM (Greater Birmingham Ministry), 53, 59, 191–192, 201

Gede, Mrs. (teacher), 85–90, 210

gender. *See* Black females; Black males

gentrification, 199–202

Georgia, University of (UGA), ix–x, 8, 10

ghettos. *See* Black poverty; downtown neighborhoods; public housing
Glass, Thelma, 64
Goldthwaite, Dionne, 210
Goldthwaite, James, xiv, 68–69, 103–104, 203–204, 209
Goldthwaite, Leola, xiv, 68, 203–204
Gordon, Lewis, 227n1 (chap. 16)
"Gospel Train, The" (song), 87, 221n9
governments. *See* Birmingham, Ala.: city government; United States government
Grandmaster Flash and the Furious Five, 73
Greater Birmingham Ministry (GBM), 53, 59, 191–192, 201
Greater New Antioch Baptist Church, 122, 129
Green, Brenda (aunt), xv, 17, 128
Green, Ms. (teacher), 83

Hamlet, Greg, 210
Hardie Tynes Foundry, xiv, 17
Harris, Elizabeth Leonard (Ms. Liz), 75–77, 100, 209
Harris, Joe (Sugar Man), 6, 99, 100, 104, 195, 209
HBCUs (historically Black colleges and universities). *See* colleges and universities: historically Black
Help Me to Find My People (Williams), 218n1
Henderson, Tenn., 136–137
Henley, William Ernest, 139
high schools. *See* schools
Hines, Lois, 59
hip-hop, 98, 157–158
historically Black colleges and universities (HBCUs). *See* colleges and universities: historically Black
history, Black. *See* Black history
Hitachi City, Japan, 3, *117*
HOPE VI policy, 183–184, 193–194, 199–202. *See also* cities, U.S.; downtown neighborhoods; public housing
housing. *See* Birmingham, Ala.: public housing communities; public housing
How Capitalism Underdeveloped Black America (Marable), 157
How Europe Underdeveloped Africa (Rodney), 159
Hurley, Ruby, 13

Hurricane Katrina, 182
Hype (drug dealer), 164–165

illegal activities. *See* Birmingham, Ala.: police; drugs; incarceration
illegal drugs. *See* drugs
Immaculata Catholic High School, 21, 22
Impressions, 64
"I'm So Glad" (song), 105
incarceration: of author's relatives, 3, 48, 49, 166, 176–177, 205; of Black people, 58, 153, 155; families affected by, 165–166, 177; of neighbors, 55, 114–115, 165; paying police to avoid, 26; prison labor and, 47. *See also* Birmingham, Ala.: police; drugs
inner cities. *See* downtown neighborhoods
integration. *See* desegregation
"In the Mornin'" (Dunbar), 88–89
"Invictus" (Henley), 139

J., Ms. (niece's family member), 205
Jackson, Emory, 13
Jackson, Rosie Lee, 30–31, 209
jail. *See* incarceration
James (playmate), 42
Jerald (neighbor), 66
"Jesus Met the Woman at the Well" (song), 118, 119
Jimmie Hale Mission's Thrift Store, 113
JJ (Johnathan), 113, 114–115
Joann (mother). *See* Morris, Joann Steele
Job Corps program, 125, 156–157, 227n5
Joey (neighbor), 68–71
John Herbert Phillips High School. *See* Phillips High School
Johnson, James Weldon, 87, 88
J. O. Johnson High School, 100, 131
Jones, Eva Hardy, 95
Jones Valley Urban Gardens, xiv, *xvii*, 200–201
Jordan (country), 3–4, 122–123, 129–130
joy: of Central City residents, 202; of Joy Bus evangelists, 120–121; of niece's birth, 130; pain mixed with, xi–xii, 10, 121; of sister's birth, 125, 127. *See also* pain
"Joy and Pain" (Maze feat. Frankie Beverly), 10

Kelly, Nate, Jr., 210
Kelly, Nate, Sr. (coach), 100–101, 104, 107–108

Kerr, Ann Zwicker, 146
Kerr, Malcolm H., 3, 146
Key Club, 115, 144
King, Martin Luther, Jr., 27–28, 169
Ku Klux Klan, 56, 61–62

Lafayette, Bernard, 148
LaMonte, Ruth, 210
Lawley, Preston, 210
Lawson, James, 148
Leonard (neighbor), 63
Lewis, John, 148
Lewis, Walter, 131
Lincoln Elementary School, 84
Liz, Ms. (Elizabeth Leonard Harris), 75–77, 100, 209
Lockett, Johnnie, 210
Lomax, Mark, 124
"Love's in Need of Love Today" (Wonder), 179
low-income Black communities. *See* Black communities, low-income

Madhubuti, Haki R., 157
magnet schools, 90–91
Majors, Richard, 67
Malcolm H. Kerr Scholarship Program, 3–4, 146
Malcolm X, 147; *The Autobiography of Malcolm X* (with Haley), 160, 161, 228n3
males, Black. *See* Black males
Mama (grandmother). *See* Collins, Oceola Steele
Marable, Manning, 157
Marconi Park, xi, xiii, *xvii*, *xviii*, 6, 200
Marley, Bob, and the Wailers, 71
Mary (spouse). *See* Muse, Mary
masculinity, Black. *See* Black males
Maxine, Aunt. *See* Wright, Maxine Steele Collins
Maze feat. Frankie Beverly, 10
McNair, Carol Denise, 1
Memphis, Tenn., 27
men and boys, Black. *See* Black males
"Message, The" (Grandmaster Flash and the Furious Five), 73
Metropolitan Gardens. *See* Central City public housing community
Metropolitan Interdenominational Church, 123

middle-class Black people, 17, 90, 115, 216n3. *See also* Black poverty
milk, chocolate versus white, 170
Million Man March, 123, 173
Mis-education of the Negro (Woodson), 68
Missouri–St. Louis, University of, 10, 205
ML (classmate), 88
Mock, James, 146, 160
Monroe, Uncle. *See* Wright, Monroe
Montgomery, Ala., Black activism in, 2, 64
Moon, Warren, 141, 226n14
Morris, Jerome E. (author), xv, *149*, *180*; "All the Same," 182; family history, 19–26, 46–48; *Troubling the Waters*, 96
—childhood (1968–1980): attends church, 118–120; birth and infancy, 2, 25–26, 28; fights with Joey, 69–71; seeks out father, 40–44; visits brother Michael in juvenile, 176; welcomes baby sister, 125; witnesses fights and conflicts, 35–37, 54–55, 65, 73, 75–76
—adolescence (1981–1986): baptism of, 122; Black consciousness reading group joined by, 159–160; connects with Clency family, 44–45, 50; at grandmother's funeral, 121; hides woman in Tokyo hotel room, 115–116; neighbors and, 113–114, 162–163; niece's birth, 130; prom attendance and fight with classmate, 92–93; siblings' challenges and, 125–129, 156–157; works at summer jobs, 109–112
—adulthood (1986–): assaulted by police, 151–153; at brother Michael's funeral, 177–179, 181; Clency family history research by, 51–52; gets to know Mary, 135–137; has operation, 142–143; at Million Man March, 123; moves to Nashville and marries, 7–8, 148, 150; plays in Turkey Bowl game, 186; reminisces with Donovan, 54–56, 57–58; returns to live in Birmingham, 6, 148; supports mother and siblings, 166, 184–185, 187–189, 190; undergraduate activities and activism, 5, 137–141, 146–148
—career: Central City research project, ix–xii, 193–194; substitute teacher, 7, 95, 148, 151; University of Georgia, ix, 8, 10, 187; University of Missouri–St. Louis, 10, 205; Vanderbilt University Television News Archives, 7

Morris, Jerome E. (*continued*)

—characteristics: appearance, 40, 48, 87, 152; fighting abilities, 66; football playing style, 131; nonuse of profanity, 69; reputation for going all out, 143

—education: Austin Peay State University, 4–5, 131–135, 142, 147, 225n5; daycare, 79–81; internships, 5–6, 146, 154; Phillips High School, 2–3, 44–45, 94, 100–107, 112; Powell Elementary School, 83–84, 85–89; Saint Louis University, 7, 148; study-abroad programs, 3–4, 113–114, 115–116, 122–123, 129–130; Vanderbilt University, ix, 8, 83–84, 95–96, 150, 168–173, 177–178, 184

—football: Central City teams, 97–98, 99, 100, 186–187; Phillips High School, 100–107, 108; throw-up tackle, 75; university, 4–5, 141, 144–146

—relationships: with Clency relatives, 40–45, 50–52; fellow teachers, 169–172; football coaches, 100–101, 107–108, 141–142, 143; football teammates, 103, 105–106, 137; mother, 138, 144; neighbors, 38, 75–76, 103–104, 114; nieces and nephews, 165, 187–189; Preston, 112; siblings, 74, 75–76, 98, 137, 155, 156–157, 179, 187–189; stepfather, 34

Morris, Joann Steele (mother), xiv, *39*, 209

—characteristics: academic skills, 22; appearance, 23–24, 35; cleanliness, 28; love of comic books, 23, 81; love of music, 34, 35, *39*, 118; religious side, 118–120, 121; use of profanity, 69

—life events: early life and education, 20–22; enrolls sons in daycare, 79–81; family and community event attendance, 59, 104, 121, 122; fights and conflicts, 35–37, 65, 73, 74–77; final illness, death, and funeral, 190, 203; hospitalized, 71; later years, 184–185, 187–188, 189; learns author is leaving football team, 144; legacy, 195; moves into Central City, 28–29; pregnancies, marriage, and children, 17, 22–26, 37; raided by police, 151–152; shares news of daughter's pregnancy, 126–127, 128, 130; takes children to church, 118–120; visits incarcerated sons, 166, 176; Willie's Super Market boycott, 62–64

—relationships: children, 138, 144, 176–177, 187–188; children's fathers, 22–23, 24–26, 34–35, 36, 37, 45; grandchildren, 165–166, 188; neighbors, 35–36, 38, 53, 59, 75–77; parents and sister, 20, 23, 121; rent office staff, 185

—views: on ass-kissing, 46; author's father, 45; Central City, 28; daughter's pregnancy, 128; disrespect, 63–64; first pregnancy and interrupted education, 22–23; hitting back, 29; sons' challenges, 72, 84, 177

Morris, Kenneth (brother), xv, *180*, 209; life events, 37, 72–73, 84–85, 179

Morris, Maurice (brother), xv, *180*, 209; adulthood, 125, 151–153, 154–155, 156, 157, 165–167, 190; characteristics and skills, 74–75, 156, 157; childhood and adolescence, 41–44, 73, 75–76, 118–120, 176; education, 79–80, 83, 85–86, 125, 156–157

Morris, Michael (Big Meaty; brother), xv, *180*; adulthood, 55, 175; characteristics and skills, 175–176, 178, 179; childhood and adolescence, 70, 72–73, 162–163, 176–177; education, 72, 83, 179; final illness, death, and funeral, 178–179, 181, 190

Morris, Richard Lee, Jr. (brother), xv, *180*, 209; adulthood, 186, 189, 190; childhood and adolescence, 25, 28–29, 71, 81, 82, 83, 138; death, funeral, and legacy, 203; relationships, 81–82, 85, 98, 159

Morris, Richard Lee, Sr. (stepfather), xv, 17, 24–25, 28, 34–35, 179

Morris, Santana (niece), 209; life events, 50, 130, 151, 152, 187–189, 204–205

Morris, Shelda (sister), xv, *180*, 209; adulthood, 151, 152, 187–189, 190–191, 204–205; childhood and adolescence, 37, 65, 83, 118–120, 125–127, 130, 176; younger children of, 205

Morris, Steve (brother), xv, 37, 179

Most Segregated City in America, The (Connerly), 60

Muse, Mary (spouse), *149*, 209; community involvement, 173; early education, 136–137; family events and, 50, 51, 179, 186; gets to know author, 135–136; graduate education and later research, 187, 188, 206; marriage and children, 8, 150, 190; religious interests of, 123–124; undergraduate education and experiences, 7,

139, 143, 146–148; views of, 136–137, 138, 144

MuseMorris, Amadi (daughter), 107, 190, 205, 207

MuseMorris, Kamau (son), 107, 205–206, 207

music. *See specific styles, artists, and song titles*

Nash, Diane, 148

Nashville, Tenn., 7–8, 147, 148, 173

National Council on U.S.-Arab Relations, 3, 5, 129, 146

neighborhoods. *See* Black communities, low-income; downtown neighborhoods; *and specific neighborhoods*

"New Life" (song), 108

New Orleans, La., 154, 182–183, 214n13

"nigger," use of term, 69

Nursery, the (daycare), 80–81

OC, Ms. *See* Collins, Oceola Steele

One Stop Convenience Store, xiv, 68–69, 103

opportunities: benefits of, 3, 5, 8–9; color-ism and, 24, 216n24; racism and, 15, 31; uneven distribution of, 8–10. *See also* Black poverty; survival

pain: of author's family, 21, 39, 120, 121, 126–129, 179; of Black students, 137; of Central City residents, 163, 202; of crack-cocaine epidemic, 6, 154–156; of fra-ternity fight, 139; of intergenerational trauma, 8–10, 213n17; joy mixed with, xi–xii, 121; of leaving football team, 145; of poverty, 9; replaced by joy, 130. *See also* joy

Panky (Charles Clency; brother), xv, 48–50, 209

Papa Slim (brother's father), xv, 22–23, 25, 73

Parker, Vanessa, 210

Parker High School, 20, 21, 56, 89–90, 102–103, 104–107

Park Place housing complex, ix, xi, xiii, *xvii*, 191, 198, 202

Parks, Rosa, 2, 64

Patterson, Orlando, 228n9

Payne, Kathleen, 146

Pee Wee (play cousin), 99

Petro (football player), 100

Phillips High School, xiii, *xviii*, *14*; author's experiences at, 44–45, 91–94, 100–101, 112–113, 129; author teaches at, 7, 148; brothers and, 85; closing of, 184; con-verted to Phillips Academy, 200; deseg-regation of, 2, 30, 55–57; dressing style at, 160; football victory over Parker, 101–107; free meals served at, 72

"Please Come Home for Christmas" (C. Brown), 34

police, Birmingham. *See* Birmingham, Ala.: police

Pollard, Alton B., 124

postsecondary institutions. *See* colleges and universities

Pot (neighbor), 53

poverty, Black. *See* Black poverty

powell, john a., 201–202, 232n7

Powell Elementary School, xiii, *xviii*; au-thor's and brothers' experiences at, 81, 82–89, 91–92; author teaches at, 7, 148; closing of, 184, 199–200; desegregation of, 30, 54; as support for Central City residents, 94–95, 166, 190

Preston (body shop owner), 110–112, 138

Price, Sarah, 53–54, 59–60, 203, 209

primary schools. *See* schools

prison. *See* incarceration

projects, housing. *See* Birmingham, Ala.: public housing communities; public housing

Pruitt, Shawn, 146

Public Enemy (hip-hop group), 157–158

public housing: Black poverty and, 2; de-segregation of, 31; history of, 12, 214n2; HOPE VI and, 182–184, 189–191, 199–202; Red Mountain Expressway protest and, 60; stigma of, 9, 193, 195, 196. *See also* Birmingham, Ala.: public housing communities; Black communities, low-income; Black poverty; downtown neigh-borhoods

public schools. *See* schools

racism: adaptive vitality in face of, 217n8; Black consciousness and, 160, 227n1 (chap. 16); of Black people, alleged, 171; in businesses, 21, 62–64, 110; colorism and, 23–24, 216n24; in educational set-tings, 133–135, 137, 147–148, 225n5;

racism (*continued*)
    gender and, 21, 67, 230n2; housing/
    neighborhoods and, 10, 12–13, 15–17, 27–
    28, 31, 33, 57, 62–64, 216n13; incarcer-
    ation and, 47, 48; incidents of, 1–2, 61–
    62; intergenerational effects of, 8–10, 15,
    213n17; targeted universalism to address,
    201–202; teaching about, 169–172, 173–
    174; in U.S. history, 67–68, 121; in U.S.
    military, 35. *See also* enslavement; segre-
    gation; whiteness
Red Mountain Expressway, xiv, 15, 58–60
Rev. (pastor), 119–120
Robertson, Carole Rosamond, 1
Robinson, Jo Ann, 64
Robinson, Johnny, 211n2 (chap. 1)
Roderick (neighbor), 159–160, 210
Rodney, Walter, 159
Roots (TV series), 161
Ruth (school official), 112, 113

Saint Louis University (SLU), 7, 148
Sanders, Eugene, 210
Sandra, Aunt. *See* Collins, Sandra
Sands, George, 61–62
Sankofa symbol, 52
scholarships, athletic. *See* athletic scholar-
    ships
schools (*see also specific schools*):
—Black (legally segregated): Black history
    and culture taught at, 90; Black teach-
    ers at, 17, 90; closing of, due to desegre-
    gation, 136–137, 225n6; lack of resources
    for, 56, 78, 89–90. *See also* Black stu-
    dents: school; colleges and universities:
    historically Black; desegregation; segre-
    gation
—Black Catholic, 21–22, 215n19
—magnet, 91–92
—predominantly Black: Black history and
    culture taught at, 86–89, 169–171, 173–
    174; Black students and communities
    supported by, 91–92, 95–96, 201–202;
    Black teachers at, 83, 91–93, 94–95, 134,
    166; closing of, due to gentrification, 199–
    200; free meals served at, 71–72, 73; lack
    of resources for, 91; white flight from, 31,
    33, 56–57, 83. *See also* Black students:
    school; colleges and universities, histor-
    ically Black; educators: Black

secondary schools. *See* schools
Section 8 vouchers, 183–184, 195
segregation: Birmingham famous for, 1–2;
    on buses, protests against, 64; in busi-
    nesses, 162, 224n4 (chap. 10); of housing/
    neighborhoods, 10, 12–13, 15–17, 31, 33,
    57, 216n3; of maternity wards, 19; public
    awareness of, 27; in schools, 55–56, 102.
    See also desegregation; racism; schools:
    Black
Seventh Court (neighborhood), xiii–xiv
Shay, Ms. (teacher), 80–81, 210
shotgun houses, *xviii*, 15, 17, *18*, 19, 214n13
Shuttlesworth, Fred and Ruby, 2, 55–56
Sims, Mrs. (assistant principal), 168, 171–
    172
Sixteenth Street Baptist Church, *xvi*, 1,
    221n2 (chap. 1)
slavery. *See* enslavement
Slavery and Social Death (Patterson),
    228n9
Slick (sister's father), 36, 37, 38
Slim (Sonny Boy) (neighbor), 98
SLU (Saint Louis University), 7, 148
slums. *See* Black poverty; downtown neigh-
    borhoods; public housing
Smith, Carter, 146
Smith, Laura, 209
Smith, Lula (great-grandmother), 20
Smithfield (neighborhood), 17
Smithfield Court housing project, 13, 90,
    196
Sneaky (neighbor), 186–187
solidarity, 147–148, 159
soul food, 162
Souljah, Sister, 171
soul(s): Central City as formative of, 11, 159;
    food as nourishment for, 162; incarcer-
    ation as isolation of, 58; inner-city, Joy
    Bus mission to save, 121; in poetry, 88,
    139; stories from, xi–xii. *See also* African
    American spirituals; church(es)
Souls of Black Folk, The (Du Bois), 10,
    227n1 (chap. 16)
southern United States: Black commun-
    ity life in, Central City as example of, x,
    xii, 3; Black education tradition in, 96;
    Black genealogy in, 51–52; Black hous-
    ing/neighborhoods in, 15–16; Black mi-
    gration within/away from, 30, 46, 48, 50,

57; drugs in, 6, 154; hip-hop in, 98; Joy Bus Evangelism in, 121; outsiders' views of, 1–2; racial caste system in, and illegal activities, 47; shotgun houses in, 214n13. *See also* Birmingham, Ala.

South Side (neighborhood), 13

Southtown Court, 196, 231n4 (chap. 20)

spirituals, African American, xi, 86–87, 105, 119–120, 122, 124. *See also* church(es); soul(s)

sports. *See* athletic scholarships; coaches; football

Steele, Joe, Jr. (grandfather), xv, 20

Steele, Joe, Sr. (great-grandfather), 20

Steele, Ronald (brother), xv, *180*, 209; adulthood, 127–129, 177, 190, 191, 204–205; characteristics and interests, 25, 73–74, 81–82, 85, 98; childhood, adolescence, and education, 17, 24–25, 28–29, 65, 81, 82, 83, 138; quoted, 25–26, 28–29, 43–44, 62

Steele, Stephanie, 146

St. Louis, Mo., 205–206

student-athlete, use of term, 142, 226n16

students, Black. *See* Black students

Sugar Jets football team, 97–98, 99, 100, 104

Sugar Man. *See* Harris, Joe

Summer, Ms. (teacher), 83–84

survival: author's, in police assault, 151–153; Black consciousness and, 159, 167; of Black students, 136–137; in crack-cocaine epidemic, 6; of enslaved people, 9; of families, mothers working for, 21; supports to ensure, 3, 16. *See also* Black poverty; opportunities

survival mode, young Black males in, 112, 157, 164–165

Tabatha (friend), 193, 194–196, 205, 210

"Take Me to the Water" (song), 122

targeted universalism, 201–202, 232n7

Taylor, Breonna, 202

teachers. *See* educators

teaching, sacredness of, 94, 172

Tennessee State University (TSU), 133, 147–148

Terminal Station, xiv, *xviii*

"Them Belly Full (But We Hungry)" (Bob Marley and the Wailers), 71

Thomas, Adella, 19

Thomas, John, 168, 169–170, 171

Tokyo, Japan, 115–116

Tony (football player), 132–133

Treble Middle School, 168–172, 173–174

Troubling the Waters (J. E. Morris), 96

TSU (Tennessee State University), 133, 147–148

Turkey Bowl football game, 186

Turrentine, Lucille H., 91–92, 210

Tuxedo Court housing project (the Brickyard), 189, 190–191, 204

Twenty-Ninth Court (neighborhood), xiii–xiv, *xviii*, *18*, *43*; about, 16–17; author's family history in, 15, 17, 19, 24, 25, 40; relationships built in, 38, 51, 99. *See also* Alley, the

United States: Birmingham as most segregated city in, 1; Black poverty in, 2, 9; Black rebellion following MLK's assassination, 27–28; Central City as poorest zip code in, 8; crack-cocaine epidemic in, 6, 153, 154, 155; education in, 56–57, 68–69, 83–84, 91–92; in global context, 3–4, 5–6, 10–11, 115; history of, views on, 41, 67–68, 86, 169–172, 173–174; immigrants in, 15–16; incarcerated population of, 58; public housing in, 60; racial divisions in, xi–xii, 10, 15–16, 31, 32, 33, 166–167; targeted universalism needed in, 201–202; violence in, 67–69, 71, 171. *See also* cities, U.S.; southern United States

United States government: food programs of, 71–72, 74; housing policies of, 12, 27–28, 31, 33, 59, 182–184, 191, 199, 214n3; income assistance programs, stigma of, 230n2; Job Corps program, 125, 156–157, 227n5; military, 3, 5, 34–35; Red Mountain Expressway supported by, 58–60; violence and, 67–68, 71, 171; war on drugs, 58, 153, 154–156, 184. *See also* Birmingham, Ala.: city government

universities. *See* colleges and universities; *and specific universities*

University of Georgia (UGA), ix–x, 8, 10

University of Missouri–St. Louis, 10, 205

Up From Slavery (B. T. Washington), 90

urban areas, U.S. *See* cities, U.S.; downtown neighborhoods

Urban Institute, 183
U.S. cities. *See* cities, U.S.

Vanderbilt University, ix, 7–8, 150, 168–169,
   172–173
Vann, David, 61, 62
Ventress Correctional Facility, 166
Vivian, C. T., 148
Vulcan Kiwanis Club, 115, 129

Walker, Robert, 27
Ware, Virgil, 221n2 (chap. 1)
war on drugs. *See* drugs
Washington, Booker T., 95; *Up From Slavery*, 90
Washington, Ms. (neighbor), 30
Watt, Mrs. (librarian), 86
"We're a Winner" (the Impressions), 64
Wesley, Cynthia, 1
West, Irene, 64
West and the Rest of Us, The (Chinweizu),
   159
white educators. *See* educators: white
whiteness, 9, 15, 31, 134, 216n24. *See also* racism
white people: Black consciousness and, 159,
   160; Christianity and, 120–121, 123; economic privilege and, 9–10; flight from
   Black residents, 31, 33, 57, 82, 83, 216n3;
   housing and, 12–13, 15, 28–30, 199–201;

names of, as slave owners, 218n1; opi-
   oid abuse and, 155; racism and, 24, 171,
   216n24; teaching Black history and, 169–
   170, 173; violence of, 1, 56, 67–68. *See also*
   Birmingham, Ala.: residents, white; edu-
   cators: white; *and specific individuals*
Wilbur N. Daniel African American Cultural Center (APSU), 146–147
Williams, Heather Andrea, 218n1
Willie's Super Market, xiv, *xviii*, 63–64
Winbush, Raymond, 147
women and girls, Black. *See* Black females
Women's Political Council (WPC), 64
Wonder, Stevie, 179
Woodson, Carter G., 90; *Mis-education of
   the Negro*, 68
WPC (Women's Political Council), 64
Wright, Maxine Steele Collins (aunt), xv,
   209; death and legacy, 204; family re-
   lationships, 19, 23, 186, 204; life events,
   19, 21, 23–24, 135–136, 176–177, 178–179;
   other relationships, 23, 76
Wright, Monroe (uncle), 135–136, 176–177,
   179, 204
WW Lounge, 35–36

X, Malcolm, 147; *The Autobiography of
   Malcolm X* (with Haley), 160, 161, 228n3

Yuzuki (Japanese woman), 115–116

Printed in the USA
CPSIA information can be obtained
at www.ICGtesting.com
LVHW040100221123
764610LV00006B/156

9 780820 365756